FEMINIST PERSPECTIVES ON LAW & THEORY

Cavendish
Publishing
Limited

London • Sydney

FEMINIST PERSPECTIVES ON LAW & THEORY

Edited by

Janice Richardson, MA, LLM
Senior Lecturer in Law
Centre for Critical Legal Studies
Staffordshire University

and

Ralph Sandland, BA, M Phil
Senior Lecturer, School of Law
University of Nottingham

Cavendish
Publishing
Limited

London • Sydney

First published in Great Britain 2000 by Cavendish Publishing Limited, The Glass House, Wharton Street, London WC1X 9PX, United Kingdom

Telephone: + 44 (0)20 7278 8000   Facsimile: + 44 (0)20 7278 8080

Email: info@cavendishpublishing.com

Website: www.cavendishpublishing.com

British Library Cataloguing in Publication Data

Feminist perspectives on law & theory
1 Women – Legal status, laws, etc – Great Britain
2 Women's rights – Great Britain   3 Feminist jurisprudence – Great Britain
I Richardson, Janice   II Sandland, Ralph
342.4'1'0878

ISBN 1 85941 528 8

Printed and bound in Great Britain

SERIES EDITORS' PREFACE

We are very pleased, indeed proud, to be able to publish this volume as part of our *Feminist Perspectives on Law* series. As the editors of this volume say in their own introduction:

> One thing about legal feminism that has not changed is that it remains a deeply political, would-be transformative, project. Part of our political mission, as editors of this volume, has been to attempt to provide the reader with an example of the necessity and benefits of broad ranging dialogue to this wider project.

This volume firmly situates an exploration of current theoretical debates within the feminist project of engagement with law. In so doing, the editors have drawn together contributors, from within law schools as well as from other disciplines, who display the diversity and richness of contemporary theoretical work. The volume can be read as an accessible introduction to this range of material but, further, is explicitly concerned with pushing the ideas, and methods employed, forward. As such, we believe that it will prove to be an invaluable contribution, not only to work within law schools but also in the broader academy. Here is a volume which does not purport to simply introduce 'theory' to a broader readership, but rather displays an active engagement with theoretical ideas which invites us to partake in that engagement.

The editors' introduction (Chapter 1) draws together themes which resound throughout the volume, themes which make clear just how far the project of feminist thinking has developed and the extent to which those committed to the project have been using, and reworking, key ideas taken from the 'grand old masters' of philosophy, not in a gesture of fealty but rather in a spirit of creative and imaginative thinking for a purpose. This is not a search for final answers. This volume displays the move beyond conventional concerns with epistemology, moving instead towards the creative and careful consideration of what tools are available to help us think with greater clarity about ourselves, law and what we might mean by feminism.

Our thanks to Janice and Ralph for taking on what, to many, would have seemed such a daunting project. They have managed to produce a volume of sophisticated work in an accessible way. We have no doubt that it will provide a challenge to many who have purported to 'know' what feminist jurisprudence is about, as well as to those who have, to date, doubted what feminist theoretical work has to offer. However, the major importance of this volume will be in offering to feminists working within, and on, law a very substantial range of material which, we hope and believe, will enhance their (our) own work.

Our thanks also, as always, to all the people at Cavendish who have worked on this project and on the series as a whole, especially Jo Reddy, whose support and enthusiasm has made this volume, and the series, possible. At a recent conference on Women and Law (University of Westminster, June 2000), it was made clear just how far the series has had a real impact in giving a forum for, and profile to, feminist work in law schools in this country as well as others. We have no doubt that this volume will enhance both the series and that work. Meanwhile, our thanks to those who have been reading and using the series. We have found your comments as valuable as your support and we look forward to hearing your views on this volume!

Anne Bottomley and Sally Sheldon

CONTRIBUTORS

Sara Ahmed is currently Co-Director of the Institute for Women's Studies, Lancaster University, with Jackie Stacey. Her first book, *Differences that Matter: Feminist Theory and Postmodernism*, was published in 1998. Her most recent book explores the relationship between strangers, embodiment and community and is entitled *Strange Encounters: Embodied Others in Post-Coloniality* (2000).

Alison Assiter is Dean of Economics and Social Science and Professor of Feminist Theory at the University of the West of England. She is author of a number of works, including *Enlightened Women: Modernist Feminism in a Postmodern Age* (1996), *Althusser and Feminism* (1990) and *Pornography, Feminism and the Individual* (1989).

David Bell teaches cultural studies at Staffordshire University. **Jon Binnie** teaches human geography at Brunel University. They are authors of *The Sexual Citizen: Queer Politics and Beyond* (2000), and both have written extensively on sexuality, space and politics.

Anne Bottomley is Senior Lecturer at the Law School, Kent University. She is a series editor of the Cavendish *Feminist Perspectives in Law* series and author of many papers exploring and developing feminist perspectives on law. Anne is also editor of the English journal, Feminist Legal Studies.

Penelope Deutscher is Senior Lecturer in Philosophy at the Australian National University. She is the author *of Yielding Gender: Feminism, Deconstruction and the History of Philosophy* (1997) and co-editor, with Kelly Oliver, of *Enigmas: Essays on Sarah Kofman* (1999). She is currently working on a book about the later work of Luce Irigaray.

Qudsia Mirza teaches law at the University of East London. She is the author of *Race Relations in the Workplace* (1995). Her current research interests lie in feminist Islamic legal theory, critical race theory and discrimination law.

Ewan Porter is a PhD student in the Philosophy Department of the University of Warwick. His research focuses on what he considers to be the revolutionary thinking of both Luce Irigaray and Walter Benjamin. He has also published a chapter entitled 'Story-time and image-time' on Walter Benjamin, in *Art in the Making* (forthcoming).

Judy Purdom is a PhD student in philosophy at the University of Warwick, working on Deleuze and painting. Publications include work on hybridity for Third Text (1994, 1995), an *Essay in Deleuze and Philosophy* (1997) and articles on Mondrian, Bacon and Nancy Spero. She is co-editor of *Going Australian* ((2000) 15(2) Hypatia (special issue)).

Janice Richardson is Senior Lecturer in Law at the Centre for Critical Legal Studies, Staffordshire University. She was previously a trade union solicitor. She has published in the area of feminist philosophy/legal theory in Feminist Legal Studies, Law and Critique and Women's Philosophy Review.

Ralph Sandland is Senior Lecturer in the School of Law at the University of Nottingham. He has published in the areas of feminist legal theory, family law, health care law and the legal treatment and construction of travellers. His text, *Mental Health Law* (with Dr Peter Bartlett), was published in 1999.

ACKNOWLEDGMENTS

The idea for this book came from the series editors, Anne Bottomley and Sally Sheldon. We are extremely grateful to Anne and Sally for trusting us with the task of editorship. We hope that the finished product does justice to their faith and inspiration. In Jo Reddy at Cavendish we found a publisher second to none. We are proud that this book is part of Jo's broader project to extend the boundaries of legal publishing. Ruth Massey at Cavendish has overseen our project with much appreciated humour and enthusiasm. Our contributors have excited and inspired us with the depth and breadth of their scholarship and their tolerance of our editorial 'style', such as it is.

Janice is grateful for the support that she has received from Staffordshire University, particularly from David Kelly of the Centre for Critical Legal Studies; from everyone at Warwick University's Feminist Philosophy Society; from insidious Deleuzians such as Jon 'you only love me for my Word skills' Rubin; and, of course, from Tom Huggon.

Ralph would like to thank Julie being there; Pauline Rolf and Phil Ulanowski for the start; and Thérèse Murphy and Peter Bartlett, whom I am fortunate to have as colleagues.

Janice Richardson and Ralph Sandland
October 2000

CONTENTS

TABLE OF CASES

TABLE OF STATUTES

TABLE OF ABBREVIATIONS

Br J Soc	British Journal of Sociology
CLP	Current Legal Problems
FS	Feminist Studies
FLS	Feminist Legal Studies
JLS	Journal of Law and Society
LC	Law and Critique
LS	Legal Studies
SLI	Social and Legal Issues
SLS	Social and Legal Studies
SPP	Social Philosophy and Policy
WPR	Women's Philosophy Review

CHAPTER 1

FEMINISM, LAW AND THEORY

Janice Richardson and Ralph Sandland

INTRODUCTION

By the middle of the 1980s, 'second wave' feminism could be said to have 'arrived', and to have secured a foothold, in many law schools. It was now a decade since the work that had been done in the 1970s, which, itself taking its cue from early second wave feminist writers – De Beauvoir, Friedan and, later, Firestone, Greer, Oakley and many others – had begun to ask why law fails to provide 'equality'. In the interim, this demand had itself been subjected to critique from within feminism, which had asked: What does it mean for 'women' to want to be 'equal' to 'men'? Is the project of legal feminism to ensure that 'women' are treated 'like men' by law? Feminism was divided as to the true answers to these questions. The divide, broadly, was between radical feminism, with its revolutionary agenda of a law which recognised women *as* women, rather than only 'seeing' women who were 'like men'; and liberal feminism, with its rejection of revolution and preference for gradualism and reform, and a continued emphasis on the demand for 'equality' before the law.

However, as the 1980s turned into the 1990s, feminist legal theory began to exhibit greater diversity. It became apparent that, despite the differences between radical and liberal feminism, between the politics of 'difference' and the politics of 'equality', between legal revolution and legal reform, the whole debate was nevertheless underpinned by a number of shared assumptions. Some of the more important of these concerned the relationship between legal change and social change (the assumption was that legal change, whether in the shape of revolution or reform, would lead to social change), and the relationship between theory and practice (the assumption was manifold and complex, but was basically an elaboration of a simple cause and effect model). But perhaps the most important was the assumption that 'law' is, always and everywhere, 'male'. In an important sense, the debate between radical and liberal versions of legal feminism, between 'difference feminism' and 'equality feminism', distills down to the question of whether 'male law' could accommodate 'the female'. Radicalism thought not; liberalism tended to be more optimistic.

Seeking to find a way through this theoretical deadlock, legal feminists began to scrutinise these underpinning shared assumptions. For example, what did it mean to argue that 'the law' – seen as a singular, monolithic entity – was 'male'? In seeking answers, feminists found little assistance from traditional jurisprudence, which was, and has largely remained, resolutely unwilling even to admit the questions, notwithstanding that (or perhaps, precisely because), like early second wave feminist theories of law, it is grounded on the same unspoken assumption about the sexed (male) 'nature' of law. So, legal feminism increasingly looked elsewhere, to philosophy, to cultural and women's studies, to postmodernism, poststructuralism and deconstruction. The result is that, by the turn of the new millennium, legal feminism, at least at the level of theory, has worked through and beyond the limitations of the 'radical or liberal?' paradigm and has recognised that the either/or choice that it posited was false and misleading. Feminist legal theory today is sophisticated, pluralistic, more incisive and careful in its arguments, more aware of its own limitations and deficiencies, less dogmatic and more tuned into the dangers of dogmatism; more aware, too, of the dangers of 'theory' and of the confusion that can result from mistaking 'theory' for 'truth'. As Anne Bottomley argues in Chapter 2 of this volume, we have to be aware that 'theory' does not provide 'truth', so that 'better theory' does not, of itself, produce 'better truth'. We have also to remember that 'theory' is not 'truth'. None can speak for all. Nor can one simply adopt a theoretical 'position' in the expectation that a ready made set of answers-for-all-occasions comes as part of the package.

It is this insistence on, or at least awareness of, the dangers of 'grand theory' or 'meta-theory' that marks out much of the feminist work that has been done since the mid-1980s from what had gone before. Of course, the new scepticism about the potential of theory was by no means a development that occurred only within feminist theory. But that feminist theory has played a prominent role in the development of this scepticism is what allows the argument that legal feminism has developed a 'third wave' of perspectives, which in some sense start 'beyond' the search for absolute Truth and Justice. This shift amounts, in part, to the admission that feminism has failed to speak equally to or for women of all races or all classes; in part also to the recognition that this 'maleness' of law has in fact excluded many men, for example, by reason of race or sexuality, from sharing in its privileges. Things were not as simple as earlier versions of feminism had supposed. One cannot simply choose between 'difference' and 'equality', nor is the male/female distinction the only pertinent consideration. Other dynamics are also at play. This can be a scary idea, since it is not just that things may be more complicated than it was thought, it is also that *there may not be 'an answer' to be 'had'*. For feminism, and other identity-based political movements, the role of 'provider of truth' was also implicitly brought into question: if there is more at stake than sex/gender, what is the role of feminism? To suppress these other dynamics by insisting that sex/gender is, 'in truth', the most important of them? It is for these sorts of reasons that it can be said that third wave feminism is a political movement with an identity crisis. But, on the other hand, to question ideas and assumptions about Truth and Identity provides an opportunity and motivation for experimentation, diversity, innovation, dialogue and originality. Certainly, there is a pressing agenda of questions concerning the relationships between feminism, theory and law.

This book aims, on one level, to provide a snapshot of the diversity of thought that now lies at the intersection of law, feminism and philosophy. But our aim is not merely to catalogue contemporary developments. It is also to push them forward. Part of this project is to break down further the institutional and disciplinary barriers that surround law and law schools. Lawyers, even feminist lawyers, as Bottomley notes,[1] can be introspective and uncomfortable with debates and ideas that occur outside their familiar intellectual environment. We hope that this volume, which contains contributions from those both within and outside law schools, will demonstrate that feminist lawyers have much to gain – as well as to give – in these interdisciplinary debates. One thing about legal feminism that has not changed is that it remains a deeply political, would-be transformative, project. Part of our political mission, as editors of this volume, has been to attempt to provide the reader with an example of the necessity and benefits of broad ranging dialogue to this wider project.

Perhaps the key feature of this project of exploring diversity rather than pursuing one truth concerns the need to reconcile diversity with commonality. To abandon the idea of 'one truth' does not mean that there cannot be significant points of commonality – of history, of experience, of interpretation, of purpose and of spirit, in amongst the differences; similarly, to acknowledge commonality in any of these ways is not to attempt to deny diversity. As such, no apology is made for the fact that the contributors to this collection adopt very different – and often seemingly mutually incompatible – frameworks. Nor do we intend here to attempt to provide the reader with some sort of map by which these differences can be reconciled. But we do want to illustrate that difference and commonality are not mutually exclusive. Whilst we are content to let the differences speak for themselves, common areas of concern do flow through the chapters of this book, and these reflect the contemporary position of feminist legal theory. We want now to draw out these common themes in order to illustrate the way in which they interweave through the contributors' chapters, whilst also highlighting the original insights that the contributors bring to bear on these areas, derived from within their varied disciplines of law, philosophy (including a flourishing of contemporary feminist philosophy) and cultural and women's studies.

---

1   Chapter 2, in this volume.

The first common theme is concern about the relationship between theory and practice, which includes an analysis of the impact (and meaning) of the philosophical imagination and the role of utopia and of the 'impossible'. Along with an analysis of what is meant by theory, there is an awareness of the diverse meanings of 'the law' and the way in which feminism has successfully challenged narrow definitions of law. (Feminist legal studies, along with the critical legal studies movements – with influences from Marxism and poststructuralism – and critical race and queer theory, has been successful in highlighting not simply law in context, but a further analysis of the social context itself.) Our second theme, widely debated and linked to the first, is the question of the meaning of the self and the relationship between self/other and subjectivity. In legal theory, one way in which the influence of poststructuralism has manifested has been as an attack on the assumption that women form a group with stable characteristics. So, the stereotyped images of women that influence legal judgments – and are then disseminated within the media – continue to be interrogated. However, the shift of theoretical framework, with a rejection of the idea that theory is a tool in a search for truth in favour of the view that, when theory is used in this way, it in some sense *produces* truth, means that theorists tend to focus upon the way law *constructs* women – rather than simply *reflecting* a fixed category that exists prior to the operation of law. The stereotype is a fiction, a story, but, through its repeated re-telling, it can seem to become 'true'. The issue then becomes a question of 'the politics of truth' (whose truth is this?) rather than a case of right or wrong (truth or untruth). Many contributors, who take up different positions on this issue, discuss this shift. Contemporary work within feminist metaphysics is used to rethink the way in which we consider what it is to be a woman or to have (or exist as) a 'self' and the relevance of this to legal theory. Our third theme, again linked to what has gone before, concerns the relationship of feminist theory to other critical theories, such as critical race theory and queer theory. How are such relationships mapped in terms of the grid of possibilities delimited by the more general self/other relationship? What are the implications of such self-imposed boundaries and divisions? Some contributors explore these questions within the context of 'minority' politics. Others are more interested in the broader theoretical issues at stake and their practical implications.

THEORY/PRACTICE

The common themes sketched above are drawn from the influence of feminism, with its emphasis upon the practical impact of 'law' on women's lives. This may appear to be a curious claim, given that theory, particularly contemporary feminist theory, often influenced as it is by the continental philosophical tradition, appears to be esoteric. There has also been a long standing feminist concern about the way in which theory has often been used to justify a status quo, oppressive to women. Against this, we would argue that there are always assumptions made about, for example, what is meant by theory/practice (employed in that instance!); what is understood by law; what it means to be a woman or a person. Without an analysis of these basic assumptions it is likely that the accepted worldviews are adopted in an unquestioning manner. From experience, we know that these are more likely than not to be conservative. In the face of this, the role of theory must be to provide the means to question and challenge such conservatism (and the role of 'theory' in its maintenance); and this is a deeply 'practical' project, which aims for tangible effects. There has been a flourishing of feminist philosophy,[2] producing tools that greatly contribute to a rethinking of legal theory and, with it, legal practices.

One of the cluster of issues surrounding the theme of the relationship between theory and practice, therefore, is to do with the relevance of theory, with many contributors questioning the role of images of utopia and of the philosophical imagination in producing social change. Interestingly, the recent history of philosophy provides an object lesson in the importance of theory to practice and practice to theory (or, perhaps, in the illusory nature of the divide between them). The rejection of the idea of 'one truth' discussed above began to take shape at least partly as a reaction to debates within Marxism and the rejection of the intellectual as being in the vanguard of the revolution, a reaction generated itself in part by the continuing influence of the events of 1968 (the year of widespread, politically charged civil disobedience and public (dis)order around the world, but notably in the US and France), particularly upon contemporary French philosophy. This has also resulted in a challenge to the question of what 'theory' is and what it does. Various contributors to this volume draw from within this tradition to consider – or employ – work, for example, derived from Luce Irigaray (Penelope Deutscher and Ewan Porter) and from Gilles Deleuze (Anne Bottomley and Judy Purdom). Irigaray and Deleuze not only share a rejection of the idea of the intellectual who affects society in a top-down manner. Both also want to use theory instrumentally, to provide new concepts and new ways of thinking and living. This proceeds from a very different view of the potential of philosophy to 'tell the truth' about ourselves and our world from the contribution by Alison Assiter, which aims to use human need to define 'the good' as a basis for law. However, as discussed above, the aim of this book is not to present the reader with 'contemporary feminist legal theory' as a pre-packed unity, but to allow contributors to further develop their varied theoretical positions. Readers can then appreciate the diversity of feminist legal theory that exists today and judge for themselves between conflicting assumptions.

---

2   In the UK, see, eg, Women's Philosophy Review, as well as the specifically legal Feminist Legal Studies and the new journal, Feminist Theory.

As a sub-set of the question of the relevance of theory, the role of utopia is a recurring theme. Whilst utopian thought has been dismissed by those who view it as an attempt to impose an ideal upon the rest of us, the thinking of utopias is defended by many of the contributors. Even those writing within the continental philosophical tradition and chary of the role of the intellectual as truth teller are interested in interventions at the level of the imaginary. The two chapters that deal with Irigaray's work, for example, focus upon the practical impact of her proposals for legal change. These include a number of separate rights for women, such as safeguards that give legal recognition to virginity, which may appear bizarre to us. The question posed by the two contributors is whether this call for legislation is 'merely' a rhetorical strategy that Irigaray does not really 'mean', and, if so, does it work, and how?

It is an interesting approach to claim rights as a rhetorical strategy. It appears even more curious as it represents a mirror image of the position in the UK. Here, it has been debated whether the effect of taking legal claims is a bad strategy. This is based upon an analysis of the way that issues are filtered through the legal framework. It is argued that it damages individual women – such as those taking sexual harassment claims – and that the courts produce a stereotyped image of women, which is disseminated by the media. It will be seen whether Irigaray's looking glass world can provide images that can free up any blockages in the way in which we think about 'the law'.

'LAW'

Just as the contributors' theoretical frameworks differ on the central question of what is meant by 'theory', along with its relationship to feminist practice, so they differ as to what is meant by 'law'. The two intersect because of feminism's overriding concern with social change. The issue is whether theory can usefully predict where – and whether – legal interventions of any kind can be successful or, perhaps less ambitiously, how it can provide tools with which to consider problems (or law) differently, to try to unblock areas of domination, which may entail a more sophisticated understanding of the idea of 'domination'. As many of the contributors emphasise, there is more to law than simply a logical, coherent, unyielding patriarchal edifice.

Feminism has been very successful in challenging the meaning of 'law'. Within the law school, an aspect of this has been a move away from the view that the study of law is concerned primarily with an analysis of cases and statues, with 'successful study' defined as being able to solve legal problems in a separate legal universe. The 'law in context' movement and socio-legal studies have emphasised that students should be made aware of the social context in which law operates. So, for example, the student of family law may learn of the availability and scope of court orders for the protection of women from domestic violence. But, unless the legal rules are studied in their context, the student may never learn that such orders very often do not work. The feminist and critical legal studies movements have gone further, and have generally been more theoretically informed, in analysing the social context itself. Continuing with the above example, the issue would be *why* such orders do not work, which entails an analysis of the gendered reality into which such orders attempt to intervene. Both approaches have been useful in focusing upon the changing practice of law, rather than assuming that it exists in an unchanging ideal world of Platonic forms. Foucault famously described French law as being like a machine, and, as Rose expressed it, this should be understood to be 'more Heath Robinson than Audi'.[3] The image evokes the sense in which different types of things form parts that are fitted together in a haphazard manner. Parts may no longer do the work they were supposed to do – if they ever did – but may have adopted some other function. For example, the marital rape exemption was initially engineered to protect men from liability for raping their wives. But this function was overtaken by events such that, before its abolition, the exemption provided an unintended disincentive to women to marry, offering greater legal protection to those women who lived with, rather than married, their male partners. Before Foucault, feminism illustrated the 'messy' way in which law operates. This goes beyond pointing out that it is not simply driven by case law and that changes in case law do not derive from logic within the law itself. (Few would now adhere to such a naïve view of law.) The wider view of law and its operations and practical (and often unpredictable) outcomes lend themselves to a feminist analysis that has emphasised that the 'the personal is political'. From this perspective, feminists have avoided the assumption that power should be viewed in a top-down manner as emanating from the State, preferring to view power as actively permeating daily relationships. Similarly, they have been interested in the way understandings, and misunderstanding (such as the status of the legally non-existent 'common law wife'), of law can affect everyday life in the home, workplace and street.

Following from a common theme of the relationship between theory/practice, then, one shared concern is how to think about 'the law' and its role in social change. There has been much feminist theory in recent years that have focused upon 'discourse' or rhetoric. For example, in her contribution to this volume, Sara Ahmed employs a Derridean analysis to think about the possibility of global justice for women; the analyses of Irigaray illustrate how she aims to intervene rhetorically to change the everyday imaginary. Nevertheless, these approaches are concerned with, and aim to effect, the material conditions of women's lives. Other theoretical positions, from both within and outside the continental philosophical tradition, start with an analysis of the importance of the material conditions (without feeling

---

3   Rose, N, 'Foucault, government and power', paper presented at the 1994 Foucault Anniversary Conference.

the need to bring these within an extended definition of 'discourse') under which one lives, for shaping both one's beliefs and one's identity.

For example, the work of Spinoza and of Deleuze, discussed by Judy Purdom and Anne Bottomley, emphasises a materialist approach to social change that perhaps has more in common with Marx than Derrida. It is interesting to note that Irigaray, Spinoza and Deleuze discuss 'imagination', and yet Irigaray's conception of the imagination differs from that of Deleuze and Spinoza. For Irigaray, coming out of – but radically reworking – Lacanian psychoanalysis, imagination is formed at a certain stage of development and is pre-linguistic. For Spinoza and Deleuze, imagination represents the initial perception that we have of an object – for example, that the sun is close by. Even though we may discover that our perception appears false, it still affects the way in which we react. So, our imagination is influenced by our everyday experiences. This Spinozan imagination is used by Judy Purdom, for example, applying the work of Moira Gatens, to consider the role of judicial experience in forming their images of women and the shame that is attached to this image.

SELF/OTHER/SUBJECTIVITY

A linked theme is the question of subjectivity: what it is to be a person or subject, and what is the relationship between the self and other. Within legal theory, this has sometimes taken the form of asking what it means to be a subject of law or a citizen. All contributors agree with the rejection of the image of the supposedly neutral or universal subject. It is common ground between contributors that, when theorists have discussed 'the subject' in the abstract, they have usually had in mind as an image of a typical person as being male – with a male body and traditional (for example, heterosexual) male lifestyle. Within law, women have been accorded rights to the extent to which they could show that they were like men. (This is the logic of sex discrimination legislation in both the EU and the US, for example.) As mentioned above, it is this type of dilemma which fostered the so called 'equality/difference' debate. There are a number of different ways in which contemporary feminist philosophy can contribute to the furtherance of this debate. Alison Assiter argues for a conception of common human nature based upon an analysis of need. In doing so, she therefore supports a conception of 'the good', rather than the liberal argument that this necessarily employs value judgments and that rights should be left without content.[4]

---

4   See, eg, Drucilla Cornell's attempt to use rights for a 'socialist feminist agenda', discussed in Chapters 4, 5 and 6 of this volume. Assiter's position is a typically modern one and is attacked by the poststructuralism that is drawn upon by many of the other contributors. This focuses upon the constructedness of what we mean by 'nature'. See, eg, the discussion of Judith Butler in Purdom, Chapter 11, in this volume.

Assiter agrees that the 'universal subject' has been conceptualised as male (and white and heterosexual) but argues that this does not invalidate her argument – that it is still possible to conceive of 'common qualities of human beings' based upon common needs. She then moves to a view of 'the subject' in which certain needs are based upon having a specifically female body. However, these are needs which, she argues, can be commonly understood and form a basis for argument in law. So, whilst Assiter, along with other contributors, rejects the abstraction of the disembodied 'universal subject', she avoids employing an image of a universal subject by focusing upon bodily needs. The 'common humanity' becomes an awareness of the fact we all have some needs and not the specific needs themselves.

Many feminist theorists have drawn attention to the way in which philosophers have linked the ability to reason with being a man.[5] As Assiter points out, Descartes proposed that his method of reasoning could be adopted by anyone, including women. Further, it has been a common move within contemporary feminist theory to make the link between the Cartesian mind/body split and to map this onto the male/female split. The argument has been that men have represented 'mind' and reason, whereas women have been used to represent 'the irrational', the body, and nature. Against this, feminist philosopher Christine Battersby (discussed by Richardson, Chapter 6, in this volume) positions Kant (rather than Descartes) as proposing the image of the self that is more widely accepted as standard within modernity. Rather than having a simple mind/body split, the Kantian self is more complex, but the important point here is that, in this version of the self, the connectedness of mind and body is more heavily emphasised. An important point for Battersby is that the transcendental self (for Kant) is defined against the transcendental object. To put this more simply, I define myself against objects in the world. The transcendental self is that which, in Kant's system, organises the world into grids of meaning, imposing order upon it. Battersby's radical move is then to think what this philosophy would be if the bodies of women were taken as the norm rather than as an aberration. Richardson's argument is that this also provides a useful approach to law. This applies not simply as a method, but also in terms of a way of conceptualising law and of focusing upon the material impact of law on the day to day reality of women's lives.

---

5   See Lloyd, G, *The Man of Reason*, 1984, London: Methuen. For an analysis of the way in which 'femininity' has been valorised in male bodies but not in female bodies, see Battersby, C, *Gender and Genius: Towards a Feminist Aesthetics*, 1989, London: The Women's Press. This traces the way in which the use of reason has not always been valued above emotion. At these times, it has been emotion that has been associated with males. Sometimes, behaviour which is classed as feminine has been valorised in the male genius, but this has never been the case when displayed by women. So, it is not *feminine behaviour* that has been despised, but women's bodies and their actions.

The emphasis on Kant rather than Descartes also allows Battersby to draw out similarities between conceptions of the self in Kant's work with those of Lacan and Derrida, and, in so doing, draw out the radical nature of Irigaray's project. Irigaray shifts from a model in which the self is defined against that which it excludes, to thinking of a self that can be both, and simultaneously, with and apart from the other. Battersby places these images of self within a historical context and further develops a conception of a self that can be understood as emerging out of otherness and yet is not radically separate from it.

The usefulness of Irigaray's work, discussed within Penelope Deutscher and Ewan Porter's chapters, is that she questions both sides of the 'equality/difference' debate – in which men tend to be viewed as a neutral measure against which women either are or are not similar. In doing so, she echoes many feminists, including De Beauvoir,[6] who ask why it is that men are able to claim neutrality. (De Beauvoir illustrates this by pointing out that it is possible for men to argue, 'you only think this because you are a woman', but it is not possible to turn this round and say to a man, 'you only think this because you are a man'.) Irigaray goes further in stressing radical alterity, that is, that women are not simply different from men but that they cannot be judged by this measure. In her vocabulary, they are not 'other of the same' but 'other of the other'. In other words, just as the female sexual organs cannot be captured by the definition 'not-penis' but are something more than simply 'not that', so women cannot be defined as 'not-men'. 'Man' can be the measure of neither 'Woman's' equality nor her difference(s).

As discussed above, the way in which Irigaray reworks the construction of what it is to be a self from within psychoanalysis involves a radical shift away from thinking of a self that is formed only by being cut off from the other. The 'other' here stands for that which is not the self. Within psychoanalysis, this is often viewed as the child forming a sense of self by cutting himself[7] off from the mother. Irigaray conceives of a self that can emerge from what is other to the self but does not depend upon a radical cut with the other in order to keep that identity stable. This difficult idea can be more easily understood by thinking about the body and the way in which it is not cut off from its environment. Irigaray has privileged the image of the foetus and,

---

6   De Beauvoir, S, *The Second Sex*, 1953, London: Cape.

7   The subject is always viewed as being paradigmatically male within psychoanalysis. For a discussion and reworking of this, see Irigaray, L, 'Any theory of the "Subject" has already been appropriated by the "Masculine"', in *Speculum of the Other Woman*, Gill, G (trans), 1985, Ithaca: Cornell UP.

contentiously, the heterosexual lovers, in order to convey the image of bodies that can maintain their own identity but which do not depend upon a split from the other.[8]

A different concept of the self is proposed by the legal theorist Drucilla Cornell, and is discussed widely within this volume. Whereas Irigaray proposes specific women's rights – even if this is to be understood only as a rhetorical strategy – and Assiter continues a line of modern ethical thought that demands specific universal definitions of 'the good' – Cornell would reject both because they give specific content to legal claims. In other words, Irigaray and Assiter both have a specific image of what it means to be a person and what laws – or what system of laws, *if any* (as this may not simply suggest a reformist project) – should follow as a result of this conception of what it is to be a person. For Cornell, as a 'socialist feminist' but coming out of the liberal tradition, this is wrong. It is central to her argument (for rights rather than a conception of 'the good') that space should be left in order to allow people to define for themselves what it means to be a person. Like Assiter, she is suggesting a framework of law which is 'universal', in the sense that women are not added into law 'as women' (as in Irigaray's model). Cornell argues that it is dangerous to give women rights simply *as women*, because this allows the State to define what it means to be a woman. Traditionally, women have been defined in terms of their relationships with men. As Purdom puts it in her discussion of Gatens, she is '"utilised" under male authority and given a specific form and function that defines her in relation to men; she is wife or mother, virgin or whore'.[9]

Like Assiter, Cornell is then faced with the problem of how to avoid the 'universal person' simply being viewed, in practice, as a male subject by those who operate the law. Cornell attempts to avoid this by making her concept of the 'person' open ended. This is discussed in detail in the contributions of both Sandland and Richardson. Like Battersby, Cornell is radically reworking an aspect of Kant. In Cornell's case, it is the Kantian 'person', rather than the 'transcendental self', that is being reworked. Cornell manages to derive a legal test from a theoretical analysis of the self by emphasising the question, 'would free and equal people agree to this (piece of legislation or the impact of this case law)?'. Their own image of what it is to be a person is central to this test.

---

8   It is important not to confuse the work of Irigaray (or Battersby) with that of Carol Gilligan, whose work has been influential within law. Both Irigaray and Battersby have an image of a self that emerges out of difference and does not emerge by defining itself against otherness (or what it is not). Gilligan has a more straightforward image of the self that is more like that of Kant. Like Kant, Gilligan emphasises the difference between the way in which women have been socialised to be empathetic, whereas men have been viewed as employing rules and using reason. Gilligan's women are already conceived as separate from others (in contrast to an image of the self that emerges out of otherness but is never cut off from it) but able to be empathetic to others.

9   See below, p 215.

One would not willingly agree to a law that would interfere with one's own 'project of becoming a person'.

It is a credit to the strength and ingenuity of Cornell's position that it has sparked so much debate. Richardson compares this work with the position of Battersby and expresses concern about the extent to which Cornell's 'project of becoming a person' fits within the US image of the person as being 'an enterprise'. The courts are then set up as neutral arbitrators that judge between competing projects. One is supposed to work on oneself as an enterprise. In the vocabulary of the right, the aim to increase one's own 'capital', for example, by buying education as if it were a fridge. Whilst this is far from Cornell's socialist feminist approach to law, Richardson argues that it can too easily be co-opted within this model.

Similarly, Sandland argues that the radical intentions within Cornell's project are undermined by her faithfulness to the liberal framework from which her work is derived. There is potential for her work to be strategically deployed within the US, and yet, in Sandland's view, it fails to go far enough to challenge the status quo, particularly in areas of race and of sexuality. This is unfortunate, given that Cornell appears to be very conscious of issues of race and sexuality. Sandland's criticism is not that she is guilty of neglect in these areas, but that she centres on the way in which her position on legal (non-)intervention, involving a simple transposition of a complex theoretical framework into 'law', can lack political acumen and endorse conservatism. As such, Sandland's paper can be seen as an application of and complement to Bottomley's thesis – that theory cannot serve as a 'shortcut' to the legal answer to political, social or cultural problems raised by the tensions between identity and difference, self and other.

FEMINIST THEORY AND OTHER 'MINORITY' POSITIONS

Sandland's chapter is also concerned with the way in which different critical perspectives can become blind to that which is 'other'. He considers, for example, the way in which Moran's[10] discussion of the tests for homosexuality within the military fails to critique the extent to which they are predicated upon a link between homosexuality and a stereotyped view of 'feminine' behaviour. The relationship between feminism and other forms of oppression is a further reoccurring theme within the book. Sandland brings out the difficulty of conceptualising the interaction between different forms of

---

10 Moran, L, 'The homosexualization of English law', in Herman, D and Stychin, C (eds), *Legal Inversions: Lesbians, Gay Men and the Politics of the Law*, 1995, Philadelphia: Temple UP.

oppression and of resistance. Similarly, Porter considers concerns that have been directed at Irigaray over this issue. Irigaray's work has been controversial because of the way in which it prioritises sexual difference rather than issues such as race, sexuality and class. In Irigaray's defence, Porter points to the arguments for radical alterity, particularly in her earlier work, and the way in which this has offered a potential model for thinking about racial difference.

The possibility of using too general a model and ignoring the historical specificity of particular struggles is obvious. This is linked with the subsumption of woman within, or as representative of, a generalised 'other' or 'minority' in a manner which elides, for example, the specific problems of black women. Sara Ahmed discusses the way in which third world women are positioned as 'a symptom of underdevelopment' in her deconstructive reading of the Beijing Platform for Action 1995. Similarly, Deutscher illustrates the problem of applying arguments for representation of those who historically have a common culture (derived from race theory) to women. She argues that these well meaning attempts to have 'women's voices' heard is problematic. This is not simply because women do not have a common culture. Both Ahmed and Deutscher draw upon the poststructuralist argument that women (and other groups) do not exist as a fixed group prior to the operation of law. They make the point that law (and other legal discourses, such as the Beijing Platform for Action and legal constitutions) is involved in actually producing images (frequently overlapping and conflicting) of what it is to be a woman.

Purdom, employing the work of Gilles Deleuze, employs the term 'minoritarian' to describe any oppressed 'minority' group, even when (paradoxically) that minority can be numerically larger than the so called majority. Although she employs a very different framework from that of Battersby (discussed by Richardson), she also wants to draw upon the 'minority' status of women and their failure to fit within a system that has been defined by male standards. She uses the position of women – and other minorities – in order to question the very act of judging. David Bell and Jon Binnie also draw upon the position of a 'minority', using queer theory to outline and explore the varied contemporary concepts of sexual citizenship and the potential to mobilise such concepts in the context of consumption, marriage and military service.

SUMMARIES

We hope to have illustrated some of the common threads that run in and out of this diverse collection of work. Whilst using these categories for heuristic purposes, it is clear that they are interdependent. In a sense, all the chapters deal with these issues and have, therefore, been discussed broadly to bring out these central themes. We have divided them into sections in order to emphasise particular themes. However, chapters that appear under one heading could, with a slightly different emphasis, inform the debates within other sections.

Theory and practice: utopia, impossibility and the philosophical imagination

Anne Bottomley's paper discusses the uses and abuses of theory by feminists in law schools. Bottomley is concerned that the current relationship between feminist legal studies and feminist theory is awkward and problematic, with discussion of the role and importance of theory likely to drive a wedge between feminists in terms of those who feel comfortable 'doing theory' and those who do not. Bottomley feels comfortable 'doing theory' but not about the fact that 'theory' can be so divisive.

Moreover, Bottomley argues, the solution is not for all simply to embrace theory. Part of the problem of theory lies in its seductive qualities. Law has historically been seen as less academic and more vocational than the social sciences and the humanities. For lawyers, therefore, part of the 'seduction of theory' is that its use can give academic credibility (gendered male) to legal research and writing. In addition, this buys into the view that academic knowledge is disinterested and apolitical, which is a problem for a movement like feminism, which is overtly political in nature. At another level, 'theory' can seem to hold out the promise of intellectual fulfilment, with the importation of theory into law schools bringing us closer to discovering the truth about law. Here, the seduction of theory is more nefarious and opaque: it is the seduction of the easy answer, the problem solved. It is the false promise of the quick fix.

Bottomley is also concerned at the way in which the dynamics of this process are conceptualised. The notion of the 'importation' of theory 'into' law schools and legal analysis is dangerously conservative of a particular conception of legal study and relevant materials. Theory is 'brought to' the statutes and cases that are taken by lawyers to be the staple legally relevant materials. This tends to confirm both the 'revelatory model' of legal research (which assumes law is a secret to be unwrapped), and the view that these *are* the only relevant focus of 'legal' research. For Bottomley, this is the 'passive' use of theory, by which she means 'the tendency to "use" and "apply" theory, rather than explore it'.[11] In the later stages of her argument, Bottomley turns to Deleuze to help articulate an approach to theory which does not deny its politics in fruitless (and counter-productive) pursuit of 'objectivity' and which

---

11 See below, p 36.

does not start from the presumption of a 'lack' in feminist legal studies which theory can fill. Instead, she argues for an approach that looks to 'theory' to engage with the politics of 'feminism' and the practicalities of 'law', which starts somewhere beyond the assumption that we will be faced with 'either/or' choices, and beyond the assumption that the role of theory is to provide for us the 'truth' that we 'lack'. On this view, theory is part of a process, a constant interaction between discrete, if overlapping, parts, not an end in itself, nor the means to any 'end' as such.

In her chapter, Sara Ahmed deconstructs the rhetoric used in the Beijing Platform for Action 1995. She considers the way in which women are entered into the rhetoric of global justice *as women*. For example, in Hillary Clinton's address, in which she talks about human rights as a preface to the UN conference, she argues that, if women are healthy, then their families will flourish. Here, Ahmed argues, the term 'their families' is working to link women's concerns and those of international politics. So, the woman's traditional position within the family closes down the gap between private and public, local and global.

Ahmed draws upon Derrida's influential essay, 'Forces of law: the mystical foundations of authority'.[12] In the essay, Derrida points to the fact that the US Constitution starts with 'We the people', and yet its creation represents the moment at which they are to be constituted as a people. So, it performs an act of creating this conception of 'the people' by purporting to describe them as already existing as a group. Similarly, Ahmed looks at the way in which 'global women' are to be constituted at and by conferences such as that in Beijing. She considers its performative function. Further, Derrida argues that 'deconstruction is justice'.[13] By this he means that the fact that it is impossible to decide whether or not a judgment is just, at the time when it is decided, means that it is impossible to actually define precise rules for justice. Justice is something that must be aimed at. This is what is meant by his argument that 'justice is an experience of the impossible',[14] that (*contra* Kant) it is impossible to know that a judgment is made justly by an appeal to rules.[15] It is this impossibility that opens up the possibility of justice.

Ahmed uses Derrida but is also concerned with a constructive project. She interprets the failure of international conferences to vocalise one voice of woman as positive. By failing to define one voice, justice remains possible. She

---

12 (1990) 11 Cardoza L Rev 921.

13 *Ibid*, p 945.

14 *Ibid*, p 947.

15 It is this aspect of the essay that Cornell (whose work is discussed in this volume by both Sandland, Chapter 5 and Richardson, Chapter 6) has used to justify her utopian position, by arguing (to put it crudely) that we do not know that justice is impossible to attain.

speculates about the chance encounters in corridors and uses the work of Spivak[16] to argue that the possibility of global justice occurs, not necessarily in the corridors of power *per se*, but in the intimacy of face to face encounters with singular women. This involves trying to think of social activism in a way that avoids the reification of a group. So, alliances do not depend upon pre-existing identities. Work is done to shape identities and alliances through these meetings. She argues against 'universalism or cultural relativism (where one either assumes one knows in advance what is justice, or one assumes that it is impossible to make judgments)'[17] to stress a politics of action, involving this work with others.

Penelope Deutscher's chapter, like Ahmed's paper, is concerned with a framework in which identities are not defined prior to their treatment in law. She is also concerned with the question of 'impossibility'. Whereas Ahmed focuses upon the impossibility of defining specific rules to ensure justice (which then opens up the possibility of justice), Deutscher considers the impossibility of Luce Irigaray's claim for specific women's rights. It is the impossibility of this claim, she argues, that makes it so important.

Like Sandland's chapter, discussed below, this chapter deals with the question of myths and the philosophical imaginary. Deutscher notes that Irigaray has been relatively neglected as a theorist and focuses, in particular, on her usefulness for a consideration of the politics of recognition. Claims for recognition derive mainly from work within race theory, in which a cultural group is viewed as having different characteristics from the majority, which demand representation. As discussed above, Deutscher shares Ahmed's disquiet about the idea of a fixed identity being represented and the specificity that is lost by this move. The problem is perhaps even clearer when the case of women is considered, because women could not be viewed as sharing a common culture at all. Nevertheless, Tully has used work by Gilligan to argue that there may be ways of thinking and acting that are specific to women as a group. Like Ahmed, Deutscher uses Derrida to make the point that 'what is proper to a culture is to not be identical to itself'.[18] In other words, this idea of a fixed identity that should be given expression by the constitution is rejected in favour of a consideration of the ways in which constitutions are productive in actually defining a group – by focusing upon certain characteristics of its members to the exclusion of their individual specificity. Deutscher goes on to develop her argument that Irigaray offers a useful way of reworking the politics of recognition. This is done by considering an aspect of Irigarayian sexual difference that is often neglected: its status as impossible.

---

16 Spivak, GC, 'Claiming transformations: travel notes with pictures', in Ahmed, S *et al* (eds), *Transformations: Thinking through Feminism,* 2000, London: Routledge.

17 Below, p 69.

18 Below, p 75, citing Derrida, J, *The Other Heading: Reflections on Today's Europe*, 1992, Bloomington: Indiana UP.

In his chapter, Ralph Sandland points out that, within feminism, one role of utopian thinking is to maintain a radical aspecificity of the subject, to keep 'the self' open as a place where constant reinvention is possible. But, he argues, feminism has so far been less willing to apply these ideas to its own constitution as some sort of a 'self'. What are the gains and losses that accrue from the division of critical approaches into camps labelled, for example, 'feminism', 'queer theory' or 'critical race theory'? Sandland argues that thinking utopianism at this level implies that these borders be interrogated and rendered problematic, and seeks to show how, if this is not done, various critical perspectives can conspire in maintaining the system of normative classification in which male, white, straight men are defined as the measure of neutrality. Of course, it has long been acknowledged that this is 'the problem'. Sandland's argument is that feminism, along with other critical theories, has yet to understand fully its own part in its constitution.

However, Sandland argues that this project must be thought of as distinct from the project of critical intervention in law. The former amounts to the call to resist 'closure', or constantly to challenge the assumption that the words and ideas we use rest on some sound footing. Since, for example, 'feminism' implies an 'other' – that which is not 'feminism', we need constantly to be vigilant about what gets counted in and what gets counted out, and with what effects, in this process. In the context set as part of intervention in, or dialogue with, law, legal concepts, ideas, procedures and possibilities, different considerations apply. Sandland argues that, if intervention in law is to have any purchase, it must be in the form of, albeit temporary, contingent, and strategically deployed, 'closures'. In other words, it is necessary to form arguments in terms of right and wrong, using legal ideas and concepts such as 'justice' and 'rights': to talk, for example, of 'women's rights', even if, in theoretical terms, we would want to resist such concepts. For Sandland, this is not to betray theoretical insights into the contingency or dangers of 'identity' as the basis for politics, but is to remain true to the utopian impulse as an injunction to 'do justice', to do the best we can in the situation as it is with the means available to us, even though we know that this strategy is inherently problematic. The error, he argues, is to conflate the two projects, rather than let each inform the other through the development of a reflexive dynamic.

Legal subjectivity: the person, self and other

In her chapter, Janice Richardson considers the questions: What does it mean to be a person or to have (or to be) a 'self'? What is the relationship between this image of being a person/self and the law?. This is done by considering the work of two contemporary feminist philosophers, Drucilla Cornell and Christine Battersby, both of whom radically rework different aspects of Kantian theory.

Historically, women were not classed as 'persons' in law. The common wisdom is that, as women now have legal personality, they should be satisfied. Yet, as discussed above, the way in which women are to be viewed in law has led to the equality/difference debate. For example, women have (pragmatically) claimed equal rights with men by claiming to be like men, but then faced problems when dismissal for reasons of pregnancy, for example, was originally viewed as being without a remedy because there was no male comparator. In other words, women lost unfair dismissal claims on the grounds of pregnancy because they could not show that pregnant men would not get sacked!

Cornell avoids the problem of women being 'added into' law, in so far as they are like men, by keeping open the image of what it means to be a person. In a move that concerns Richardson, law is called upon to defend and 'to keep open space' in which people can be allowed to define themselves. Richardson argues that this view of law is too 'top-down' and that it does not have the ability, in practice, to keep open space. This space in which, for example, a woman who has been sexually harassed aims to defend herself, is filled with paperwork, speeches and stereotypes.

For a different model of the self and, potentially, of the law, Richardson turns to the work of a contemporary feminist philosopher, Christine Battersby. In Battersby's work, the self emerges out of difference in a manner that lays emphasis less upon the 'imaginary domain' of Cornell than upon repeated bodily habits and rhythms. The use of this model is to produce a more 'bottom-up' model of both the self and the law.

In Ewan Porter's chapter, the questions of equality/difference and models of the self continue to be discussed. Here, Porter compares the early and later work of Luce Irigaray and draws a different conclusion about the later work from that of Deutscher.[19] He argues that Irigaray's earlier work is particularly useful in thinking about the equality/difference debate. Irigaray reworks philosophy and psychoanalysis to illustrate the ways in which they have been grounded upon the exclusions of women. As discussed above, Porter outlines and supports her early work, which questions the way in which women are measured against male standards. It illustrates how philosophers have considered universal notions of person and self which, when examined, turn out to assume the male body and lifestyle as the norm. Porter illustrates this with a sketch of the way in which Irigaray deals with Lacan and Kant and, later, with Hegel.

However, he is critical of the way in which she later starts to use the heterosexual couple as a model – compared to her earlier work, in which she was interested in women amongst themselves. She appears to set up a hierarchy of differences, so that sex differences count more than issues of

---

19 See Chapter 4, in this volume.

sexuality or race. In discussing the rights that are suggested by Irigaray, he points to the argument by Gail Schwab[20] that Irigaray proposes a principle of equivalence, and considers her influence upon Cornell and upon the question of recognition.

Drawing from a very different framework, Alison Assiter argues for a conception of 'the good' and of 'common humanity' based upon needs. Whilst starting with a conception of 'the human' that is necessarily embedded within culture, she argues that it is possible to go too far in viewing the identity of individuals as being 'constituted' in different communities or by 'discursive practices'. Against the contemporary trend within feminist theory, she argues for the concept of objective human needs, examining four arguments against this position. She concludes that:

> Far from the existence of 'objective' non-expressed needs which are incompatible with individual liberty, then, on the contrary, the satisfaction of basic needs is a precondition of anyone being free to do anything at all.[21]

She defends her argument against any claims that it is so broad as to cover other animals by expressing her sympathy with more ecological – and less anthropomorphic – approaches. In other words, she is sympathetic to calls for animal 'rights' on the grounds of need. Against much contemporary theory, including Irigaray (discussed in later chapters), she links a 'universal human nature' with the possibility of 'universal values' based upon need. She further suggests that our 'cultural imaginary' is only 'contingently plural'. She implicitly takes issue with much contemporary theory, derived from Nietzsche and Foucault, to argue that, even if powerful groups have falsely been able to argue that their needs and desires represent rationally grounded principles, this is not necessarily always the case. In other words, she suggests that an objective morality can be derived from needs and, further, argues that needs can be separated from values.

In the final section, she turns to a discussion of the position of women, who have been traditionally viewed as outside 'humanity'. She points out that femininity has been linked with nature, and masculinity with reason. Whilst Descartes did view his method as applying to everyone, including women, Assiter argues that to base 'common humanity' upon reason is to generalise from the experiences of certain men. In contrast, she argues for a generalisation based upon material needs; that is, we are all beings with certain material needs, for example, for air, food and shelter. She then shifts this 'common humanity' to argue that, just as there are specific material needs of all humanity, there may be specific needs of women as a group linked with

---

20 Schwab, G, 'Women and the law in Irigarayan theory' (1996) 27 Metaphilosophy 152.
21 See below, p 158.

maternity. She recognises the historical danger of this 'difference approach' to law but clearly feels that more can be gained by this approach.

'Minoritarian politics'

The term 'minoritarian' is deployed to describe groups whose position is not viewed as the 'norm or universal' within society, irrespective of their number. In their chapter, David Bell and Jon Binnie discuss the notion of 'sexual citizenship', bringing together issues raised within both feminist and queer theory. Again, the central questions are concerned with the practical implications of the use of the term. They ask, 'Is the concept of citizen the best way to mobilize sexual politics? Who is a sexual citizen? How can we use the notion to begin to interrogate the intersections of law, politics and identity?'.

Bell and Binnie start by critically discussing various proposals for thinking about sexual citizenship. They then draw out their own position by looking in detail at three areas in which 'sexual citizenship' has been used: within the 'pink economy'; the issue of gay marriage; and, finally, the issue of gays in the military. They note the way in which some commentators have viewed lesbian and gay rights as commodities to be bought and sold on the open market. Naïvely, some have welcomed this, with capitalism being viewed as opening up the possibility of rights! This illustrates the way in which liberal gay rights theorists, just like liberal feminists, are not necessarily critical of other forms of exploitation, not only in terms of race, but also in relation to class.[22] However, the queer movement, in common with feminism, has tended to have a much more radical agenda than simply aiming to be just as exploited as (that problematic construction) straight white men.

Similar questions of assimilation are raised by asking whether it could ever be useful to promote marriage, that outmoded institution that relates to the safeguarding of property, even in the form of gay marriage. Bell and Binnie contrast 'gay liberation's utopian social project', in which gay culture leads, with the pro-family agenda of liberal reform. They consider the argument that gay marriages can destabilise the meaning of marriage by illustrating its constructedness and whether this is ultimately recouperable. The discussion about 'gays in the military' raises debates, in common with feminist theory, about the construction of identity. They consider Judith Butler's arguments[23] that it is the military that set up the definition of being

---

22 See Coole, D, 'Is class a difference that makes a difference?' (1996) 77 Radical Philosophy 17.

23 It should be noted that Judith Butler has a different model of identity from that of the other theorists discussed in the other chapters in this volume. (See, eg, Benhabib, S, Butler, J, Cornell, D and Fraser, N, *Feminist Contentions: A Philosophical Exchange*, 1995, London: Routledge.) This has not been expanded upon in detail because it is not central to Bell and Binnie's argument. Butler's position is also discussed in Purdom, Chapter 11, in this volume.

gay (a point also considered within Sandland's chapter). In their conclusion, they return to the relationship between theory and political practice, stressing the need for theory to be attentive to 'the lives and experiences we theorise about'.

There are at least two senses in which the following chapter, by Qudsia Mirza, could be classified as minoritarian. First, women within Islam could clearly be viewed as being positioned as a 'minority'. Mirza considers the arguments for an interpretation of Islam and Islamic law derived from the *Qur'an*, which views women as equal and acknowledges their lost position as active interpreters of the Islamic texts. Secondly, the position of Islam itself can be viewed as a minoritarian position in the West. For Western lawyers and feminists, it takes a leap of the imagination to think oneself into the framework of the legal system described by Mirza and the debates that she raises. It is for these reasons that the chapter can be situated within the final section.

However, like the other chapters, this contribution could also be viewed as overlapping with other themes. It picks up the question of the role of utopia and the philosophical imagination raised within Part I of this volume. This is raised in an unusual manner. Whereas the earlier contributors were concerned about keeping open a future utopia, which is to inform our law, Mirza discusses the way in which Islam looks back to an *earlier* utopia. The role of law is, then, to attempt to recreate this utopia in the present. Her concern with not only utopia, but the historical position of women, resonates with some of the discussions about the work of Irigaray.

In the final chapter, Judy Purdom draws upon the work of Moira Gatens, through Spinoza and Deleuze, to think about shame. Shame is used in order to focus upon misogynist images of women, the act of judging and, ultimately, as a way of mobilising dissent. Purdom starts by asking, 'Why is it that rape is equated with degradation and shame? What conception of women and the body does rape assume?'. She points out that shame is attached to the female body as much as it is to women's behaviour, and links this shame with the paradoxical position of women within liberal democratic societies. They are viewed as free citizens, and yet are still treated as if under the natural authority of men. Purdom extends Gatens' arguments to discuss the shame of women within rape trials, arguing that shame is symptomatic of their exclusion from the body politic. She quotes Deleuze, who argues that 'it is shame that forces philosophy to be political philosophy'[24] and asks whether this shame could be 'a source of strength and a possible impetus to exposing and then resisting the paradoxical exclusion of women from the body politic'.[25]

---

24   Deleuze, G and Guattari, F, *What is Philosophy?*, 1994, London: Verso, p 110.
25   See below, p 213.

Citing Gatens, she points to the way in which judges' imagination (in the Spinozan sense as that which is derived from experience) is coloured by their experience of women (normally in subordinate roles as secretaries or wives) and how this informs their decisions to women's detriment. Employing Deleuze, she problematises the broader activity of judging itself:

> Judging consists in treating the entirety of the visible as material for surveying rather than educating, always relating it to something else, the memory of a latent content that explains it, the pre-existent values according to which it is assessed.[26]

Purdom uses this to think about the way in which judging (in the specific sense of judicial decision making) involves concern with *minutiae*:

> It is as if the more one surveys, the more one knows, the more accurate the assessment against transcendent norms and the more 'reasonable' the judgment. But what is clear from the institutionalism of sexism within liberal democracy is that such 'surveying' is an inquisition that can only exacerbate women's failings.[27]

She does not use this as an argument simply to dismiss struggles for legal recognition, but to argue that this should not define the extent of the struggle.

Deleuze stresses the importance of what is 'minoritarian' (the position of 'minorities' that include women, lesbians and gays and racial minorities, amongst others) and their ability to resist 'capture'. Purdom mobilises this idea to think what it would be for women to be unashamed. In this final utopian image, which also engages with theories of identity and the relationship between theory and political practice, 'minorities', including women, are viewed as less invested in conventional fixed ways of behaving and can use this position to experiment and to invent different ways of living. But, of course, it is not truly a final image. The logic of minoritarianism, it must follow, is also relevant to those of us who tend to be constituted as part of the 'majority'. However each of us is mapped onto the grid of possibilities constituted by what might be termed 'majoritarianism', there is always scope for reimagination; and in this there can be no finality.

---

26 Gatens, M, 'Through the Spinozist lens: ethology, difference and power', in Patton, P (ed), *Deleuze: A Critical Reader*, 1996, Oxford: Blackwell, p 165.

27 See below, p 216.

PART I

THEORY AND PRACTICE: UTOPIA, IMPOSSIBILITY AND THE PHILOSOPHICAL IMAGINATION

CHAPTER 2

THEORY IS A PROCESS NOT AN END: A FEMINIST APPROACH TO THE PRACTICE OF THEORY

Anne Bottomley[1]

My paper is not, initially at least, concerned with engaging with theory *per se*; rather, it is concerned with an exploration of the idea of theory and its use by feminists in law schools. I want to address a broader audience than those who feel comfortable, and conversant, with current theoretical developments. Whilst many of these developments reflect the ease with which an increasing number of academic lawyers engage with theory, we are in danger of reproducing a division, which is familiar in all law schools, between the theorists and 'the rest of us'. To a great extent, this will always be the case, but there is a general issue for critical lawyers in relation to trying to militate against a division between work on theory and work on law, and a specific issue for feminists, who, I would argue, cannot, for political reasons, refuse an engagement with law and must, therefore, strive to relate theory with law.

However, there is an extra difficulty which I need to explore in my analysis of 'our present condition': it is my contention that much work in/on law by feminists, whilst drawing on theoretical insights, remains entrapped in heritages which are reductive in their use of theory and, therefore, of their insights into law. I shall refer to this work as sustained by 'the feminist imperative' and 'passive' in its use of theory. I shall argue that part of the problem lies within the idea of 'theory' as something to be used rather than a process of use in itself. My major point here is not to assert another theoretical structure, another theory to be applied; it is rather to use the insights made possible by Deleuze to argue for a new engagement with the project of theorising, which, I hope, will be of value to feminists working within law.

There are clearly developments in legal work which are progressive and enabling. Part of my task is to signal these developments and to argue that they can be seen as the harbingers of a new engagement with the enterprise of theory, which offers very rich possibilities for feminists. However, in order to fulfil this potential, we have to overcome (let go of) a number of expectations that many of us still hold about the idea and use of theory.

---

1   My most immediate thanks go to Ralph and Janice for their patience and support – in particular in pointing out to me that recovering health was more important than trying to keep going against the odds. The long genesis of the ideas expressed here was helped, and at times usefully hindered, by conversations with Chris Stanley, Andrew Dart and Nathan Moore; I acknowledge my debt to all three of them. My thanks also, as ever, to Belinda and Derek Meteyard and, finally, to Hilary Lim, Joanne Conaghan and Beatrice Bottomley, who have all encouraged me more than they realise.

My starting point is to reflect on the fact that, whilst feminism might hold us together in an increasing number of feminist activities – from courses to conferences, from journals to books – as both lawyers and feminists, we have inherited a very problematic attitude towards, and engagement with, the idea of 'theory'.

A group of women, all academics working in law schools and all of whom would identify themselves as feminists, were sitting on a grassy bank, enjoying the sun. The conversation, as with so many post-prandial conversations, was rather desultory, but became animated when one of the women (a visitor from overseas) began to lament the lack of theoretical work amongst feminists in law schools and to say how impoverished, in particular, she found the English. This theme was enthusiastically taken up by a small number of the group, whilst others fell silent. It was as if we were suddenly divided between those of us who could 'share' the perspective of the critique, and the rest of us, who somehow represented the failure and were silenced by that failure. I really do not know how the others were experiencing this scenario – I have not talked to any of them about it since. What I experienced was an overwhelming sense that this was all somehow very wrong, anger with the way in which the scene was being played out in front of me and frustration that I could not begin to verbalise why it was all so wrong. In the end, I withdrew, rather rudely and pre-emptively, having realised that I could not ignore my overwhelming sense of alienation but neither could I usefully verbalise it, because I simply, at that stage, did not understand it. Could it be that I was simply feeling defensive in the face of such a vehement attack? Or that I was feeling protective towards a group of women whose discomfort with the critique was palpable? As I went away and initially 'worried through' my reaction to the scene, I had to consider both of these possibilities as reasons for my response – but the level of anger I felt suggested something much stronger and deeper than either of these factors; a frustration which came from, it seemed, an emotive recognition that the whole discussion was deeply flawed and that this had something to do with the way in which the idea of theory was being used and, especially, the idea of feminist theory. I didn't know what it was that made it so flawed – my response was entirely emotional. I simply felt an overwhelming sense of negativity and a compelling need to try to understand, intellectually, why I had responded in this way.

I look back on this scene as the beginning of an intellectual (and political) struggle within myself that led me to a series of difficult questions and a necessary period of absenting myself from entering into debates within/around feminist-legal-theory. It was an epiphany which, initially, distanced me, in a very radical way, from so much of what was going on around me. Why had the idea of theory, and specifically feminist theory, had such a negative effect on a group of women who were all articulate, active academics and feminists? It was not simply the force with which the critique of the lack of theory had been put; it was the response to the critique which interested me, and the fact that the whole event had been so divisive.

As I began to work through my own responses to the scenario, and tried to ground them intellectually, a sense of disjuncture developed. It was a strange experience to be surrounded by evidence of an increasing presence of feminist work in law schools, and yet to feel distanced from so much of it. To many feminists, this has been simply a time to celebrate and to push forward, welcoming new developments with an increased assurance and momentum. I did not feel the same confidence, and the speed of some of the developments simply left me feeling isolated, as well as worried. But the depths of my concerns, as well as the fact that I had such difficulty articulating them, effectively silenced me. To begin to try to give voice, to find voice, in this context seemed at best downbeat and at worst heretical. Yet the scene on the bank revealed one great disjuncture – between feminist work on law and a forceful critique of lack-of-theory.

Now, looking back, it is difficult to untangle a personal journey from a more generalised sense of dissatisfaction and concern with 'feminist work'. I think that it is relevant that my early academic life was formed within the context of a very active women's movement and that the dissipation of that movement has left me without a location outside the academy. Equally, I think that it is very relevant that the younger women working as feminists have a very different sense of, and experience of, the politics of feminism. Further, my own academic history covers periods in which the study of law was contested within the academy – periods in which being 'a lawyer' was regarded as academically suspect and 'lawyers' were not at all sure about their academic identity. This colours my own sense of an academic project for law, but, equally, there is an emerging generation of academic lawyers who do not bear quite the confused heritage which was (is) my burden. So I am aware that much of my critique and concerns carry the marks of my generation and my own history, but I believe that this heritage does have a continuing relevance, as a context not merely to my own narrative, but also to the continuing and developing project of feminist work on law. The purpose of my paper is to explore this project and, initially, to argue two points:

(a) that the idea of feminist-legal-theory can, too easily, become a seductive trap, a place into which we project our desire for answers, in order, we think, to complete a feminist project;

(b) that the allure of feminist-legal-theory is made possible by our encounter with theory as external to ourselves, as lawyers, and is required by our faith, as feminists, that we have a specifically feminist project.

I shall argue that, by understanding the allure and seduction of the idea of feminist-legal-theory, and the many institutional factors which feed this process, we can begin to use theory in a more productive way. By emphasising the use of theory, we can give greater theoretical credence to the major strength of feminist work on law: an engagement with law which explores feminism, law and theory as ongoing and continuing projects.

There are three threads to my argument, which I will draw out and then weave together in my exploration of the tapestry of feminist-legal-theory:

(1) the problematic division between theoretical work and work in/on law;

(2) how, in the use made of 'theory' in current work in/on law, which I will characterise as 'passive' work, certain expectations are placed on the idea of theory, as opposed to

(3) an active engagement with theory/law, which problematises the very idea of theory.

SEDUCED BY THEORY

Track one: the lawyer's story

I want to suggest some of the factors which I think made possible the 'scene on the grassy bank'. Primarily, these factors derive, I believe, from the fact that all of the women present were academic lawyers. [2]

Lawyers have a difficult relationship with the rest of the academy – it is not merely that we are associated with the teaching of degrees, which are viewed by many as essentially vocational, but rather that it is presumed by other academics that we are somehow limited to (and by) a study of law which is content-based (a learning of rules), or, at its best, method-based (an exposition of how those rules were reached and how they are now to be applied). Lawyers are not seen as making an academic contribution to the larger academy – despite brave attempts in periods of institutional growth to context legal work within a cross- (or even multi-) disciplinary approach, in periods of institutional constraints, the value of lawyers is simply in the numbers of students we can recruit. Under the pressure of limited resources, lawyers have colluded in reproducing an image of law schools as essentially training grounds for lawyers, recruiting large numbers of students, thereby commanding limited resources and protecting our jobs more successfully than our more 'academic' colleagues.

But, behind these institutional trends, the question is, what is actually going on in law schools? And here, one has to admit to the fact that, despite a great deal of good and innovative work, there are still three predominate features in the majority of law schools. First, a great deal of boring, undigested, uncontextualised doctrinal detail constitutes the major part of the

---

2   I began to explore these ideas in a paper given in 1993 and published as 'Feminism, the desire for theory and the use of law', in Barnett, H, *Sourcebook on Feminist Jurisprudence*, 1997, London: Cavendish Publishing, pp 84–91.

diet of most undergraduates and, therefore, of most of their teachers. Substantive law teaching has changed little. Secondly, where interesting work does find a place, it tends to be on the margins of the curriculum and taught by people who feel that they have 'escaped' the stasis of substantive material and then do their best to keep a distance from this material, fearing entrapment should they come too close to it. Thirdly, for lawyers who are really interested in theoretical work, we suffer a strange triangulation. The traditional theoretical site for a lawyer is the study of jurisprudence, but here, despite valiant efforts, it is difficult to break free from a presumption that one is working within a terrain which is limited by Austin to the study and understanding of law; by positivism to the study of (or rather search for) certainties; by liberalism to the pinning down of the key concepts of equality and justice; and by the teachers of jurisprudence to a geography of key ideas to which one simply adds chapters of knowledge areas to the established canons of the texts. If one moves out of jurisprudence to a study of broader philosophical ideas (perhaps encountering some history and even, possibly, literature), then one is in the terrain marked 'humanities': please apply to the AHRB for funding. If, however, one's interest is in the operation and practice of law, then this is the terrain of the social sciences: please apply to the ESRC for funding.

Lawyers who are working with theoretical ideas could be working within, or over, any of these three sites. It is even more problematic when one remembers that doctrinal work is deemed 'humanities'. This division does not impede work which neatly fits a humanities/social science divide or does not require funding! But it does carry two important messages for lawyers: first, that we do not have one 'place' in which to develop our work. In fact, it reminds us that, whilst, historically, we were viewed as one of the liberal arts, it was the dominance of the social sciences in the mid-20th century which enabled, but also constrained, a great deal of work on law. This dual heritage has created a rather mixed message for much contemporary work on law, especially for feminists, and, more importantly, the immediate heritage of the social science/law encounter has severely curtailed work on legal doctrine. Secondly, the binary of humanities/social sciences has, I think, effectively reproduced the most significant result for lawyers: a sense of the externality of theory to law and, at another level, the lack of identity for lawyers as academics and, therefore, as theorists.

Our heritage is a complex story, which tends to be rendered, in a very one dimensional account, as a story of 'lack': the lack of a sense of authenticity of ourselves as academics and of our subject as academic.[3] This means that, for many of us, our encounter with 'theory' is rendered problematic from the beginning. It is encountered as an 'addition': an addition to the knowledge of an area of legal rules or an addition to our own identity as 'lawyers'. This trope is made more difficult by the fact that we are still torn between being offered 'method' by the social sciences and 'theory' by the humanities.[4] And, for many of us, that is what it feels like – being offered methodology or theory developed in other subject areas and then seeing how far we can apply it to our own work. Even today, it remains a trajectory of looking outwards and bringing in – rather than finding theory or method implicated in everything we do. And the most deeply embedded aspect of our heritage is a series of presumptions about the idea of theory itself – an idea which we have failed to grapple with because, I believe, we have presumed that theory is a given, an identity constructed in another place, about which we, as mere lawyers, simply seem to have one choice: whether or not to use it.

This condition is the condition of the majority of legal academics – feminists do not escape it, we work within it. Indeed, a major problem which many feminist academic lawyers have faced in the past is a critique of their

---

3   See, further, Bottomley, A, 'Lessons from the classroom: some aspects of the "socio" in "legal" education', in Thomas, P (ed), *Socio-Legal Studies*, 1997, Aldershot: Dartmouth, pp 163–84. See, also, the trenchant comments of Goodrich, P, 'The critic's love of the law: intimate observations on an insular jurisdiction' (1999) 10(3) LC 343.

4   I am well aware that these divisions between subject areas (and the false division between the idea of methodology and the idea of theory) are constructs which are increasingly contended, and that the major thematic ideas of the last decade(s) have permeated all the subject areas and challenged subject boundaries. However, institutional constraints have often limited a full transformation of the way in which we think and designate ourselves in relation to our subject areas. Despite the growth in the new universities of such subjects as 'cultural studies', one still has, for instance, geographers and sociologists writing very similar material in very similar ways but publishing their books under the designations of 'geography' and 'sociology', even when chapters of the books worry about why they are so designated. Furthermore, lawyers tend to remain isolated from much of this and still reach out to the academy, using presumptions about the core identity of the social sciences or the humanities subjects; rather as 'they' make presumptions about what 'we' are doing without encountering and recognising the diversity within law schools. The puzzle of social science/humanities is interestingly played out in the dilemma faced by the Socio-Legal Studies Association (see *ibid*, Bottomley). Equally, many critical lawyers tend to presume that they are working within the humanities; but the divisions are becoming increasingly blurred and unsustainable.

work as lacking theory because they are lawyers, thereby rendering their work problematic as feminists as well as as scholars.[5]

Initially, I recognised that my emotional confusion and anger stemmed in large part from my sense of being put into a place of choice. I was being offered a chance to identify with the 'theorists', as opposed to the 'non-theorists', who, in the terms of this conversation, represented the majority of feminists in law schools. It was quite clearly implied that the lack-of-theory, for whatever reason that there was a lack, was a demeaning factor: these were feminists who were not truly academic because they were not 'doing theory'. And, as represented by the women present that day, this 'lack-of-theory' was a rather shameful fact that one didn't like to admit to. However, it was clear that it was not sufficient to declare oneself 'for-theory', unless one could display that one 'had it'. In other words, we were being divided into the 'theorists' and the 'non-theorists' and the claim to ownership of theory was a claim to be displayed. It was a 'place of choice': a place in which to declare one's self, to declare which side of the line one was on. And yet, crucially for me, it was no 'position of choice'; I knew the terrain but the map was not one with which I could identify, nor one which I wished to use. It was, in fact, doubly crucial for me: I wanted to be able to lay claim to theory. I wanted to for two reasons: first, because I myself had often lamented the lack of theoretical perspective both in law schools and in feminist work; and, secondly, because, in the immediate scenario, I could then be with the angels! But to side with the angels would be to refuse not only the other women but also my own sense that this was all wrong. The 'place of choice' had to be vacated: because of the strong divisions it created between us, but also, more importantly, because it was premised on an assumption of 'theory' which was unexplored. Those who 'had it' simply asserted the lack of it in others. Those who lacked it simply felt that lack, and, with that lack, a sense of lack of self-worth.

---

5   See, eg, Smart, C, *Feminism and the Power of Law*, 1989, London: Routledge, and 'The women of legal discourse' (1992) SLS 29. She argues that lawyers take law too seriously, in that it is centre stage for them/us, but also that there is too strong an imperative to always be engaging with law, struggles within law and issues of law reform. These factors militate against the development of theory, but a way forward can be found by appreciating, and undertaking, the study of law as a social science. This critique remains important, not only because it represents a classical, social scientists' view of legal academics and reproduces the socio-legal approach established from the 1970s (that is, that the way forward is through the social sciences), but also because it speaks directly to feminists who, by implication, through their engagement with law, are caught not merely by their lack of theory, but by their implicit adherence to the values of law, legality and liberalism. The problem with some of her earlier work especially is that it privileges 'context' and 'process' over doctrinal analysis and does not problematise social science method; see, in particular, Smart, C, *The Ties That Bind: Law, Marriage and the Reproduction of Patriarchal Relations*, 1984, London: Routledge. For a response to her work from within law schools, see Bottomley, A, 'Feminism, the desire for theory and the use of law', in *op cit*, Barnett, fn 2, pp 84–91; Drakopoulou, M, 'Post-modernism and Smart's feminist critical project', in 'Law, Crime and Sexuality' (1997) 5(1) FLS 107; Sandland, R, 'Between "truth" and "difference": poststructuralism, law and the power of feminism' (1995) 3(1) FLS 3.

Track two: the feminist's story

The most significant aspect of this approach to theory is the sense of 'lack'; and, as with all movements which begin with the notion of lack, or absence, the promise (hope, fear) is that, by finding and seizing/embracing the object, we will become complete. Of course, as our crass understanding of psychoanalysis has taught us, there is a double-bind here. Our desire to embrace the other is confused by the fact that the other has been constructed by our own projection. What we experience as lack, we construct as possible to overcome by our encounter with the other.

This is where we begin to encounter the process of seduction as an aspect of desire. Seduction can operate in two ways. First, there is the seduction of the promise – the possibility of being made complete. This form of seduction is most dangerous when we seize the first possibility of seeming completeness and hold on to it for dear life in order to try to maintain a sense of completeness. We defend it with vigour, because it seems that we have secured a place from which we assert 'theory'. Secondly, there is the seduction of imminence. This is even more dangerous territory – we have found an entry point to the place of theory, but we haven't yet finally, quite, caught the actual theory we want. In fact, we have now joined a very selective game which proves just how good we are 'at theory': we can say why others lack quite-the-right-theory and suggest that we have a greater grip on what it might be. We are in play – but our play is based on very clear ground rules. They are still constituted around lack and the promise of final fulfilment.

Feminists have, understandably (given that they are also (in this context!) legal academics), entered into this game with alacrity by adding another twist – the notion of feminism. To law we add theory, and now to theory we add feminism. Feminism, using theory, can interrogate and expose law. Interrogate and expose, because we 'know' that law is not 'feminist' (I will explore this notion later); but what we need is 'theory' (or 'a theory') to identify this cogently, logically and systematically, possibly to explain it (this generally means to find the causal patterns and, for some, original cause(s)), and, through such explanation, to find projects for reformation and to dream of real transformation.

The paradox of feminism, namely, that it is both a strength and a weakness in the academy, is that it is essentially a political project. It is about wanting change – whether in small steps or grand leaps. It is about saying that what we have at present is not enough for us. We, of course, divide on how we think change should be brought about and to what extent it has already been brought about. We also divide on what we think are the most important aspects on which to focus in our desire for change. But one thing holds us together, firmly, and that is the simple truth that all of us continue to see and experience a society in which we, as women, feel discriminated against and (albeit for some of us rarely directly, but often in more general terms) oppressed.[6]

It is trite to recognise that the term 'feminism', as with the term 'feminist', must both be used with care and not be over-generalised. I have tried to find an all-encompassing way of holding together the disparate voices within feminism, but my next move is more difficult. I suggested above that feminism is a political project which tends to presume a critique of law which fulfils the expectation of law as oppressive to women. I do not, cannot, contend that all feminists work on this presumption – indeed, many so called liberal feminists look to law as a potential tool for emancipation, and much contemporary feminist work tries to work with a much more pluralistic and fragmented account of law, in which law is neither a wholly oppressive nor a simple emancipatory tool. But too much work is still caught in a presumption that one is simply seeking theory to reveal that feminist truth that law works against us and never, or only rarely, for us.

I think that there are a number of factors which feed this approach. The first is the experience of theory as external and simply to be applied to legal data. The theory that one tends to look for in these circumstances is one which will confirm the second factor, the expectation that feminism is about revealing the fundamentally flawed and problematic nature of law. These two factors did emerge from, and address, a crucial period in our academic history: when the gendered nature of law was denied by a refusal to consider doctrinal studies in relation to either their social context or consequences, or in relation to emerging theoretical work in other disciplines, most notably the social sciences. However, in too much of what I will term 'passive' work, they have remained defining features past a time when they have any real respectable academic (or political?) credence. Crudely, I would suggest that this work is characterised by a continuing adherence to positivist thinking and, crucially, limits the development of feminist work *on* law by taking very partial legal data to confirm both feminism and the theoretical model being employed, rather than thinking more cogently about law *per se* (or, indeed, the project of feminism and the use of theory!).[7] Certain areas of law are taken as

---

6   I have had three experiences (this academic year), all in relation to work (but not all at my place of work), which left me feeling silenced and belittled. I experienced them as not only incidents of discrimination and sexism, but as very oppressive. Interestingly, in such status ridden times as our own, I held (institutional) seniority in each case but gender was obviously more relevant. Perhaps I should simply characterise these incidents as happening in the last century! But, unfortunately ...

7   See Drakopoulou's concern that too much feminist work is marked by an adherence to an ontological project: 'Women's resolutions of laws reconsidered: *epistemic* shifts and the emergence of feminist legal discourse' (2000) 11 LC 47. Joanne Conaghan explores similar themes and issues but expresses them through a concern with feminist adherence to normative theoretical work: Conaghan, J, 'Revisiting the feminist theoretical project' (2000) 27 JLS 351.

connoting law more generally and then, within these areas, what is extrapolated over and over again are the familiar themes of the revelation of oppression and the failure of the legal system to be able to address the concerns of women. All law can then be condemned and all prejudices and expectations confirmed. This type of work is very satisfying – hence its continued strength and longevity.

I have purposely over-written the previous paragraph. My purpose is not simply to condemn such work,[8] but to argue that it is actually very difficult to escape the complex formed by the lawyers' heritage[9] and the feminist imperative, and that, further, such work is actually welcomed by a (feminist) audience who feel that they can identify with such work.[10]

Susan Edwards, in her book, *Sex, Gender and the Legal Process,*[11] recognises in her introduction that there are many feminisms and says that there is not one 'method' for feminist research, but her critique of law (to be followed in chapters forming case studies) is summed up as an:

> ... endeavour ... to examine law's claims, law's essentialism, law's masculinism and exclusion of women[12] ... [in order to] render masculinity, masculinism, structures of patriarchy – heterosexism as open to account and challenge[13] ... [for] the inexorable fact remains that *inter alia* law is holistically, root and branch, viscerally, temporally male ...[14]

She concludes in her introduction that, in order to survive, we must:

> ... challenge, engage and transform.[15]

This is all brave and powerful political rhetoric (although the very closed image of law she presents leaves one wondering how feminists are to begin to 'engage and transform' beyond the project of revelation and critique); but it remains at the level of rhetoric, for what is asserted here is a feminist

---

8   Indeed, it has produced, and still produces, some very good material; the problem is that this too quickly becomes 'the whole story'.

9   I have written this from within the legal academy – I would, however, add that one of the problems of the isolation of the legal academy is that women from other academic disciplines tend too often to presume 'lack-of-theory' amongst lawyers and are all to ready to offer theory, but with little grounding in, or understanding of, law. This further amplifies the problem.

10   I do not think that this perhaps uncomfortable factor can be ignored. This is what many feminists, particularly students, want; therefore, this work is cited and used with such frequency that it becomes rather like a 'canon' of feminist work on law and feeds the presumption that, from these revelations, feminism can be confirmed and law, necessarily, denied. It is not helped by the fact that so many of our male colleagues also presume that this is 'the feminist academic project', which limits their expectations of our work as feminists.

11   Edwards, S, *Sex, Gender and the Legal Process*, 1996, London: Blackstone.

12   *Ibid*, p 4.

13   *Ibid*, p 6.

14   *Ibid*, p 7.

15   *Ibid*, p 8.

'knowledge' of law which can only but be confirmed in the case studies focused upon. Both theory and law become subsumed in an overwhelming feminist critique.

Nagire Naffine gives a much more considered account of feminist use of theoretical material.[16] It is presented as having moved through first and second stage feminist theory to a third,[17] which:

> ... resists the notion that law represents men's interests in anything like a co-ordinated or uniform fashion ... law is not coherent, logical, internally consistent and rational ...[18]

And, although she cites as 'central to third phase feminism ... an explicit rejection of grand theory',[19] she goes on to add: '... and a commitment to the study of particular instances of women's oppression.'[20]

Therefore, the study of law will concentrate on revelation of oppression (usually, this work focuses on criminal law, family law and work on the 'body of women') through law as the 'truth is that law reflects the priorities of the dominant patriarchal social order'.[21]

Thus, law is confirmed as no more than an oppressive tool and used to confirm the existence of the 'patriarchal social order'. What rejection of grand theory is there in this? 'Law' and 'the patriarchal social order' are, in the final analysis, closed systems.[22] A final example is the rather different project of Hilaire Barnett's introduction to feminist jurisprudence.[23] Here, although she valiantly tries to bring together feminist theory (and methods!) and feminist critiques of traditional jurisprudence, and emphasises the plurality of feminist approaches, a major part of her text is then taken up with the usual case studies and she does not take the opportunity to 'revisit' her 'theoretical material' in any kind of concluding remarks.

---

16 Naffine, N, *Law and the Sexes*, 1990, Sydney: Allen & Unwin.

17 I always worry about accounts which map feminist work through progressive stages. It certainly helps the student to situate material and become aware of the temporal context: it offers an introduction to a range of material and, hence, is attractive as a text. But it feeds two presumptions: one, that we can fit all work into neat models by identifying common, core features; and two, that later work not simply builds on earlier work but builds by a process of lineal development – it gets better and better, a kind of fem Whig version of history.

18 *Ibid*, Naffine, p 12.

19 *Ibid*, Naffine, p 13.

20 *Ibid*, Naffine, p 13.

21 *Ibid*, Naffine, p 13.

22 Even the much more sophisticated Bridgeman, J and Millns, S, *Feminist Perspectives on Law: Law's Engagement with the Female Body*, 1998, London: Sweet & Maxwell, illustrates the difficulty of not becoming entrapped into an elision that the case studies illustrate 'all' law, leaving little, if any, space for an 'engagement with law', which is particularly visible in their conclusion.

23 See *op cit*, Barnett, fn 2.

All of these books offer some valuable material for feminist work, *but* we should differentiate that from a presumption that the trajectories they follow are necessarily the most productive for feminists. The theoretical input into each of them is uneven and I would not want it thought that I am suggesting that they share a common core which allows me to 'frame them' within one group and then critique their shared failings. Rather, I want to read the texts as a disparate grouping which, however, do share a common problem arising from working within the same tropes. The first of these tropes is that they are written and marketed as 'feminist texts', for use (with the possible exception of Edwards) as textbooks on student courses. The most obvious point to make here is that this is welcomed by publishers as assuring sales. But it carries other implications. These texts are primarily marketed to law students; therefore, the introduction to theoretical ideas takes a certain form: here it is, you can use it too. Here are examples, you can add your own. There is no imperative to reveal any deep theoretical problems; rather, what is expected is neat packaging and ease in application – models for use. Therefore, arguably, to cite such texts as problematic in theoretical terms is unfair if the context in which they were produced is not taken into account. However, such texts do become benchmarks of feminist work[24] and can begin to draw not merely directions, but boundaries to feminist work: they feed a culture of expectation. It is at this point that the second trope does become very problematic.

Despite[25] the 'feminist imperative' visible in the work, I have characterised such work as 'passive' in its use of theory. By 'passive' I mean the tendency to 'use' and 'apply' theory, rather than explore it. This passiveness is, I believe, the product of our heritage as lawyers, as well as a consequence of the 'feminist imperative'. The passiveness tends to reproduce a picture of theory which is essentially positivist. It also, despite gestures to the contrary, finds it difficult to break from 'grand theory', despite a recognition of muddle and unevenness, because what is being asserted is the hidden truth of law as part and parcel of a 'patriarchal social order'.[26] The claim to reject grand theory and, rather, look to instances of oppression in law does not work at another level either: the separate instances become a confirmation of 'law', a series of case studies, and, therefore, explicitly or implicitly, a closed model of law is used.

---

24 There really is a sense in which the arrival and acceptance of 'feminist work' in law schools is marked by textbooks, rather than in the plethora of journal articles; it is rather like becoming part of the establishment. Encoded within such publications is the factor of relevant courses existing, established publishers recognising this existence and a feminist 'coming of age' by authors who can sustain material for the length of a book.

25 I was tempted to write here 'because of' rather than 'despite', but this would be to presume a necessary causal link and I shall argue later that this is not necessary at all. The 'despite' should be read as a clue to the later argument.

26 *Op cit*, Naffine, fn 16.

I am reminded, although it comes from a very different direction, of Carol Smart's criticism of legal work as resistant to theory:

> ... a form of resistance to all theory ... based ... on the argument that, because law is a practice which has actual material consequences for women, what is needed in response is counter-practice, not theory. This constituency demands 'practical' engagement and continually renders (mere?) theoretical practice inadequate ... These ... elements present a major obstacle to proponents of feminist legal theory as they (we) are met with the frustrations of being ignored or seen as outmoded in and by law and are simultaneously moved to renounce theory by the oral imperative of doing something in or through law.[27]

This critique was aimed at the interface between political activism and academic work. I have cited it here because it was a critique taken very seriously at the time and, in many ways, the texts I have cited above could be seen as an attempt to answer that critique not by becoming caught in a reformist, incremental, responsive approach, but, rather, by trying to link material together and find patterns in the data, as well as useful theoretical tools with which to explore the data.

Smart argues for a 'clearer vision of law',[28] which moves from a general and totalising theory of law – from which one might try, but will fail, to predict outcomes to specific legal reforms – to, rather, an engagement with law at a different level:

> Law cannot be ignored precisely because of its power to define, but feminism's strategy should be focused on this power rather than on constructing legal policies which only legitimate the legal forum and the form of law ... It is important to resist the temptation that law offers, namely, the promise of a solution. It is equally important to challenge the power of law and to insist on the legitimacy of feminist knowledge and feminism's ability to redefine the wrongs of women which law too often confines to insignificance.[29]

I think that this is very much the project of the texts I have cited – especially Bridgeman and Millns.[30] However, I also think that most of us who have engaged in this type of work do not have any problem with 'resisting the temptation of law'. It may seem that we are open to it because we write on law and are lawyers, but I do not think that that is our problem. What I do think is a problem is having a 'clear vision of law'. So much feminist work is concentrated on the 'revelatory' model that we risk presenting a closed model of law. We limit the possibilities of engagement – we become, in a crucial way,

---

27 *Op cit*, Smart, 1992, fn 5, p 29.
28 *Op cit*, Smart, 1989, fn 5, p 165.
29 *Op cit*, Smart, 1989, fn 5, p 165.
30 *Op cit*, Bridgeman and Millns, fn 22.

passive in the face of the law.[31] I shall argue that this is not merely problematic for the feminist project, but that it is reductive (and passive) in its use of theory. But, before I do so, I want to tease out another implication in Smart's analysis: that is to do with the role of theory.

TAKING THEORY SERIOUSLY

The most obvious, and yet most problematical, response to a critique of work as passive in its use of theory is one which insists on a greater 'purity' in theory; that is, a concern to struggle out of the constraints of the feminist imperative and to engage with theoretical work on, if I can put it this way, its own terms. In an important sense, this also seems to require, initially at least, a distancing from work on law. At its best, this work can be seen as an important corrective on previous work: insisting on a more careful engagement with current theoretical work, as well as exposing the pitfalls of an unthinking adherence to the feminist imperative. However, such work can also reproduce some of the binary divisions to which lawyers, in particular, are prone, and can be a source of division rather than an enabling move forward. This 'call to theory' can be too often used to chastise and discredit feminists who still address law and still find some purchase in the revelation of law's inadequacies. As such, it can become deeply apolitical – not so much because of the project of an engagement with theory, but because of its consequences. But there are other implications in such a move which I find problematic at another level.

Lawyers have been prone to accepting a division between 'theory' and 'practice', 'jurisprudence' and 'law'. Within the legal academy, theorists have been accredited with a grudging respect, but a position on the margins. Indeed, for many 'theorists', this margin is one they have willingly inhabited: a place of safety, away from the perils of engagement with substantive law. From this place of safety, an élitist image of theory is reproduced. at its best,

---

31 One of the problems, ironically, is that the 'power of the law' begins to be taken too seriously. Smart, Edwards and Naffine all recognise that a presumption of coherence in legal doctrine is no longer tenable and, therefore, seem to recognise muddle and unevenness in law. However, their shared response is to move to a more abstract model of law's 'power to define', as if the deep structure of 'law' is now to be found in a rather different place, requiring a little more work at 'revelation'. This is rather like the defeated doctrinal lawyer trying to find logic and coherence in principled patterns behind the confusion of doctrine. All are still searching for, and are expecting, deep structural patterns. All remain wedded to the positivist project. None of this is to argue that there are not patterns in law and that these patterns have often been used detrimentally against women's needs and expectations – but it is to refuse to accept any suggestion of deep structural determinism. The point is to recognise contingency – and then to tease out those patterns which, in certain circumstances, in certain times, might be of value to the feminist project.

one day, somehow, if you care about this at all, theoretical work will trickle down and permeate the rest of the academy; which is usually taken to mean that, once a theory has been worked on sufficiently, it can be used by others who are concerned with 'application' rather than theory for its own sake. At its worst, theory remains within an abstract terrain. What, therefore, may be being reproduced here is a position for theory which simply conforms to, and confirms, the position of theory as the pinnacle of the academic project and the theorist as the 'true' academic/scholar. I think that this was probably what was at the root of the divisive character of the 'grassy bank scene': a division between those who embraced theory, becoming theorists, and those who were not comfortable with theory in its most abstract character, finding it alien, an arena into which they had not entered and, possibly, an arena which they felt neither well prepared for nor, perhaps, saw as immediately relevant to their own work.[32]

A much more radical 'take' can be presented in this context. Have we forgotten that a major aspect of feminist critique (and also of much radical critique in general) was the challenge to the abstract voice of the theorist speaking from above – securing a dominant and dogmatic stance from the very ability to distance and taking authority from the dispassionate voice of reason? Surely, challenging this was a major imperative in feminist work? So, what we have to face today is the difficulty in finding ourselves possibly reproducing a divide – but with other women/feminists claiming the high intellectual ground.

A major project for feminists has been to 'use' theory, rather than become subservient to the very constraints we challenged. Again, there are many institutional factors which militate against trying to keep this approach open, one of which, I am afraid, is wanting to become 'one of the boys'. This is a difficult temptation to resist for many of us – especially when the boys still seem to be so firmly in control. A great deal of feminist theoretical work is caught between addressing two audiences – addressing the 'great men' on the crucial aspects they have missed because of their lack-of-feminist-insight and, at the very same time, addressing feminists in terms of the usefulness of using the 'great men'. These women attempt to stand as inter-locators, but one cannot help but feel that their major (and, in institutional terms, understandable) imperative is to join the academy. But what might that entail? Perhaps, more than anything else, that their work is recognisable to the establishment as what is expected 'of theory' and that they can meet on the established terrain and play by the rules of that terrain:

> I do not include feminism in this list of conceptual schemes. Clearly, if the issue was one of themes and influences, one would have to – feminist concerns, indeed, intrude in relation to each of the developments sketched below ... I

---

32 See, also, *op cit*, Goodrich, fn 3.

simply don't see much by way of conceptual innovation or influence here, with the limited exception of Luce Irigaray. It is rather a matter of opening up the realisation that in unleashing any, or at least most, of these conceptual frameworks to fields of application, there are always gender implications to which attention needs to be paid.[33]

Feminism here is reduced to 'gender implications'[34] when theory is applied, and otherwise 'themes and influences', but not that crucial marker of 'concepts'. Now, many feminist theorists would clearly wish to challenge this as a 'write off'[35] (or may strive to prove that feminism can deliver in these terms). I would take a slightly different tack, first noting that Murphy decontextualises the authority of these 'concepts' by citing male authors who themselves may have been addressing, or at least have been influenced by, 'feminist themes'. The pattern of his paper is to privilege concepts and authority, and then only allow for feminism in the process of 'application' (and, indeed, further, he does not really address how his reading of the key conceptual patterns might have been influenced by feminism – although what I am about to say would suggest that, at one level at least, he has not been so influenced). Secondly, I would suggest that one of the products of feminist thinking on theory could be to challenge his very use of the idea of theory as 'concept' and his subsequent marginalising of 'themes' into a kind of middle order space between theory and application. Feminist critics are here faced with a clear choice – either provide theory in these terms or challenge the terms of reference themselves.

Murphy does commit himself to what I think is the hallmark of critical theory for lawyers – that theoretical work is a tool for understanding law. For feminists, this project is, however, still a deeply political one. For many commentators, this has been one of the very problematic issues for feminist work in theory – for Goodrich (writing in the same volume as Murphy), it is a strength. I suspect that, for Murphy, it is seen as a weakness.

TAKING FEMINISM SERIOUSLY

We continue to need to refuse to allow our feminism(s) to be read only within an academic terrain: this is a recognition that, whilst our feminism informs our

---

33 Murphy, T, 'Britcrits: subversion and submission, past, present and future' (1999) 10(3) LC 237, p 245.

34 Perhaps one consequence of allowing 'women centred' questions to drift into 'gender issues'? See *op cit*, Conaghan, fn 7.

35 The most obvious contender for 'recognition' would be the very rich feminist work on 'the body'; see, eg, Grosz, E, *Volatile Bodies, Towards a Corporeal Feminism*, 1994, Bloomington: Indiana UP, and *Space, Time and Perversion*, 1995, London: Routledge. But I suspect that Murphy would probably counter this by finding the 'origins' in Nietzsche and Foucault!

academic work, it cannot be finally validated by it. We can use academic work to explore our feminism, but we cannot, and should not, seek a final identity and purpose for feminism in the academy.

Two consequences flow from this. The first is the necessity of engaging with our material, whilst recognising that we have a project which is not entirely academically based. We have to be honest about this: not to do so will result in a continuation of the production of work which I have characterised as 'passive', that is, working with law (and theory) within an unexplored 'feminist imperative'. We have to render our feminism as a given which is treated problematically rather than axiomatically; that is, we have to understand that our feminism is not a coherent, rational, intellectual enterprise, but something which continues to defy such limitations. We have to continue to explore and test our feminist instincts and, in so doing, we can, and must, bring to bear our academic credentials upon this project. But, and it is an important but, in so doing, we must recognise that it is most likely that, whilst we can to some extent ground our feminism, it (we) will not be reduced, its (our) geography constrained, to an entirely academic terrain. My first concern is, then, to underline that our feminism must inform our academic work, that our project as feminists is indeed that. But, secondly, we must look much more closely and much more carefully at how we translate that project into our academic lives. The feminist project cannot be used as an excuse for poor theoretical work.[36]

To write a paper on theory, to write a theoretical paper; what does this entail? What expectations does a reader bring to such a paper? By what standards do my/our colleagues judge the validity of such a paper? 'Validity': strange word to use. What words have I heard used recently to describe papers we wish to commend – 'good', but more often, now I come to think of it, 'strong'. Strength – I must think more about that word. It is a judgment usually expressed along with a cluster of other criteria: well grounded, robust in argument, clarity of thought and expression, etc. To what extent does 'strength' also involve the criterion of innovative thinking? And to what extent must innovative thinking be presented in a pattern or form which signals the presence of the other criteria? When can 'strength' be stretched to giving expression, or exploring innovative thinking, in different forms of written presentation? This might be 'brave', but when does 'brave' become foolhardy, a weakness rather than a strength? These questions have become particularly pertinent for those of us writing in the shadow of the 'Research Activity Exercise'. As we approach the third round of this exercise, the word 'strong' often now resonates with the use of another interesting term: 'scholarly'. Now, what expectations do we bring to a judgment of work as

---

36 I am reminded of a friend saying of a well known feminist 'scholar' from the States: 'She does not have a theoretical bone in her body.' It is not enough to claim authority, or authenticity, simply from the identity one can assert and the place from which one purports to come. This becomes the tyranny of the high moral ground.

'scholarly'? What does it mean to me, now, to think about the presentation of a paper on feminism and theory with the words 'strong' and 'scholarly' hanging in the ether?

What marks in/on a text suggest a 'scholarly' approach? I could have begun my paper by following one fundamental principal in scholastic work – begin within another text. Ground this text through the citation of others – this suggests three functions. First, it lends authority to one's own work. Secondly, it situates one's work in such a way as to indicate that one is conversant with all the relevant material and one is able to select, from that material, a suitable beginning. Thirdly, having situated oneself, one then moves on to apply, possibly by differentiation, the previous text to one's own work.

To write theory is usually assumed to be to write 'about theory'. To find a position, one has to locate the map of theory; it is not enough to merely display analytical thinking; one has to display a familiarity with a terrain which has already been established as 'theory' and follow a pattern for the presentation of sound theoretical work. Although we are nowadays wary of the terms 'objective' and 'rational', we continue to use them as working principles – a paper must display an argument which can be followed and justified, mere assertion is not enough, and the argument must be voiced in a manner which asserts the validity of the argument – the authority must come from the argument itself, not the position of the speaker.

The development of scholarship is always portrayed in a dispassionate way[37] – although we do not 'name it' very often, we still work within a frame which suggests that we are simply seekers after the truth, or at least a better truth than the one we presently have. We know, in fact, that our scholarship is both led and curtailed by the institutional frames in which we find ourselves. The production of knowledge is not a dispassionate process; rather, it is a messy and contentious business, so messy and so contentious that it seems better that we do not think about it too often, for to do so may seem to explode our founding myths, the ones that make possible our very process of working as, and presenting ourselves as, scholars. In fact, it can be a serious jolt to be asked to explore one's theoretical premises or admit to the market forces which influence the production of scholastic work.

Nevertheless, I think that we would all agree, as feminists, that certain traditions of scholastic work are valuable. The question is one of when those traditions have been used to constrain, or even deny, the potential in the development of work which is important to us, especially inchoate, exploratory work which is reaching out into difficult territories, in which we

---

37 On the traditions and effects of the 'dispassionate voice' (and the distanced observer) I particularly like the work of Gillian Rose; see *Feminism and Geography*, 1993, Cambridge: Polity.

think we glimpse new horizons of possibility, but we find we have no maps readily at hand.[38] We sometimes find ourselves working on dangerous margins – and playing safe, especially when we face being graded in our published work, is very tempting. So we have to try to find devices which allow us to explore and begin to find voice(s) but which also allow us to engage with each others' material and establish modes of engagement which do not silence us but allow us to evaluate.

We have to think clearly about the idea of theory, so that we can begin to find other ways of engaging with, using, theory. For instance, I think that one of the problems with an idea of feminist-legal-theory is that the term implies theory about law which is feminist. Further, the process of linking individual terms of reference on a regular basis produces, at some point, a presumption that the linkage now forms a category. The individual terms become melded into one. An identity is formed. However, using such an identity or category holds within it certain prerequisites and makes, operationally, certain presumptions. The major prerequisite, I would suggest, is that the core of the identity is signalled by the first term used – in this case, feminism. The presumption is, therefore, that feminism is the key marker of specificity. But, further, a second presumption is made – that at least one of the terms is stable as a referent. In this case it could be the term legal-theory. We know what legal-theory is and we are simply adding the specificity of feminism. In practice, however, this referent is simply not stable enough: it actually signals very little beyond bringing 'theory' to 'law', or 'law' to 'theory'. We might try to stabilise the object by referring to 'jurisprudence' rather than legal-theory – but we are likely to meet some interesting resistance. 'Jurisprudence' too firmly connotes the central referent as being 'law' rather than 'theory'. A cursory glance at any jurisprudence text will remind us of why the break from 'jurisprudence', and the stultifying heritage of positivism, was signalled by the embracing of the term 'legal theory'. That simple change in terminology signalled a break for freedom – a chance to explore theory, *per se*, and then bring that to bear on our knowledge and understanding of law. It is that memory which now turns me back to the idea of feminist-legal-theory.

Categories, as identities, are neither unitary nor stable: they are contingent – the process of bringing together terms and melding them by naming gives the illusion of stability and the promise of delivery, but, in practice, the process by which they are linked, and the purposes served by

---

38 See Bottomley, A *et al*, 'Dworkin: which Dworkin?' [1987] JLS 47 for an example of a polemical paper trying to 'make people think', rather than conforming to the expectations of a 'paper on feminist theory'. There is clearly a role for such papers – but they can become dangerous enterprises when our work is judged for its scholastic credentials in terms of the RAE or even used by others to demonstrate a lack of theoretical rigour in feminism, which totally fails to appreciate the project or to take account of the context of such interventions.

that linkage, are transient. It is a process of coupling and de-coupling, and in that process we can take the opportunity to examine, and re-examine, each of the terms used. In practice, we do this all the time – we use feminism to interrogate theory and theory to interrogate feminism, and then we use both/either to interrogate law, and so the process continues. But, and this is what really interests me for the purposes of this paper, we so rarely recognise that this is the process in which we are engaged. We prefer, for many reasons, to work by presuming axioms rather than using premises. We presume feminism and then are simply working on theory, or vice versa, or we presume feminism and are working on law, or vice versa. And then, from within the terrain marked by these didactic movements emerges a possible centre, a possible unifier, and, instead of seeing the geography from which it emerges, we turn our sight onto the new site. The terrains marked 'feminism', 'law' and 'theory' become a possible feminist-legal-theory. And we are seduced into making possible that site by presuming it – we lose the sense of imminence and of contingency by speaking (of) it as a thing-that-already-exists. But it is a trap. A trap, because, once we begin to try to build in it, we actually build on it. Then we cannot afford to look at, or reveal, shaky foundations. Instead, we set our sight on a new horizon – finding/creating feminist-legal-theory. The object rather than the process is rendered visible, and further, what easily becomes lost is the purpose, the project – it becomes taken for granted and then too easily subsumed.

ALTERNATIVE MAPPING[39]

This is about process and context. It is about movement and direction. And, at this point, I need to be much more direct about my own theoretical project:

> At this particular moment of feminist theory, it is urgent to think about the nature and the status both of thinking in general and of the specific activity known as theory.[40]

I was first brought face to face with this challenge to 'thinking' by Alice Jardine's seminal book.[41] Jardine was my first encounter with thinking about

---

39 'The map does not reproduce an unconscious closed in upon itself; it constructs the unconscious ... The map is open and connectable in all of its dimensions; it is detachable, reversible, susceptible to constant modification ... A map has multiple entryways, as opposed to ... tracing, which always comes back "to the same". The map has to do with performance, whereas ... tracing always involves an alleged "competence" ... The tracing should always be put back on the map ...' (Deleuze, G and Guattari, F, *Capitalism and Schizophrenia: A Thousand Plateaus*, 1987, Minneapolis: Minneapolis UP, p 12.)

40 Braidotti, R, 'Towards a new nomadism', in Boundas, C and Olkowski, D (eds), *Gilles Deleuze and the Theater of Philosophy*, 1994, New York and London: Routledge, p 160.

41 Jardine, A, *Gynesis: Configurations of Women and Modernity*, 1985, Ithaca: Cornell UP.

thinking in the flesh; of situating ourselves, our desires and our potentials (in all their glorious and fragmented, plural ways) by finding images which would help us enter the territory of thinking by beginning to think for ourselves (the many selves of us). It was in her work that I first encountered the benefits of using visual techniques to explore abstract ideas – and found that these techniques could render visible movement and horizons, as well as situate place. From her I first learnt the usefulness of the imagery of mapping and the many different ways in which maps can be formed and used. This is my personal account – I do not pretend that she was the source or authority for these ideas; she was simply the place where I encountered them and they made not merely sense to me but suddenly made so much possible in places where I had so badly struggled before.[42]

Later, and partly through the work of Braidotti,[43] I began to engage directly with the work of Gilles Deleuze. At this point, I could easily slide into the use of a figure of authority to justify my work – and male authority at that! I want, rather, to try to achieve a rather different movement. Here is a body of work in which I have found, as a feminist, key themes and imaginative techniques which have helped me in exploring my own concerns and issues. I do not try to authenticate my material by reference to another – but I do find it enabling, and scholastically useful, to be able to hear resonances and find a sense of familiarity, an aspect of recognition, in work which comes from such a different place. I am well aware that, in writing this way, I am radically challenging the usual mode of scholarship. I seem to be looking only for confirmation and I am willing to 'pick' from Deleuze (or others) that which is useful to me, rather than accepting (and testing) the wider corpus[44] of his work. I could argue that this is what much 'use of' key figures usually is anyway – even though it pretends to be more. In practice, however, I have found my relationship with Deleuzian material to be interactive – I have been forced to test a great deal of my feminism through my encounters with Deleuze, as much as my feminism has proven resistant to certain elements of Deleuzian thinking. I think that the key to an encounter with Deleuze is process – a functional account of what he makes possible by making us think much more concretely and cogently about the process (and purpose) of thinking. His scholarship is not, in my opinion, designed to ask us, the

---

42 Some traces can be seen in the Introduction to Bottomley, A and Conaghan, J (eds), *Feminist Theory and Legal Strategy*, 1993, Oxford: Blackwell.

43 See, especially, Braidotti, R, *Nomadic Subjects*, 1994, New York: Colombia UP.

44 But, see the Deleuzian notion of 'the body'! I have not the space to investigate the Deleuzian figuration of the body here (or the often cited feminist concerns with the Body-without-Organs), but see Gatens, M, 'Through a Spinozist lens: ethology, difference and power', in Patton, P (ed), *Deleuze; A Critical Reader*, 1996, Oxford: Blackwell; *op cit*, Braidotti, fn 40; Grosz, E, 'A thousand tiny sexes: feminism and rhizomatics', both in *op cit*, Boundas and Olkowski, fn 40.

readers, to simply accept and apply – it is designed for use, for engagement.[45] Therefore, my purpose is not to say, 'here is Deleuze', or even, 'here is my reading of Deleuze'. It is rather to say, 'here are (some of the) ways in which I locate in my work the influence of Deleuze'.

What are the major features of Deleuzian work[46] which have influenced the way in which this paper has developed?

Three features are most important:

(1) A recognition of the authenticity of having a project which is neither defined nor contained within 'theory' but upon which 'thinking' and, therefore, 'theory' is brought to bear.

One of the major features of Deleuze's work is to challenge the Freudian presumption that desire is necessarily premised on 'lack', which has so dominated our perception and understanding of desire, and to think of desire as affirmative (following Spinoza and Nietzsche):

> ... as immanent, as positive and productive, a fundamental, full, and creative relation. Desire is what produces, what makes things, forges connections, creates relations, produces mechanic alignments. Instead of aligning desire with fantasy and opposing it to the real ... for Deleuze, desire is what produces the real ...[47]

The feminist imperative can be validated as a desire, but must not then be lost in desire-as-lack; rather, it should be read as a productive force for what it can make possible.

(2) Thinking desire as lack sustains a fixation on 'other' and feeds the myth that completeness can be found and, indeed, should be sought by unity with the 'other'.

45　There is another point to be made here – I often think that those of us brought up in the positivist tradition still tend to approach all texts as 'authority', a kind of flat mono-tonal plane which we will judge on its merits and then adopt or dismiss. What we often miss is the open textured nature of work which draws on other traditions – we do not 'hear' subtle shifts in the way we are being addressed, appreciate the different voices being used or 'read' the differing placements, which, as 'reader', we are being offered by the movements of the author. This is visible in the way in which some Anglo-Americans respond to Deleuze; it is also very visible in the way in which Luce Irigaray, for instance, is often 'flattened out' by her Anglo-American critics (see, eg, Lacey, N, 'Feminist legal theory: beyond neutrality' (1995) 48(2) CLP 1). It is better to think in terms of an 'encounter' and, in Irigaray's case, I think that it helps to recall the therapeutic movements between analyst and 'client'. For an interesting analysis of both writers, see Richardson, J, 'Jamming the machines: "woman" in the work of Irigaray and Deleuze' (1998) 9(1) LC 89.

46　The books I have found most useful are *op cit*, Deleuze and Guattari, fn 39; and Deleuze, G, *Difference and Repetition*, 1994, London: Athlone.

47　*Op cit*, Grosz, fn 44, p 195.

Even within the context of a challenge to the idea of the unitary subject, and an understanding of the 'other' as a projection from ourselves in order to try to sustain a sense of self, the trope of 'other seeking' remains compelling. Deleuzian thinking pushes us to rid ourselves of this longing and to realise what a trap (a return) it actually is. To do so, we need to take seriously the challenge to the unitary subject; to understand the positive nature of multiplicity and not to try to reduce this to a centre, a whole or a unit.

Therefore, keeping feminist/legal/theory as separate sites is crucial – as is keeping open each of these sites. Keeping them separate does *not* mean presuming that each, or any, has an integrity or boundary which defines them. Sites are not cored, bounded places – there is no interiority; they are surfaces upon which, and within which, we move. The surfaces meet and mingle – but nothing, in any final sense, merges. Therefore, no system is closed – no knowledge final and no 'place' a place of authenticity which can be used to interrogate and judge other sites. We move within, and use, each, in as far as each makes possible our desires. This movement through and between is visualised by the key Deleuzian figuration of the 'rhizome', as opposed to 'arborescent' modes of thinking.[48]

This deep challenge to the notion of the unitary, as well as the fragmentary seeking unity, is linked to the third imperative in Deleuzian thinking.

(3) The challenge to binaries:

> ... feminist theory and Deleuzian rhizomatics share a common target – the reversal of Platonism – a reversal that problematizes the opposition, so integral to Western thought, between the ideal and the real, the original and the copy, the conceptual and the material, and, ultimately, between man and woman, it may in fact turn out ... a (provisional, guarded) alliance ... of real strategic value.[49]

The most important binary which I have wanted to challenge in this paper is theory/practice or theory/law. A binary means a place of choice which must force us into one side or the other. The challenge is to refuse that choice – not to pretend that it has not been set up, which would be to conflate it, but to actively refuse it.

The refusal is signalled by insisting on movement – but not what used to be called praxis (this term carries too much baggage to really convey what I mean by movement).[50] The movement I am talking about does not indicate

---

48 A good introduction to rhizomatic thinking is found in *op cit*, Grosz, fn 44.

49 *Op cit*, Grosz, fn 44, p 190. In modern terms, it is the challenge to Hegelianism.

50 I think the weight of this baggage is visible in Pather, P, 'On foreign ground: grand narratives, situated specificities, and the praxis of critical theory and law' (1999) 10(3) LC 211.

any kind of stability to two sites which we move 'between'; because we are also moving through those sites themselves, there is no closure. The movement is a movement over and between surfaces.

These are the three key features which have informed the construction and development of this paper – but, in outlining them in this abstract way, I am all too aware that I may seem to fall into the trap of now 'revealing' my theory, having 'revealed' the limitations of others. If I say that this is simply because of the difficulty of my project, I have subverted and denied the hope I expressed that such an approach is actually enabling to the development of feminist theoretical insights. I offer three pleas in mitigation. First, that it is my own failing to be unable to express these ideas with clarity, but I continue to struggle with that; secondly, that it really is so difficult to find new ways of scholarship that do not fall into the pitfalls of the old; and, thirdly, that it is in the practice of the project, and what that makes possible, rather than in trying to render an abstract account of it, that this approach must finally be evaluated.

I have been writing so many student references recently that I feel an impulse to end by simply saying: I commend him to you. But this is nowhere near sufficient! There is so much in Deleuze which I have not used here, in any overt way, but which has informed my work. But there is also much in Deleuze which does not speak to me and which I do not use. Am I trying to simply ignore what I find difficult and therefore not merely being partial but also not a 'good Deleuzian'? Well, I do not pretend to be a good Deleuzian – I use from him what I find enabling and, further, I am willing to say that I think that this is being 'faithful' to Deleuze: I believe that, within 'his' project, he has created space for people like me to use what is useful for me.[51] But it would be wrong to give any impression that to be 'faithful' is to have become a 'believer', or not to recognise that many feminists have had great problems with aspects of the work of Deleuze.[52]

Neither do I want to be either territorial or, even worse, imperial, in what I finally want to suggest.

---

51 'It is thus no longer appropriate to ask what a text means, what it says, how to interpret or decipher it. Instead, one must ask what it does, how it connects to other things (including its reader, its literary and non-literary context).' (*Op cit,* Grosz, fn 44, p 199.)

52 See a resumé in *op cit,* Grosz, 1994, fn 35, Chapter 7.

EMERGING HORIZONS

Earlier in this paper, I alluded to 'progressive and enabling work'. I do not want to claim this work for, or as, a Deleuzian approach, but I do think that this work parallels it and indicates the kinds of way in which we can move forward. Hilary Lim finds strategies for refusing a binary between a woman's body and that of a foetus by using Donna Haraway's work.[53] Thérèse Murphy argues for a careful analysis of sex/gender – neither dichotomised nor collapsed.[54] In this volume, Ralph Sandland engages, very directly, with the problem of finding a way to express and theorise futures beyond the immediacy of engagement and critique. Meanwhile, Joanne Conaghan considers the slippage of feminist work into 'gender studies',[55] and the influence of the careful theorising of, for instance, Judith Butler and Elizabeth Grosz, has become more evident in work on law.[56]

Developing the theme of 'strategic' lawyering has led to more consideration of the potential use of both legal strategies and legal principles – not in any abstract way, but in a situated concern with engagement with law.[57] Being proactive involves a concern for trying to utilise emerging legal patterns – for instance, the attempts being made by the House of Lords to develop themselves as a constitutional court, as well as the recent introduction of the Human Rights Act 1998.[58] At another level, it is about being much more aware of the heuristic/cognitive possibilities of utilising certain ideas or trends without being caught in the trap of having to, in some final way, believe in them. Even binaries can be useful in their time – as long as we see them as establishing fields of debate and sharpening thought rather than presenting us with choice – equality/difference was a productive debate, as

---

53 Lim, H, 'Caesereans and cyborgs' (1999) 7(2) FLS 133.

54 Murphy, T, 'Feminism on flesh' (1997) 8(1) LC 37.

55 *Op cit*, Conaghan, fn 7.

56 See, eg, Loizidou, E, 'Sex at the end of the 20th century – some re-marks on a minor jurisprudence' (1999) 10(1) LC 71.

57 Cooper, D, 'Fiduciary government: decentering property and taxpayers' interests' (1997) 6(2) SLI 235.

58 This development is seen not only in the mode of reasoning in which so many of their judgments are now cast, but also in their development of the use of *amicus curiae* briefs. We will, I think, at this juncture have a lot to learn from the Canadian experience in particular. Rethinking our use of 'rights' language in an immediate and strategic way is quite different from the very disappointing approach taken by Aileen McColgan. See McColgan, A, *Women Under the Law: The False Promise of Human Rights*, 2000, Harlow: Pearson.

long as we did not think that we had to come down on one side or the other.[59] These are devices for mapping terrains of engagement and for signalling warnings about absolutes and extremes: they remain useful until they effect any form of closure. Then, there are the 'empty words' which are so replete in possibilities – do any of us really want to lose the space which 'justice', that quintessential reference to our desire(s), signals? We are all now well used to the need to sustain our notions of 'subject' and 'rights', not merely because we cannot afford to lose their strategic usefulness, but also because they still speak an aspect of our desire(s), however imperfectly.[60] We still value rational debate and the tools which allow us to evaluate our work.[61] Critique does not end any of our needs for any of these things – it simply cautions us about their use. Central to all of this – central to our politics as feminists and our work as academics – is the recognition that the process we are engaged in is an exploration of our desire[62] and the tools (in thinking and in thinking about law) which help us towards the expression of this.

POSTSCRIPT

This paper has become, I hope, an argument for a recognition that 'process', rather than 'product', is the lodestone of 'theory' and that, although this statement is easy to write, it is much more difficult to understand what it actually means, as well as to try to achieve it. My argument is that this idea, so simple and yet so difficult, holds the key to what was wrong with the dynamics of the scene on the bank in the sun. In small ways, we can begin to 'see', grasp towards, the importance of it, and we can engage with it incrementally – but to write it in an abstract form remains, necessarily, difficult. It is, for me, an essential, and essentially, feminist project – I try to find ways and means, amongst abstract theorists as well as in pragmatic engagement, to tease out and test the dynamics of it and to try to convey these

---

59 Deleuze's figurative device of 'the fold' seems to me to be full of potential for feminist work; folding, refolding, unfolding – to bring surfaces into relation or play with different configurations through the imagery of folds. See Deleuze, G, *The Fold, Leibniz and the Baroque*, 1993, Minneapolis: Minneapolis UP. For an interesting, albeit brief, encounter with 'the fold', see Nancy, J-L, 'The Deleuzian fold of thought', in *op cit*, Patton, fn 44. I also like Grosz's use of the figuration of the Mobius strip – see *op cit*, Grosz, fn 35.

60 See, eg, Bottomley, A, 'Women and trust(s): portraying the family in the gallery of law', in Bright, S and Dewar, J (eds), *Land Law: Themes and Perspectives*, 1998, Oxford: OUP, pp 206–28.

61 See, eg, Braidotti's careful review of the value of 'philosophy' in *Patterns of Dissonance*, 1991, Cambridge: Polity.

62 I have written 'desire', but the word should be read as connoting a multiple, rather than a singular, expression.

dynamics to others. At another level, my intellectual instinct[63] is that this does flow with an emerging pattern in theoretical work, which will come to be seen as the demise of Newtonian models of theory and the reception of the full impact of relativity and quantum theory outside of the science of physics – a real struggle with an understanding of process (rather than substance) as being the model by which we, at present at least, try to engage with an understanding of our world and our place in that process of understanding.

63 I cannot place a footnote here to cite authority for this statement, hence my reference to an intellectual instinct. It is something which I have picked up in different ways in different places. I have talked to friends about it and have become increasingly convinced that so much of what we are at present surrounded by is a struggle out of Newtonian models – but played through in different terms and in different places.

CHAPTER 3

AN IMPOSSIBLE GLOBAL JUSTICE? DECONSTRUCTION AND TRANSNATIONAL FEMINISM

Sara Ahmed

How can global justice for women be thinkable? It will be the argument of this paper that we have to think the unthinkability of global justice for women, if it is to be thinkable. Rather than base our call for global justice on a notion of advancement, rights or development, transnational feminisms need to think about how global justice fails to be secured by the very *constitution* of women as global actors, and to *work* with the very failure of global justice to be present, or be presented by, the law. In other words, it is only by working *with* what is not named by documents such as the Beijing Platform for Action 1995, which requires that we work *on* such documents in the first place, that attempts to 'do justice' to women within international civil society will allow us to open up the 'possibility for justice'.

This possibility, this opening up of a different future, which is, of course, yet to be thought, is not simply a matter of thinking differently. Rather, in this paper, I will call for a different way of *acting* in relationship to the constitution: the constitutions which found both 'the nation' and 'the globe', as well as the constitutions which found the gendered subject of and in law (that is, the subject whose 'coming into being' involves a subjection to the law). This understanding of activism, which works with the failure of constitutions, will be informed by a deconstructive notion of justice, whereby the question of justice is only thinkable if we give up a certain notion that it can be found within a legal judgment or, indeed, within the law in general. My contribution to the debate on the relationship between deconstruction and justice, and feminism and the law, will be to suggest an intimate relationship between constitutionality and judgments and, hence, between justice, transnational activism and the failure to be constituted by the law.

DECONSTRUCTION AND JUSTICE

In his powerful and much cited contribution to the conference, 'Deconstruction and the Possibility of Justice', Derrida pronounces that 'deconstruction is justice'.[1] How can we understand this pronouncement? What does it say about deconstruction and about justice to define them as the

---

1   Derrida, J, 'Force of law: the mystical foundation of authority' (1990) 11 Cardoza L Rev 921, p 945.

same thing? How can we, that is, understand the status and function of the 'is'?

In this article, Derrida begins with the very question of the deconstructability of 'the law', a deconstructability which exceeds the very opposition between foundationalism and anti-foundationalism precisely insofar as the origin of the law cannot be the law, and yet the law, having already arrived, posits itself as originary:

> Since the origin of authority, the foundation or ground, the position of the law, can't by definition rest on anything but themselves, they are themselves a violence without a ground. Which is not to say that they are in themselves unjust, in the sense of 'illegal'. They exceed the opposition between founded and unfounded, or between any foundation or anti-foundationalism.[2]

Now, this thinking of the law as the impossibility of founding itself as the law recalls Derrida's earlier work on constitutionality. Here, he discusses the status of the American Declaration of Independence as itself bringing into existence the very subject-category of 'the people', who supposedly were the foundation of the 'right' embedded in the constitution: 'this people did not exist. They do *not* exist as an entity, it does *not* exist, *before* the declaration, not *as such*'.[3] As a result, the origin of the Constitution is itself an effect: this reversal of temporality, suggesting not simply that the Constitution has no foundation, but that its foundation is produced by the very rhetorical act of declaring itself to be found.

In 'Force of law', the emphasis on the performative aspect of constitutions is more clearly linked to its deconstructability:

> The Structure I am describing here is a structure in which law (*droit*) is essentially deconstructible, whether because it is founded, constructed on interpretable and transformable textual strata (and that is the history of the law (*droit*), its possible and necessary transformation, sometimes its amelioration), or because its ultimate foundation is be definition unfounded.[4]

Here, deconstructability is a sign, not simply of the failure of law to found itself in an originary moment, but of the strategic effect of that failure: the law is open to transformation, an openness which, like enforceability, becomes structural rather than incidental to the law itself.

The deconstructability of law, Derrida suggests, is another name for justice. That is, justice is possible only insofar as the law itself is impossible as a ground that can determine an outcome or resolution which is, already in its proper moment, just:

2   *Op cit*, Derrida, fn 1, p 943.
3   Derrida, J, 'Declarations of independence' (1982) 15 New Political Science, p 10.
4   *Op cit*, Derrida, fn 1, p 943.

> I'm preparing to demonstrate that one cannot speak directly about justice, thematise or objectivize justice, say 'this is justice' and even less 'I am just'.[5]

Justice cannot be found in a decision, judgment and, in a very precise sense, within law itself, conceived as the groundless nature of violence. As a result, 'Justice is an experience of the impossible'[6] – which is not to say that justice is not possible. Justice is only possible insofar as we recognise that any judgment or decision is not, and cannot be, just. The deferral of justice is hence the condition of possibility of justice, a deferral which does not require that we 'give up' the constitutions that allow us to make judgments, or to take for granted certain rights or certain subjects, but that we give up an assumption that justice can be achieved or found within the constitution of law itself.

In order to think through the implications of this, we need to think about the relationship between justice and historicity, understood as a responsibility to the past or to memory as the trace of the past in the present. Derrida considers the common axiom that one must be free and responsible for one's actions in order to be just or unjust.[7] But, at the same time, this freedom or decision of the just must follow a law, prescription or rule, having the power to be of a programmable order.[8] In relationship to questions of legality, then:

> ... to be just, the decision of a judge ... must not only follow a rule of law or general law, but must also assume it, approve it, confirm its value, by a reinstituting act of interpretation, as if ultimately nothing previously existed of the law, as if the judge himself invented the law in every case.[9]

Therefore, for a decision to be just, it must, in its proper moment, be regulated and without regulation:

> ... it must conserve the law and also destroy it or suspend it enough to have to reinvent it in each case, rejustify it, at least reinvent it in the affirmation and the new and free confirmation of its principle.[10]

The relationship between history and law which is often understood as the very foundation of law's justice (the precedent as rule of law) is here cut open and understood as just only insofar as the law cannot return to history, as if history itself was enforceable through law. The law's judgment is, rather, the making present of the memory of the law as that which is neither guaranteed by the past nor projectible into a future. As a result, the present judgment is not the making 'present' of justice: justice is precisely a time lag, a moment of deferral, which is also an opening towards an unliveable future, in which one

---

5   *Op cit*, Derrida, fn 1, p 935.
6   *Op cit*, Derrida, fn 1, p 947.
7   *Op cit*, Derrida, fn 1, p 961.
8   *Op cit*, Derrida, fn 1, p 962.
9   *Op cit*, Derrida, fn 1, p 961.
10   *Op cit*, Derrida, fn 1.

lives 'with' the need to re-justify to and for others who are always yet to come: 'It follows from this paradox that there is never a moment that we can say *in the present* that a decision *is* just.'[11]

And yet, we must judge: '... justice, however unpresentable it may be, doesn't wait.'[12] And so, we judge. The intimacy of deconstruction and justice is bound up with the trauma of this ghostly moment: one must decide about what cannot be decided, one must reach a conclusion without proper and full justification. The demand for a decision necessarily goes through the passage of the undecidable. The undecidable, as a trace or 'ghost', becomes lodged in every decision, cutting it open, as the irreducible demand that we must decide about what is impossible.[13]

We decide, we judge: it is such acts, which are necessary and yet impossible, that suggest the madness of justice. Justice is possible insofar as there is no proper justification for justice, insofar as any judgment is mad, unjustifiable by what is before the judge. All judgments are mad, even if some judgments are *more or less justified* by what is 'before' the one who judges. Certainly, if we think of the legal judgment, it would follow that no judgment can be fully justified in the present by 'the evidence', or by a set of principles for adjudicating between cases. I would suggest that, while deconstruction refuses to provide us with a positive model of justice (by declaring 'what is justice' or 'what are the proper criteria for deciding the case in a way which is just'), deconstruction nevertheless does provide us with a way of thinking about injustice: an injustice occurs when a (deconstructible) constitution is used to found a judgment in the name of justice. This injustice turns the madness of the judgment into the rule of law. Rather, for deconstruction, justice is only possible insofar as it fails to be found in the law, constitution or judgment, insofar as this failure is recognised in the very necessity of making, provisionally, here and now, a judgment. Justice is only possible in the event of its failure, in the very event of the failure of the law in general, and the legal decision or judgment in particular, to declare itself as just.

CONSTITUTING WOMEN AS GLOBAL ACTORS

Quite clearly, the gendering of subjects involves constitutional acts. While we are used to thinking of constitutions as the documents which declare fundamental principles by which a State is organised, our task is also to think more precisely about what is constituted by 'constitutions' as understood in this sense. For 'to constitute' is to give a legal and philosophical form to some-

---

11 *Op cit*, Derrida, fn 1, p 961.

12 *Op cit*, Derrida, fn 1, p 967.

13 *Op cit*, Derrida, fn 1, p 965.

thing, which, paradoxically, becomes a thing only insofar as it is already constituted. It is, hence, to establish or to form that which is yet to be formed. The constitution is thus *the act of giving form to that which is not yet*. Clearly, the gendering of subjects involves constitutional acts, that is, declarations of subjecthood that produce categories such as 'woman', and 'women' that supposedly pre-exist the act of declaration. In the context of transnational feminism, we need to consider how the constitution of gendered subjects takes place differentially around the globe, and how this differentiation works in part *by elevating certain local acts of constituting 'women' into the global*.

Rather than just thinking of the constitution as bringing into effect its own origin, we can consider how the effects of constitutions also involve judgments. What do I mean by this? The subject categories that are the effects of constitutional acts are themselves differentiated. In this sense, the effect occupies an economic register of 'more and less', as well as a moral register of 'better and worse'. For example, the subject categories such as 'the people' or 'women' are not simply found through the rhetorical act of declaring themselves to be found: they are both founded and differentiated, such that only some subjects can be declared as belonging to the subject category which is found. Within particular constitutional regimes, the subjects 'people' and 'women', themselves an effect rather than an origin, may be found(ed) through a prior act of differentiation, which would declare that there are 'more and less' and 'better and worse' people (such as men and women), and 'more and less' and 'better and worse' women (such as white women and black women). In this section, I want to examine how women are constituted as global actors, and how this constitution involves a model of justice predicated on a judgment about the differential value of women, by examining representations of 'women' within and around the UN conference in Beijing in 1995. This conference provided one imaginary and material space in which feminist activism was given a global dimension.[14]

Partly, we need to examine the rhetoric surrounding the event that made claims on behalf of the event and that constituted the event itself as the 'globalisation' of feminism. For example, we could examine the rhetoric used by Hillary Clinton in her opening speech in the conference, a speech that is available on the internet. Interestingly, her speech, which is *about* how women are in some sense *already* global agents, was, in terms of its distribution, and hence consumption, dependent upon a globalised mediascape to confirm its object. Clearly, then, her speech is producing the very subject category

---

14 For a discussion of the use of rights discourse in and around the conference, see Chapter 1 of my book, *Differences that Matter: Feminist Theory and Postmodernism*, 1998, Cambridge: CUP. See, also, Sum, N, 'From politics of identity to politics of complexity: a possible research agenda for feminist politics/movements across time and space', in Ahmed, S *et al* (eds), *Transformations: Thinking Through Feminism*, 2000, London: Routledge.

(women as global actors, woman as global actor) which it supposedly is about. What is evident from her speech is that 'women', as subject category, comes to measure, or be the measure of, the level of social advancement of different nations:

> What we are learning about the world is that, if women are healthy and educated, their families will flourish. If women are free from violence, their families will flourish. If women have a chance to work and earn as full and equal partners in society, their families will flourish.[15]

In this public address, Hillary Clinton is talking precisely about the human rights of women across the globe as a preface to the UN conference. What is striking about this statement is the use of 'their families' as a means of closing the gap between the concerns of women and the concerns of and for international politics. That is, Hillary Clinton suggests, without reference to either nation or globe, that women's rights secure the flourishing of families and, hence, by implication, the advancement of the family of 'the nation' and 'the globe' as a 'family of nations'. Hence, women become global actors precisely insofar as they are relegated into the familial space at the very same time as that space becomes the imagined form of the globe itself.

Noticeably, in this public address, Clinton constitutes women as actors on a global stage by appealing to what women share or have in common:

> At this very moment, as we sit here, women around the world are giving birth, raising children, washing clothes, cleaning houses, planting crops, working on assembly lines, running companies and running countries.[16]

What is then listed is a series of acts that women 'around the world' are doing, or are even doing together, at the very same moment. The list begins with the acts most commonly used to bind women together as mothers (childbirth and childcare), and then moves towards acts normally associated with men as 'leaders' of nations. By positing women as leaders of nations through this metonymic chain, Clinton implies that women become global actors precisely through an *extension* of the activities within the home: women are mothers; they reproduce not only children, but also nations; while women as housewives and carers not only manage domestic space, but also global space. Significantly, then, women enter international politics by *being themselves*, a narrative which collapses the boundary line (always tenuously drawn) between their private space, and public space, and between the local and the global, through reference to very traditional notions of what women already contribute to the (re)production of the familial and social order.

15　Clinton, H, 'Remarks for the United Nations: Fourth World Conference on Women', Beijing, China, 5 September 1998, available at www.whitehouse.gov/WH/EOP/First_Lady/9-5-95.html. Thanks to Ngai-Ling Sum, whose chapter in our edited book, *Transformations* (*op cit*, fn 14) brought this speech to my attention.

16　*Ibid*, Clinton.

Certainly, Clinton's address uses the 'we' as a way of articulating the common concerns of women around the world, whether as mothers within the 'private' space of the family, or as mother figures within the 'public' space of the nation. At the same time, Clinton uses the 'I' as a way of signalling her own mobility in reaching to these other women, usually hidden from the 'eye' of international politics:

> I have met new mothers in Jojakarat, Indonesia, who come together regularly in their village to discuss nutrition, family planning and baby care ... I have met women in South Africa who helped lead the struggle to end apartheid and are now helping build a new democracy.[17]

It is the encounter between the mobility of the white Western woman, who moves across and between private and public spaces, as well as between nations, and those 'women' whom she speaks of, that is striking here. For what is at stake is precisely how *some* women are afforded agency within the global, through relegating other women into 'local' spaces, *at the very same time as that relegation is concealed under the constitution of 'global women'*. Clinton's 'I' can assert itself, by naming the encounters she had with women who inhabit the 'localised' spaces of the family, community and nation, in the very process of articulating what it is that 'we' *already* have in common (in the work that we do).

Here, the globe becomes a fetish precisely through being imaged as 'women'. Women-as-globe is only possible as an image by concealing the work that needs to be done to make it possible: it is the encounters, the meetings, between the white, Western woman, and the women in other spaces, which allow her 'I' to become 'global' by claiming their activities as 'her own'. The constitution of women as global agents clearly involves, then, a universalism predicated on a prior act of differentiation: 'we', as women, are (making) the globe, by translating the work 'they' do within families, communities and nations, into an 'I' that speaks.

Importantly, then, we can consider how the very documentation produced by the UN conference for women in Beijing participated in the constitution of 'women' as global agents. The document, *Platform for Action*, needs to be thought of as an effect of multiple encounters, both those between the participants who were present (and absent) at the conference and the encounters that are already at stake in the gendering of the international division of labour (which positions women differently around the globe in relationships of production and consumption). At the same time, however, we need to think of the Platform as making encounters possible, that is, as producing its own subject, and as *having its own effects*. Like all public documents in which subjects are defined as 'having' rights, we have a transformation of a performative into a constative: the document itself

---

17 *Op cit*, Clinton, fn 15.

produces the very subjects that it claims to re-present.[18] However, that moment of production is only possible given a prior history of encountering, which allow certain subjects to be faced, at the moment they are constituted, as such.

The Platform for Action certainly takes for granted the subject status of 'women' through the following *dictum*: women's rights are human rights. It seeks to 'ensure the full implementation of the human rights of women and of the girl child as inalienable, integral and indivisible part of all human rights'.[19] Such subject status is afforded through a discourse of potentiality: women, in some sense, must become subjects with rights by realising their full potential, a realisation that requires, paradoxically, that they already have the rights that they do not yet have (in this sense, the document presupposes that women are subjects by implying that they are *not yet subjects*, that they have yet to 'become' what they 'are'). Hence, advancement and development is deemed possible only by advancing and developing women, such that they become women and human at one and the same time:

> The empowerment and advancement of women, including the right to freedom of thought, conscience, religion and belief, thus contributing to the moral, ethical, spiritual and intellectual needs of women and men, individually or in community with others, and thereby guaranteeing them the possibility of realising their full potential in society.[20]

Here, the realisation of 'their potential' is allowed by the collapsing of a universal discourse of advancement or development (which assumes the primacy of the individual who has rights and freedoms guaranteed under law) into the advancement and development of women as such. Women both measure the advancement of the human, and themselves need to be advanced, such that they can become human.

While the declaration constitutes women as subjects insofar as they are potentially human, the documentation differentiates between women according to their advancement: by implication, *some women are defined as more advanced than others*. Thus, the call for advancement is also about bringing some women into the category of 'women' and (implicitly) other women into the category of 'human':

> ... to improve the effectiveness of anti-poverty programmes directed towards the poorest and most disadvantaged groups of women, such as rural and indigenous women, female heads of households, young women and older women, refugees and migrant women and women with disabilities.[21]

---

18 *Op cit*, Derrida, fn 1

19 UN, *Report of the Fourth World Conference on Women*, 1995, Declaration 9, available at gopher.un.org/11%2fconf%2ffwcw%2foff%2fplateng.

20 *Ibid*, Declaration 12.

21 *Ibid*, Declaration 60(a).

Throughout the document, there are repeated references to these various categories of 'other women'. By listing these different groups of women who are 'more oppressed', the document seeks to differentiate between women and complicate any simple positing of 'women' as a global or homogenous group, bound together in a shared oppression. However, at another level, what is then posited is a generalised category of 'other women' against an implicit category of women who are 'less disadvantaged' and, in the terms of the document (which conflates disadvantage with underdevelopment), more advanced. The grouping together of various forms of otherness thus does an enormous amount of work in the document: it allows the positing of 'women' as global agents, by defining them against women who have yet to advance or to develop into women. This notion of undeveloped woman as a *symptom* of underdevelopment in general thus confirms the human-woman agent – the individual who has autonomy, rights and freedom – as the proper *telos* or goal of globalised feminism. Even if collective agencies are named as contributors to the emancipation of women, the narrative of globalisation assumes the primacy of an individual – who is both gendered as woman and ungendered as human – and whose potential, when realised, becomes a sign of global advancement and development.

This assumption that the aim of global feminism is to enable individuals to realise their potential (to find a future which is already present(ed) as their nature) in the discourse of potentiality (one's becoming is determined by one's being) is hence linked to ideals of development which equate development with modernity. Throughout, the document calls for women to be given access to modernity, understood in terms of 'resources', that is, in terms of the transformation of land and 'nature' into both capital and technology:

> We are determined to: ensure women's equal access to economic resources including land, credit, science and technology, vocational training, information, communication and markets, as a means to further the advancement and empowerment of women and girls.[22]

Here, the term 'economic resources' functions as a way of gathering together a diverse range of value-laden activities: what is significant is that access becomes access to the networks of exchange, and the flow of capital within the globalised economy. As Mohanty suggests, globalisation needs to be understood in terms of the constitution of subjects and spaces through the differentiation and spatialisation of forms of labour.[23] We can also consider the networks of exchange and flows of capital as spatial forms of subject-constitution: for example, the accumulation of Third World debt and First World profit under the banner of development produces subjects with

---

22 *Op cit*, UN, fn 19, Declaration 36.
23 Mohanty, CT, 'Women workers and Capitalist scripts: ideologies of domination, common interests and the politics of solidarity', in Alexander, MJ and Mohanty, CT, *Feminist Genealogies, Colonial Legacies, Democratic Futures*, 1997, London: Routledge, p 5.

differing degrees of entitlement and agency, both within and between nation spaces. Within the narrative of advancement as access to resources, advancement becomes a means of fulfilling one's debt to modernity, or of becoming modern as an acquisition of debt.[24] Indeed, implicit in this narrative of access is that it is the 'acquisition' of debt which enables the constitution of others into subjects in the global space.

Gayatri Spivak has given us a powerful critique of how women's emancipation is coded as access to global telecommunications as such.[25] As she demonstrates, this process involves the transformation of the heterogeneity of indigenous knowledges into property. In such narratives, these technologies function not simply as symbols, *but as the very material*, of Western modernity: by having 'it', women will become 'it', that is, they will become modern and will realise their potential (they will hence become themselves – become selves – through modernity). Hence, modernity becomes a sign of what is missing for these 'other women', for what makes them 'other than women'. The United Nations itself, as an organisation that is premised on neutrality but based on notions of individual autonomy, democracy and civil society, which are ideologically inflected, hence constitutes itself as a necessary element, not only in the development of women, but also in the very constitution of women as (global) subjects.[26] In other words, the well being of 'all women' and the constitution of women as actors in the globe is assumed to be a measure of the degree to which women are 'brought' into modernity by global agencies. Although it would not be correct to say that the feminist critique of development is totally missing from this narrative – the emphasis is on giving agency to women in grassroots communities – the transparency of those institutions that are already global in reach is clearly affirmed (they are presented as 'giving' women 'the globe', rather than occupying and regulating 'the globe'). They are presented as the necessary condition for the 'development of women' insofar as they provide the mechanism that enables the individual to be 'translated' into the global and constituted as a global subject.

What is important in the conflation between individual development with global development is the notion of generation: the document defines itself as

---

24 This is not just about Third World debt – for example, debts for subaltern subjects can be accrued through local developers who have an alliance with global capital. See Translator's Preface and Afterword in Spivak, GC, *Imaginary Maps*, 1995, New York: Routledge. A fuller investigation of the relationship between subject constitution and debt than I can offer here is required such an investigation would no doubt draw on the legacy of Marxist theory.

25 Spivak, GC, 'Claiming transformation: travel notes with pictures', in *op cit*, Ahmed, fn 14.

26 For a fuller investigation of the politics of the UN in relation to development, see Kabeer, N, *Reversed Realities: Gender Hierarchies in Development*, 1995, London: Verso.

being about *allowing women to grow up*. The relationship between the signifiers of 'girl' and 'woman' is thus significant:

> The girl child of today is the woman of tomorrow. The skills, ideas and energy of the girl child are vital for the full attainment of the goals of equality, development and peace. For the girl child to develop her full potential she needs to be nurtured in an enabling environment.[27]

The temporality of this narrative is important: growing up becomes a measure of global development. The life course of the girl child hence becomes a metaphor for the life course of 'the globe' itself. In this way, the fulfilment of the girl's potential marks the course or trajectory of the globalisation of feminism.

The document therefore comes to represent itself as 'the making of a new generation': 'It will be crucial for the international community to demonstrate a new commitment to the future – a commitment to inspiring a new generation of women and men to work together for a more just society.'[28] Here, self-making becomes global-making through the positing of a 'new generation'; they will be the agents, even the *foundation*, of a new and better community, one in which 'home' becomes 'the globe' and 'the globe' becomes 'home'. This generation, posited by the document as foundational, is hence a symptom of the future: it is the girl and boy who will re-make the international community *in their own image*, that is, through an embodiment of their potential, through an embodiment of what has not yet taken form, but which takes their form. Significantly, then, the document is premised on an elided heterosexuality: the making of a new generation confirms the significance of the heterosexual couple to the international community. The new community will globalise the very form of the heterosexual couple as the (heteronormative) family. The absence of any reference to sexuality – and in particular to lesbians – within the document suggests that the new 'international community' will be reproduced through the normalising of a (supposedly egalitarian) heterosexuality: the new generation of global agents will be (re)produced from, or even through, the legislation of the heterosexual family as the proper 'form' of the international community.

The document, then, in 'making a new generation', involves forms of legislation which define global citizenship and agency in terms of the heterosexual couple and the heteronormative family, which thus also becomes the proper goal of global feminist activism. In this sense, it constitutes 'women' as global agents insofar as 'women' allow the re-constitution of this familial form, as long as women *give birth to* the very forms which measure her advancement in terms of the reproduction of the (hu)man. The work of women is, in some sense, to (re)produce the family as the image of the

---

27 *Op cit*, UN, fn 19, Declaration 39.
28 *Op cit*, UN, fn 19, Declaration 40.

'healthy world'. Such a constitution of women as agents in the globe involves a form of subjection: women become global subjects only insofar as they remain subjected to the laws of the heteronormative familial and social order.

TOWARDS GLOBAL JUSTICE

The document, of course, must be translated into local contexts and transformed into action. Given its significance as a framework for action, where the question of gender is posed, after all, as a matter of international political concern, the document names a number of actors; that is, it names those who will act upon it (it acts in part, then, by naming the actors). Actors that are named include 'all actors of civil society, particularly women's groups and networks and other non-governmental organizations and community-based organizations',[29] as well as 'the Governments and the international community'.[30] As a form of writing that defines itself as a 'platform' for action, then, the document opens up a gap between writing and action, a gap that brings into play a range of actors who have not necessarily authorised the writing, but who have been authorised by it. This authorisation itself differentiates between the actors who are named as such by the document: we have to consider not only who is the 'we' that writes the text, but also who signed it – 'the Governments' who represent 'their people' – and hence who authorised it through the proper names of the signatory.[31]

What I want to examine here is how we can build a different way of understanding how feminism can translate across national spaces, which assumes, or works with, the failure of 'women' to be constituted as global actors, and translates that failure into a form of collective activism. That is, it is where the document fails to translate – where it fails to constitute women as subjects within and subjects of 'the globe' – that a possibility for an alternative form of transnational feminist activism might emerge. In other words, in this section, I want to draw out the implications of the *deconstructability* of the constitution of women as global subjects (another way of talking about the possibility of global justice) for transnational feminist activism.

As I suggested in the previous section, the constitution of women as global actors involves forms of judgment and differentiation, where various 'other' women are named as yet to fulfil their debt to modernity. The ideal, then, of the document is the *becoming women of all women*: it is the development of all women into modern individuals, who are able to reproduce not only the

---

29 *Op cit*, UN, fn 19, Declaration 20.
30 *Op cit*, UN, fn 19, Declaration 21.
31 See *op cit*, Derrida, fn 1, p 945 for an analysis of the relationship between signing and constitutionality.

family, but the globe as a familial space. In such a model, women who are marked as different to those women who are already 'modernised', must be brought into the international community. As such, 'Third World women' become those who are already recognised as out of time with the making of a new community, and who can only be brought into time through entering the modernity promised as the family of the nations (the others whose future will be an entry into, and an affirmation of, the inclusivity of the modern and democratic 'we' of the globe itself).

The constitution of women as global actors hence involves a judgment, not only of what it means 'to be' a woman, but also about which women are the subjects who can secure justice, and which women have failed to become such subjects of the law. If this constitutional act involves judgments, then, it also produces its own model of justice, and its own universalist model of what would constitute 'justice for women': justice for women is precisely defined as entrance to modernity (the development of women into modern subjects). Given the violence of this constitutional judgment, given the very failure of this justice to be just, I would argue that we need to think of feminist transnational activism as a way of *working with what fails to be constituted by such constitutions*, that is, as a way of working with the very failure of the constitution of women as 'global subjects' to translate into forms of 'being' or 'acting' in the world. Clearly, to take for granted the constitutional status of the signifier 'global women' would perform its own injustice. The task of feminism is not, then, to refuse to work with this impossible signifier 'global women'; rather, it is to activate it, that is, to make it work insofar as it fails to secure a referent in the world. Global justice is hence not about declaring women as subjects within the globe: rather, we need to think the impossibility of this constitution in the work that we do.

Partly, this means giving up a universalist model of justice which declares that justice can be found within or through the constitution of women as modern and lawful subjects. Does this mean that such a feminism would refuse to make judgments? Does this mean that feminism *should* refuse to make any declarations about what is more and less just? That we would stop working against what we might have agreed to be injustices? Of course, this is not the case. Instead, we need to think of justice as that which we must work for, rather than being that which 'founds' the work that we do. Certainly, in the meetings that took place during the United Nations conference in Beijing, including those that were unofficial (elsewhere, I have shared my fantasies about the chance encounters that may have taken place during the conference in coffee bars),[32] discussions and arguments were had about what constitutes justice for women, some of which were reported in the Western media as

---

32 Ahmed, S, 'Intimate touches; proximity and distance in international feminist dialogues' (1997) 19 Oxford Lit Rev 19.

evidence of the failure of the conference, or of the lack of a shared agenda or understanding between women from the First and Third Worlds.[33] However, it is such dialogues, based on dissent rather than consent, which open up the possibility of global justice, precisely insofar as they admit to the failure to know what such justice would mean, that is, insofar as they fail to declare and constitute justice as Law. In such dialogues, the question of what is global justice for women is precisely what is in dispute. Indeed, working for global justice for women is, here, about working with the very failure of justice to be secured in the present.

Indeed, I would argue that, in different spaces and in the formation of local as well as transnational collectives, feminists need to have a dialogue about what might constitute justice for women in which consensus is not the goal or final outcome and in which consensus is not presumed to involve the realisation of justice. The possibility of such a dialogue is premised on a recognition that there can be no criteria for deciding what constitutes justice in advance. Indeed, what needs to be agreed is precisely what such criteria might be. Even when the criteria for deciding what constitutes justice have been agreed, to solidify those criteria into law would be to perform its own injustice. One could argue that the history of Western feminism within the international arena has precisely been about the violence of constituting one model of justice for women, based on a liberal tradition of rights and autonomy, as the law.[34] To assume that we can find global justice in a law, principle or declaration is to enforce a particular call for justice as law. It is hence to foreclose the possibility of justice.

Furthermore, what is agreed about the criteria for justice is dependent on 'who' participates in the dialogue in the first place and who may be excluded from the decision making process. Any decisions that are made about criteria for making judgments are hence partial, temporary and disputable by those who are yet to speak or judge. The very failure of feminists to speak with 'one voice' about what constitutes global justice for women during the Beijing conference (a failure which failed to be written into the *Platform for Action*) is, therefore, not a failure to find justice, but the condition of possibility for a justice which is irreducible to the law. It is in this specific sense that the possibility of justice involves the deferral of justice: the possibility of global justice depends on a recognition of its impossibility in the present (for what is presented in the present will always fail to hear other others).

It is thus of significance that, in the work of Gayatri Spivak, the scene of global justice is not so much in the corridors of global agencies such as the UN

---

33 *Op cit*, Ahmed, fn 32. Here, I discuss media reports on the conference within the UK.

34 For elaborations of this point, see Mohanty, C, 'Under Western eyes: feminist scholarship and colonial discourses', in Mohanty, C, Russo, A and Torres, L (eds), *Third World Women and the Politics of Western Feminism*, 1991, Bloomington: Indiana UP. See, also, *op cit*, Ahmed, 1998, fn 14, pp 51–58.

(though is it not *not* there); it is, rather, in the intimacy of face to face encounters with the subaltern woman, as the one whom one is working with and for:

> I have, perhaps foolishly, attempted to open the structure of an impossible social justice glimpsed through secret encounters with singular figures; to bear witness to the specificity of language, theme and history as well as to supplement hegemonic notions of a hybrid global culture with the experience of an impossible global justice.[35]

Here, the impossibility of global justice and, with it, the possibility of global justice, is glimpsed with 'secret encounters with singular figures', rather than in already public spaces or in an already constituted globality. Such secret and close encounters are not the rendering present of the subaltern woman (in the form of her being brought into the constitution of 'global women'). Rather, there is something that does not get across, something that is necessarily secret. The encounter or secret meeting is also a gift, in that it resists the structure of an exchange: there is not a proper object that moves from one to the other. The encounter involves responsibility: each other gives to other others, although what is given cannot be determined in advance or transformed into an outcome. Hence, ethics for Spivak, as for Derrida, becomes 'the experience of the impossible'.[36]

How do these singular encounters become the scene for global justice? Gayatri Spivak discusses the relationship between face to face encounters and collective activism in terms of supplementation, calling for 'a collective struggle *supplemented* by the impossibility of full ethical engagement'.[37] Here, she suggests that a collective activism, which does not involve face to face encounters with others, will fail. Such encounters, based on a proximity that does not allow merger, benevolence or knowledge (in other words, that does not overcome the distance) involve work; they involve 'painstaking labour'. Such work is differentiated from anthropological knowledge: it is not field work. Rather, as a form of encounter, it involves getting closer to others in order to occupy or inhabit the distance between us. Such encounters must supplement collective activism precisely because they prevent 'us' from assuming that we can gain 'access' to the difference of those others and translate that difference into law. At the same time, we cannot assume that the distance or difference 'belongs' to her.

Of course, such a model suggests the intimacy of the political and the ethical as ways of achieving 'better' relationships to others. But what I want to think about here is the relationship between the face to face and the collective and how that relationship needs to be thought beyond the terms of

---

35 *Op cit*, Spivak, fn 24, p 197.
36 *Op cit*, Spivak, fn 24, p xxv.
37 *Op cit*, Spivak, fn 24, p xxv.

supplementation. Certainly, the face to face encounters or secret meetings discussed by Spivak do not involve the presumption of 'privacy' – these meetings are secret only in the sense that they do not involve the revelation of the other's 'truth'. However, she is clearly also talking about meetings as involving encounters between two people (not 'the self' and 'the other', but this person and that person), which can only happen 'when the respondents inhabit something like normality'.[38] What I want to think of here is how the meetings, which do not reveal, but conceal, are not simply about two people facing each other; rather, such meetings, insofar as they are face to face, are *forms of* (and not supplements to) collective activism, but a collectivity understood in different terms, beyond the reification of the social group. In this sense, meetings are never private; they are not withdrawn from the multiplicity of public spaces (where there are always more than one or two others to be faced). They involve, in the proximity and distance of facing, an engagement with other others. The meeting is singular – it is with 'this other' – and yet also collective – *'this other' brings with her other others*. So, in getting together, and speaking to each other, we are also opening a space in which other others can be encountered, even if they are not yet faced.

So, for example, the act of speaking to an other within the improper spaces in the UN conference should not be seen as separate from the collective work done within the conference and its making of 'women as global agents'. Rather, it is such meetings that both allowed that making to occur (concealed behind the generic 'we' of the document) and, if named or declared, would represent what *does not make up* the category of 'global women'. The constitution of the subject-category 'global women' depends on the erasure or concealment of these other encounters from the document itself. Or, to put it differently, such encounters work with what is *missing from or in the formation of collectives* (and hence they cannot take place without or within the forming of collectives). These encounters or meetings in which judgments are made involve the deferral of justice, and are hence its condition of possibility.

Thinking of the face to face (or facing) as collective in their very singularity is about developing a different understanding of collective politics in which alliances are always formed, insofar as they are *yet to be formed*. Alliances, then, are not guaranteed by the pre-existing form of a social group or community, where that form is understood as commonality (a fantasy of a community of friends) or uncommonality (a fantasy of a community of strangers). So, the collective is not simply about what 'we' have in common – or what 'we' do not have in common. Rather, collectivities are formed through the *very work that is needed to be done* in order to get closer to others, without simply repeating the appropriation of 'them' as labour or as a sign of difference.

---

38 *Op cit*, Spivak, fn 24, p xxv.

Collectivity, then, is intimately tied to the secrecy of the encounter: it is not about proximity or distance, but a getting closer, which accepts the distance and puts it to work.

What I am calling for, against either universalism or cultural relativism (where one either assumes one knows in advance what is justice, or one assumes that it is impossible to make judgments), is a politics which is premised on secret encounters, on encounters with those who are missing from the constitution of lawful subjects (such as 'global women'). Such a politics assumes that 'action' and 'activism' cannot be separated out from other forms of work: whether that work is about the differentiation of tasks (globalisation as labour), ways of speaking (to others, with others), and even ways of being in the world. Indeed, this approach to activism assumes an intimate relationship between acting and writing (for example, in the very constitution of 'platforms for action'), and it also assumes an intimate relationship between ontology and politics (between being and acting). Thinking about how we might work with, and speak to, others, or how we may inhabit the world *with* others, involves reimagining a different form of political community, one that moves beyond the opposition between common and uncommon, between friends and strangers, or between sameness and difference.

Such a politics based on encounters between other others is one bound up with responsibility – with recognising that relationships of power between others are always constitutive of the possibility of either speaking or not speaking, or of judging or not judging. We are, so to speak, 'right in it'. We do not withdraw from our implication in, for example, the international and gendered division of labour by refusing the privilege of speech, or by refusing to 'make judgments'. Beginning from an 'in-it-ness', a politics of encountering gets closer to others in order to allow the differences between us, as a difference which involves power and antagonism, to make a difference to the very dialogue between others. Here, the differences between us necessitate the dialogue, rather than disallow it – a dialogue must take place precisely *because* we do not speak the same language.

It is the work that needs to be done to get closer to others in a way which does not appropriate their labour as 'our labour', or their talk as 'our talk', that makes possible a different form of collective politics. The 'we' of such a collective politics is hence what must be worked for, rather than being the foundation of our collective work. In the very 'painstaking labour' of getting closer, of speaking *to* each other and of working *for* each other, we also get closer to 'other others'. Hence, in such acts of alignment (rather than merger), we can re-shape the very bodily form of the community as a community that is always to come, as a justice made possible only by its impossibility within the constitution of the present.

The act of giving up assumptions of community as either what we have in common or what we do not have in common, in order to imagine a community that is not yet, may enable a different kind of ethical and political relation between subjects (differently and unequally positioned by the international division of labour) which is based on a more mutual encounter. Indeed, the possibility of a more mutual encounter depends on acknowledging the power differentials that make absolute mutuality or correspondence an impossibility. The emphasis on secret encounters is, here, not a refusal to recognise the power relations that frame such encounters between women, but a call for such secret encounters to *re-animate* the encounters that already exist between women. In other words, through such secret encounters, we could be moved or touched by others whom *we cannot represent*.

Here, one encounters, one has a secret encounter, when something happens that is surprising and when 'we' establish an alliance through the very process of being unsettled by that which is not yet. This is not a community whose foundation is assumed to be just. Rather, it is a community where we are surprised by others with whom we work for justice, that is, where others fail to be constituted as subjects by the law. Such close encounters are always secret encounters, where something fails to be revealed. Through such encounters, transnational feminist communities may be formed by working with that which fails to be made into a collective identity (such as 'global woman'), that is, by re-making *what it is that we may yet have in common*.

CHAPTER 4

THE DECLARATION OF IRIGARAYAN SEXUATE RIGHTS: PERFORMATIVITY AND RECOGNITION

Penelope Deutscher

But sexuate rights are impossible, isn't this the point that she's making?[1]

Myth or fiction is not simply, for Irigaray, a *reflection* of social organization, it also gives a shaping force to the conceptualization of rights and citizenship ... Plato's fiction is not just an expression of Ancient Greek class or sexual warfare; it actively contributes to women's exclusion from full citizenship ...[2]

The problem with the creation of myths, however, is that it is an aleatory process. Who can tell in advance which reworking, which creation, is going to crystallize a potential shift in the collective vision and make a new configuration possible?[3]

Surveying the extensive field of Irigaray commentary, Pheng Cheah and Elizabeth Grosz recently noted that, while she is 'probably the only living feminist philosopher today who has articulated an elaborate program for concrete sociocultural, legal and political transformation', Irigaray's 'contributions to political theory have largely been overlooked'.[4] Few commentators have considered Irigaray's place in the context of political philosophy, historical and contemporary, although some indications of how Irigaray might be so situated have been offered in the work of Iris Young,[5] Nicola Lacey,[6] Drucilla Cornell[7] and Nicole Fermon,[8] amongst others.

---

1   Grosz, E, in Butler, J *et al*, 'The future of sexual difference: an interview with Judith Butler and Drucilla Cornell' (1998) 28(1) Diacritics: A Review of Contemporary Criticism 20.

2   Whitford, M, *Luce Irigaray – Philosophy in the Feminine*, 1991, London and New York: Routledge, p 185.

3   *Ibid*, p 188.

4   Cheah, P and Grosz, E, 'Of being-two: introduction' (1998) 28(1) Diacritics: A Review of Contemporary Criticism 5.

5   Young, IM, 'Polity and group difference', in *Throwing Like a Girl and Other Essays in Feminist Philosophy and Social Theory*, 1990, Bloomington and Indianapolis: Indiana UP, pp 114–40.

6   Lacey, N, 'Normative reconstruction in socio-legal theory' (1996) 5(2) SLS 131; Lacey, N, *Unspeakable Subjects: Feminist Essays in Legal and Social Theory*, 1998, Oxford: Hart.

7   Cornell, D, 'Gender, sex and equivalent rights', in Butler, J and Scott, JW (eds), *Feminists Theorize the Political*, 1992a, New York and London: Routledge, pp 280–96; Cornell, D, *The Philosophy of the Limit*, 1992b, New York and London: Routledge; Cornell, D, *At the Heart of Freedom: Feminism, Sex, and Equality*, 1998, Princeton: Princeton UP.

8   Fermon, N, 'Women on the global market: Irigaray and the democratic State' (1998) 28(1) Diacritics: A Review of Contemporary Criticism 3.

That said, Irigaray has been a frequent point of reference in debates about the recognition of sexual difference. Most often, the reality of actual differences between men and women has been asserted, so that it can be argued that difference should be *recognisable* by our political and legal institutions. In the words of Christine Littleton, for example, equality analysis is phallocentric because 'it is inapplicable once it encounters "real" differences'.[9] For example, for US courts dealing with claims of discrimination on grounds of pregnancy, 'a generalisation of difference between the sexes that was accurate, and permanently so, was beyond the pale'. Continues Littleton, 'Legal equality analysis 'runs out' when it encounters 'real' difference'.[10] So, the problem is located as one of blindness versus recognition: can we restructure our formal and legal institutions so that they *recognise* the fact of 'real' sexual difference. In 'Polity and group difference', Iris Marion Young criticises politics of equality which define citizens in terms of what they 'have in common as opposed to how they differ' and universality 'in the sense of laws and rules that say the same for all and apply to all in the same way; laws and rules that are blind to individual and group differences'.[11] However, not all feminists see the issue of sexual difference as one of whether it can be *recognised* at law:

> ... feminists can remind judges that they too are the architects of women's work aspirations and identities. Courts can acknowledge their own constitutive power and use it to create a workworld ... To create that world, they must abandon the fiction of the female subject already-fixed 'before' the law.[12]

Schultz argues here that the role of the law is not simply to reflect social norms and traditional or conventional notions of identity. The law's role can be understood as creative or constitutive. Could we ask what sorts of identities it might be possible to legally invent? Could we understand the law as legitimately playing such a role? Could Luce Irigaray's work be assessed insofar as it contributes to an understanding of legal creativity of this kind?

I want to place under scrutiny the language of legal and institutional 'blindness' versus 'recognition', and the location given to difference – here sexual difference – as the potential object of legal, civil and constitutional fields of vision. Irigaray is assumed to have contributed to a tradition which laments contemporary political culture, public policy and legal and government institutions for their blindness to sexual difference. It is true that she sometimes uses the formulations of 'recognition' in discussing sexual

---

9 Littleton, C, 'Reconstructing sexual equality', in Kennedy, R and Bartlett, K (eds), *Feminist Legal Theory*, 1991, Boulder: Westview, p 44.

10 *Ibid*, pp 42–43.

11 *Op cit*, Young, fn 5, p 114.

12 Schultz, V, 'Women "before" the law: judicial stories about women, work and sex segregation on the job', in *op cit*, Butler and Scott, fn 7, p 324.

difference. But to focus on such formulations alone overlooks a crucial aspect of her work on sexuate rights and legal reform. This is her concurrent argument that a recognition of sexual difference is 'impossible'. In her early work, Irigaray argues that sexual difference is radically *excluded* from culture. This concept of exclusion does not undermine her simultaneous arguments for a philosophical and cultural recognition of sexual difference, for she deems hers to be a politics which militates for the impossible.[13] Many commentators[14] have discussed Irigaray's philosophy in terms of a concept of performativity. Irigaray hopes for a bringing into being, a founding or a constitution of sexual difference, rather than a politics of recognition. The status of such a founding is 'impossible', because it would 'recognise' that which would not precede the time of legal recognition, but be instituted by it.

So, one should not subsume Irigaray's support for a legal recognition of difference to provide support for the positing of women's differences as 'already-fixed before the law' and awaiting legal recognition. Such an interpretation would overlook an important aspect of her argument. While Irigaray is a frequent point of reference for those who discuss the limitations of equality-based feminist legal reform, the status of her concept of difference is complex. Apparently, Irigaray finds value in arguing, not for a legal recognition of sexual difference which would be possible, but for one which would not be. I want in this chapter to pursue the specificity of this argument and consider what kind of contribution it can make to the politics of recognition. How might debates about the politics of recognition be usefully altered by reference to Irigaray's work?

In posing this question, I will first turn to a context in which the problematics of recognition have been most thoroughly debated in recent years. This is, however, a context in which discussions of feminism are more likely to cite figures such as Carol Gilligan than Luce Irigaray.

---

13 Irigaray, L, *I Love To You*, Martin, A (trans), 1996, London: Routledge, p 10.

14 See, eg, Cornell, D, *Beyond Accomodation: Ethical Feminism, Deconstruction and the Law*, 1991, New York and London: Routledge; Huffer, L, 'Luce *et veritas*: toward an ethics of performance' (1995) Yale French Studies 87; *op cit*, Lacey, 1996, fn 6.

THE POLITICS OF RECOGNITION

In assessing the status of feminism in recent debate about the politics of recognition (debate which has fostered most notably around the work of Charles Taylor,[15] James Tully[16] and Nancy Fraser,[17] for example), Susan Wolf has rightly argued that the politics of recognition has some difficulty in contemplating its potential application to gender politics.[18] Women do not share a unique culture which might be supported and recognised by educational reform. The language of difference deployed in this debate applies better to contexts in which a marginalised people's integrity and self-respect could be consolidated by legal and institutional recognition of its cultural history and specificity. Yet, as James Tully notes, a 'politics of cultural recognition' has included, in addition to claims for recognition by nationalist movements, multicultural or intercultural movements:

> ... the demands of feminist movements for recognition ... that women should have an equal say within the constitutional institutions of contemporary societies and their authoritative traditions of interpretation. Because the constitutional institutions and traditions of interpretation were established long ago by men to the exclusion of women, it follows that they should be amended ... in order to recognise and accomodate women's culturally distinctive ways of speaking and acting, so that substantive gender equality will be assured in the daily political struggles in the institutions the constitution founds. Making this task even more difficult, women's culture itself is not homogeneous, but multicultural and contested.[19]

Here, Tully employs a formulation which refers to women as sharing distinctive ways of speaking and acting which should be recognised at law. He also recognises the problem with this formulation – there is no homogenous culture that women share which might call for this kind of recognition. Repeatedly, Tully's references to women fail with this logic, as he continues to subsume women with 'multicultural groups' and 'linguistic minorities' as a large set of those who would 'seek to participate in the existing institutions of the dominant society, but in ways that recognise and affirm ... their culturally diverse ways of thinking, speaking and acting. What they share is a longing for self-rule',[20] etc.

---

15 Taylor, C, 'The politics of recognition', in Guttman, A (ed), *Multiculturalism: Examining the Politics of Recognition*, 1994, Princeton: Princeton UP, pp 25–74.

16 Tully, J, *Strange Multiplicity: Constitutionalism in an Age of Diversity*, 1995, Cambridge: CUP.

17 Fraser, N, *Justice Interruptus: Critical Reflections on the 'Postsocialist' Condition*, 1997, New York and London: Routledge.

18 Wolf, S, 'Comment', in *ibid*, Guttman, p 76.

19 *Ibid*, Tully, pp 2–3.

20 *Ibid*, Tully, p 4.

The most obvious response is that there should be a better separation of the politics of recognition as it might apply to linguistic minorities and multicultural groups, and as it might apply to women. The problem might seem to be simply that Tully and others are trying awkwardly to fit women into a model which is conceptualised for the purposes of a philosophy of multiculturalism. On the other hand, the fact that women do not fit this model easily may make us question the model. References to 'distinctive ways of speaking and acting' ring falsely in relation to women, but perhaps they should also be reconsidered in relation to linguistic minorities and multicultural groups. In fact, I will argue that Irigaray's work can make a contribution to the problem of recognition. The solution that Irigaray has offered to the problematics of a politics of recognition may have applications beyond the obvious scope of her own work.

Tully's politics involve the affirmation of diversity. He refers to an ideal of:

> ... protecting and enhancing the cultural differences and similarities of intercultural citizens ... They are Antigone's children, the citizens of the common ground created by European imperialism and the many resistances to it ... The recognition and accommodation of these suppressed and persecuted citizens on equal footing with other members of a society marks the transition to post-imperial constitutionalism. It requires more than ... mutual toleration and respect ... It requires that the citizens affirm diversity itself as a constitutive good of the association.[21]

What Tully does acknowledge very early in his work is the problematic status of recognition once the lack of self-identity of a culture is recognised, and in this regard he cites a Derridean formulation: 'What is proper to a culture is to not be identical to itself.' Recognition can never be definitive, because cultural identities are constantly 'contested, questioned and renegotiated':[22]

> The politics of cultural recognition takes place on this intercultural 'common' ground, as I shall call the labyrinth composed of the overlap, interaction and negotiation of cultures over time. Of course, mutual recognition is not rendered unproblematic by the reconceptualisation and reclarification of the ground in which we stand.[23]

But the weight of Tully's argument falls on the point that we should not see a nation's constitution as a static, original entity. While he makes the simultaneous point that we need to recognise that identities are not static entities, this loses emphasis in his work. This is particularly seen in his comments on women.

---

21 *Op cit*, Tully, fn 16, p 177.

22 *Op cit*, Tully, fn 16, p 25, citing Derrida, J, *The Other Heading: Reflections on Today's Europe*, 1992, Bloomington: Indiana UP, p 9.

23 *Op cit*, Tully, fn 16, p 14.

Tully refers to women's 'feminine ways of speaking, thinking and acting',[24] citing Gilligan's work on the ethics of care and sexual difference and her question concerning whether women's voices are given a distorted hearing in a tradition which emphasises justice.[25] Later, he argues that, because constitutions were established without the voice of women, it is not sufficient for women to try to integrate their voice into these founding constitutions. Instead, women need to be able to have a say 'in their own voice' and women's 'culturally different ways of speaking and acting need to be recognised'.[26] So, despite the recognition that women do not share a specific culture or language, as those of a particular racial or cultural group may, Tully's comments about women repeatedly attribute to them pre-existing and stable differences. He designates the philosophical problem as regards the law, women and difference to be how constitutional negotiations might come to recognise, by constitutionalising, gender difference. Thus, just constitutional negotiations would, he writes, involve negotiating which gender differences are 'relevant and worthy of being constitutionalised'.[27] Each of these references attributes to women a pre-existing specificity and particular manners of speaking and acting:

> ... with this protection in place, women will be able to amend the political institutions they share with men so they can speak and act in their own ways on equal footing in everyday political struggles: that is, without assimilation to other ways of speaking and acting.[28]

Tully admits that 'many male and female sceptics doubt that there are identity related differences which require constitutional protection'.[29] But, at this point, he attributes the position of female specificity not to his own argument, but to the current feminist thinking:

> However, cultural feminists have brought forward sufficient evidence of their differences and their constitutional domination by men to establish that their claim warrants a fair hearing.[30]

Tully's formulation suggests that the only kind of sexual difference that the law might legitimately recognise is a sexual difference which pre-exists that

---

24 *Op cit*, Tully, fn 16, p 47.
25 *Op cit*, Tully, fn 16, pp 48–49.
26 *Op cit*, Tully, fn 16, p 178.
27 *Op cit*, Tully, fn 16.
28 *Op cit*, Tully, fn 16.
29 *Op cit*, Tully, fn 16, p 178.
30 *Op cit*, Tully, fn 16, pp 178–79.

recognition.[31] Any other kind of constitutionalisation of sexual difference would, by this argument, be illegitimate:

> If the participants [in periodic constitutional dialogues] reach agreement that no significant differences remain that cannot be recognised and accommodated in the prevailing constitutional order, then the sceptics will be proven correct. If not, then they must agree that the cultural differences that remain after the discussion ought to be constitutionalised.[32]

So, it is Tully himself who considers that the issue of sexual difference and its recognition at law is limited to recognising existing differences between men and women. It could be said that this sits uncomfortably with references to the law's powers to enhance difference and promote diversity, which imply that the role of the law may not only be to recognise difference, but also to foster it. From the point that diversity is considered to be a good, and the moment that Tully rejects the notion that constitutions are documents whose original nature and logic must be respected, then it is not clear why a politics of difference must be limited to a politics of recognition. Why should we not value legal reforms which promote, or attempt to institute, difference or play an inventive, creative role in this respect? Furthermore, not all theorists in this area do limit the scope of a politics of recognition to real differences, which must precede the legal time of recognition.[33] Consider, for example, Nancy Fraser's formulation:

> Recognition claims often take the form of calling attention to, if not performatively creating, the putative specificity of some group and then of affirming its value. Thus, they tend to promote group differentiation.[34]

---

31 In addition to references to Carol Gilligan and the ethics of care, feminist theory discussed by Tully includes Lugones' and Spelman's notion of differentiated difference, described as a notion of criss-crossing, overlapping cultural differences, something referred to as a postmodern, disintegrative notion of difference by Linda Alcoff (*op cit*, Tully, fn 16, p 49) and Genevieve Lloyd's argument that great concepts of constitution were founded in opposition to what is attributed to the feminine (*op cit*, Tully, fn 16, p 50).

32 *Op cit*, Tully, fn 16, p 179.

33 Charles Taylor's emphasis is placed more strongly on the potential for the law, in its apparent 'recognition' of identities, to allow new possibilities for those identities (*op cit*, fn 15, p 25): 'our identity is partly shaped by recognition or its absence, often by the *mis*recognition by others, and so, a person or a group of people can suffer real damage, real distortion, if the people or the society around them mirror back to them a confining or demeaning or contemptible picture of themselves. Non-recognition can inflict harm, can be a form of oppression, imprisoning someone in a false, distorted and reduced mode of being.' However, Taylor goes on to see the issue as being largely one of esteem, of whether public and institutionalised depictions of women are demeaning.

34 Fraser examines the way in which a politics of recognition has come to compete with a politics which emphases the primary importance of issues of redistribution. She argues against the bifurcation of these issues. See *op cit*, Fraser, fn 17, p 16.

From this perspective, we could think of feminist theorists who might serve as alternatives to Carol Gilligan as key references for the thinking of sexual difference. The most obvious figure, whose omission from Tully's discussion is noticeable, is Luce Irigaray.

I suggested above that feminist commentary on Irigaray has often elided a key aspect of her concept of sexual difference. This elided aspect is the one which most offers the potential to contribute to debate about the politics of recognition. What is passed over is the status of the concept of Irigarayan sexual difference as impossible. 'Impossible' does not mean that a culture which affirmed sexual difference could never come to pass. Rather, it means that we cannot identify and 'pre-fix' the identity whose recognition one might wish to see at law. Instead, the sorts of identities whose possibility is enhanced by a legal affirmation of difference would arise from that legal affirmation, rather than precede it. This means that the law is understood to play a performative role. Commentators who have underlined, in positive terms, the impossibility of Irigarayan sexual difference are generally those who have discussed it in the context of a politics of performativity, and one example can be seen in the early work of Drucilla Cornell.

DRUCILLA CORNELL, IRIGARAY AND THE PERFORMATIVE

Legal theorist, Drucilla Cornell, has been one of those commentators most attentive to that aspect of Irigaray's work concerned with the founding of sexuate rights. Cornell's early work reflects her interest and sympathy for the concept. In *Beyond Accomodation*, Cornell writes positively about the aspect of Irigaray's work whose aim is to re-metaphorise the feminine. Here, 'performativity' is a key term for Cornell. Repeatedly, she emphasises the aspect of Irigaray's philosophy which breaks with a 'politics of recognition' and, in each case, performativity is the term which serves as the reminder of this break:

> To reduce Irigaray's positioning vis à vis the 'sex' of feminine specificity to description of gender identity or of biological femaleness is to fail ... to heed the specificity of Irigaray's literary language and its performative powers to crack open what 'is' ... [T]he affirmation of feminine difference ... refigures the feminine.[35]

In 'Gender, sex and equivalent rights', Cornell presents the concept of equivalent rights, which she references to the concept of sexuate rights presented in Irigaray's 'How to define sexuate rights'. The problem with equal

---

35 *Op cit*, Cornell, fn 14, p 17.

rights, as critics have repeatedly noted, is that 'we continually have to analogize our experience to men's if we want it legally "recognized" as unequal treatment'.[36] Instead, a new formulation of equivalent rights which might apply, for example, to the right to abortion and the right to childbearing, would 'allow difference to be recognized and equally valued without women having to show that they are like men for legal purposes'.[37] On the one hand, Cornell retains the concept of the re-metaphorisation of the feminine, noting that Irigaray's concept of equivalent rights addresses feminine sexual difference, as this is *'continually reimagined'*.[38] And, as she states in a later interview, 'I did not see Irigaray at all as an essentialist. If anything, the feminine was a kind of radical otherness to any conception of the real or reality.[39]

On the other hand, the reader notes the extent to which the language of recognition repeats throughout Cornell's essay: 'Equivalent rights recognize that the human species as currently constituted is composed of two genres,' and, later, '... sexual difference is recognized and valued.'[40] But her overall discussion makes clear Cornell's appreciation of the paradoxical status of this recognition. To recognise a feminine sexual difference as reimagined has a peculiar status of recognition. It does not recognise what pre-exists that recognition; instead, it contributes to the institution of the very sexual difference that it apparently recognises. From this perspective, the language of recognition is necessary, so long as we understand the status of recognition which grounds that language: that which is recognised is not understood as preceding the recognition, despite the use of the language of recognition, which would seem to indicate the contrary.

By contrast, Cornell's more recent *The Imaginary Domain* makes very little reference to Irigaray. The work is indebted in no small degree to Irigaray's concept of sexuate rights and the crucial role that they might play in re-structuring models of civic personhood. Cornell argues for reformulated rights which include women and which protect the imaginary domain and ensure the rights to have one's sexed represented and to represent one's own sexed being. But, in so doing, she does not consider woman to be a pre-given identity with established rights and obligations. She takes as her legal reference point 'what should be', not 'what is'. As she writes, 'We are demanding that what *should be* must exist as a matter of law'. And, similarly, 'To claim our legacy as women is to remember what has yet to be, and to demand it as already "ours". That is the paradox inherent in understanding

---

36 *Op cit*, Cornell, 1992a, fn 7, p 292.

37 *Op cit*, Cornell, 1992a, fn 7, p 293.

38 *Op cit*, Cornell, 1992a, fn 7, p 281. Emphasis added.

39 *Op cit*, Butler *et al*, fn 1.

40 *Op cit*, Cornell, 1992a, fn 7, p 282.

feminism as what Ursula le Guin has called "an archeology of the future"'.[41] What Cornell considers to lie before the law is not a fixed identity, but a right to form a future identity. What should be recognised by the law is that right, rather than an identity. While a process of evaluation is demanded, this is not an evaluation of a pre-fixed identity. Instead, new identities would emerge from the process of evaluation:

> As a result, we should not demand that we *be* as women before the law; we should demand instead equivalent evaluation *by* the law of our sexual difference. Such an evaluation goes against what we have been designated 'to be' as human creatures of lesser worth rather than affirming any current designations of what a woman is ... As a demand to the law it is a demand for transformation.[42]

In sum, Cornell's account in *The Imaginary Domain* pulls back again from the notion of recognition, at least insofar as this implies the recognition of a static, pre-fixed identity. The right to representation of one's sexuate being, she writes, means that we can no longer represent a person as neuter, nor as 'something "there" ... but [as] a possibility, an aspiration which, because it is that, can never be fulfilled once and for all'. The person must be respected as part of a 'project'.[43] Though it makes virtually no overt reference to Irigaray, I think it can be argued that *The Imaginary Domain* is a work heavily endebted to an Irigarayan concept of sexuate rights.

More recently, however, Cornell has come to express considerable reservations about Irigaray's project. In the subsequent work, *At the Heart of Freedom*, Cornell's references to Irigaray are more extensive, but Irigaray is now figured definitely, and critically, as a theorist who 'naturalises sexual difference in her advocacy for sexuate rights',[44] in addition to privileging sexual difference over difference of race, nationality and the non-heterosexual. Cornell further claims that Irigaray's work on sexuate rights contradicts her philosophical work, which leaves 'the question of sexual difference ... as a question'.[45]

This position is most clearly articulated in Cornell's interview with Cheah, Grosz and Judith Butler. In this context, Cornell explains her original interest in Irigaray:

---

41 Cornell, D, *The Imaginary Domain: Abortion, Pornography and Sexual Harassment*, 1995, New York and London: Routledge, pp 235, 237.

42 *Ibid*, p 236.

43 *Ibid*, p 5.

44 *Op cit*, Cornell, 1998, fn 7, p 30.

45 *Ibid*, Cornell, p 200.

> I found someone who was deploying the feminine unashamedly in a utopian manner, saying that there is a beyond to whatever kind of concept of sense we have. And without that beyond being articulated, endlessly breaking up the real, we can't even get to a different kind of ethics.[46]

Cornell goes on to explain that, for her, Irigaray had never been an essentialist thinker. To the contrary, she found Irigaray valuable precisely because she was attempting to articulating a beyond without content. Consider the extreme contrast with the Cornell of *At The Heart of Freedom*, for whom it is precisely the way in which Irigaray refigures the imaginary which is the problem:

> ... the attempt to give rights, thought through gender difference as a universal, denies women the freedom to reimagine their sexual difference. For Irigaray, there are naturally two sexes. Her ontologisation of the two denies that women live their biology in infinitely different and original ways. In the imaginary domain, sexes cannot be counted because what we will become under freedom cannot be known in advance.[47]

Cornell's interpretation of the status of sexual difference is clearly at odds with her earlier comments. While she makes many important criticisms of Irigaray, I do think that she passes over the key aspect of Irigaray's philosophy: the close analysis that Irigaray offers of the *impossibility* of any status that sexual difference might have in contemporary culture. This concept of impossibility should, in my view, be read with Irigaray's concurrent attempt to give content to an imaginary for sexual difference. I am here merely repeating Cornell's own earlier arguments about Irigaray. To criticise her attempt to give content to that 'beyond of sense' would be a mistake, insofar as Irigaray does affirm the impossibility of these attempts.

Cornell may be underestimating the extent to which Irigaray's project does attempt to retain a kind of 'beyond of sense'. As she has done earlier in her work, Irigaray's attempts at conceptual invention piggyback onto existing and traditional concepts of femininity and maternity, in this case virginity and the uniqueness of the mother-foetus relation in terms of a specifically ethical relation whose emblem is the placenta. They are blown out, so as to become unrecognisable and culturally senseless. White Western culture is very far indeed from privileging virginity in the Irigarayan sense. Cornell interprets the project as an attempt to fix down the meaning of sexual difference. But this is a question of how one occupies the position of the 'beyond of sense'. Does one speak with no content, or offer notions whose function are to exceed sense? When Irigaray speaks in the name of a legal recognition of the specificity of virginity, should we criticise her for giving content to the senseless, or identify a formulation which must, in contemporary culture, occupy the position of the senseless?

---

46 *Op cit*, Butler *et al*, fn 1, p 20.
47 *Op cit*, Cornell, 1998, fn 7, p 122.

It is, then, quite indicative that, when Grosz prompts Cornell, 'But sexuate rights are impossible, isn't this the point that she's making?', Cornell responds, 'You see, what's interesting though is that they may not be', and then again, 'I have always read her as programmatically serious about sexuate rights, and seeing them as realizable'.[48] Certainly, Irigaray speaks in the rhetorical mode of 'programmatic seriousness' about sexuate rights. But the question is whether they function rhetorically for us as 'possible' or 'impossible'. What Cornell takes to be a mistaken attempt to give content can, I think, also be interpreted alternatively, as a program of sexuate rights for the recognition of sexual difference, formulated so as to insist on their own impossibility, however serious the spirit in which they are articulated. Indeed, the more serious the spirit, the more they will perform as 'the impossible'. While questions remain about the utility of an Irigarayan politics of impossible recognition, I do think that the assumption that their specific content works to undermine their function as 'impossible' is mistaken.

In the context of its own aspirations, Irigaray's concept of sexual difference is not weakened to the extent that she gives it specific content. Nor is it weakened by its lack of more specific content. But it is weakened if these two aspects of her approach to the concept decouple. Her aim is to retain the double notion of sexual difference as both 'impossible' (lacking sense) and as that which she would see legally 'recognised' (yet how can we think a recognition of the senseless?). It stands or falls on its ability to retain this contradictory status.

However, at times, it seems that Cornell's point is to resist not the fact that Irigaray gives content to sexual difference, but the precise content she gives, a content which, according to her argument, attempts 'to give rights, thought through gender difference as a universal' and thereby 'denies women the freedom to reimagine their sexual difference'.[49] With this comment, it could be argued that Cornell returns to the terms in which she has long assessed Irigaray's concept of sexual difference: performativity. In her earlier work, Cornell had supported Irigaray's project precisely by explaining its performative aspect. Irigaray's language, she argued, had the power to 'crack open what "is"'[50] and refigure the feminine. Now, Cornell seems to question not only the substance of Irigaray's work (that she gives content to the feminine), but also its performance. Irigaray's language acts to deny women the freedom of their imagination. These comments allow some reflection on the status, not just of sexual difference, but also of performativity in Irigaray's work. Reviewing some of the main debates which have circulated around Irigaray's work in recent years, it could be argued that performativity reoccurs

---

48   *Op cit*, Butler *et al*, fn 1, pp 25, 26.
49   *Op cit*, Cornell, 1998, fn 7, p 122.
50   *Op cit*, Cornell, fn 14, p 17.

repeatedly as a key issue in the interpretation of her project, and that performativity interconnects with a concern about instrumentalism.

Irigaray's turn to the language of rights is interesting in the context of debates over 'rights-talk' in recent political philosophy. For some, a confidence in rights is over-optimistic, placing too much faith in the idea of systematic institutional reform to achieve cultural change.[51] The concern is that one reform in one domain may not be sufficient to lead to the cultural change that it seems to aim at. What might Irigaray's own position be? I have elsewhere argued[52] against the view that her concept of sexuate rights reflects excessive confidence in the efficacy of legal reform to effect social change. I have argued that the sexuate rights need to be interpreted in the context of Irigaray's proposals for reforms to language, religion, economic reform, love, daily interpersonal relations, intergenerational relations between parents and children and relations between those in differential power relations – such as parent and child, teacher and student, man and woman, and so on. Far from a reflection of confidence in the efficacy of legal reform, Irigaray is arguing that, in order to make possible substantial social change, a reorganisation of relations between men and women and a restructuring of sexed identity, femininity and masculinity, it would be necessary for social reform to take place simultaneously on all these levels. Again, this raises the question of how the program is understood in terms of its performativity. Should we assess the rights in terms of what they might lead to (and then ask whether sexuate rights alone would be sufficient to move us to a culture of sexual difference)? Or should we ask how the rights perform? (And we might argue that their obvious inadequacy as regards the institution of a culture of sexual difference underlines the need for change at all cultural levels, rather than rights reform alone.)

Considerable literature about Irigaray's sexuate rights has tended to evince concern over the likely outcomes of a declaration of sexuate rights. One argument is that Irigaray places excessive confidence in 'rights talk'. In the words of Lacey, Irigaray 'espouses a curiously naïve and apparently instrumental optimism about legal reform'.[53] Even if Irigaray is not being

---

51 For some, confidence in rights can be misleading, distracting attention away from the real inequalities which may be present, but concealed by an apparent situation of institutionally guaranteed equity. Of course, for others – Patricia Williams is among them – it is the loss of confidence in rights which is insidious. The debate about over-confidence in rights distracts attention from the extent to which some groups have not achieved basic rights. The debate conceals differences between the very different relation to rights and the history of rights (eg, the different histories of African-American and white Americans) of those who debate the subject. See Williams, P, *The Alchemy of Race and Rights*, 1991, Cambridge, Mass: Harvard UP and Cornell, *op cit*, fn 7, p 190, discussing the material at p 154 of Williams' book.

52 In a chapter on Irigarayan sexuate rights included in Ahmed, S *et al* (eds), *Transformations: Thinking Through Feminism*, 2000, London: Routledge.

53 *Op cit*, Lacey, 1998, fn 6, p 245.

naïvely instrumentalist about legal reform, a second argument is that she is naïvely instrumental about rhetoric. Margaret Whitford has raised doubts in this regard. Whitford has argued that the utopian moments of Irigaray's philosophy should be understood 'in terms of the imaginary, rather than as literal accounts of a possible future'.[54] However, as the debate has taken place, it becomes clear that the explanation of the program as a utopian interest in a new imaginary for individual social reforms has not aided matters. Instead, debate about excessive confidence in a program for legal reform merely shifts to concerns about excessive confidence in a program of utopian visions; a politics of the imaginary.

In all of these responses, it is again the instrumentalism which seems to trouble critics – the idea that Irigaray seems to believe that, as a result of her philosophy (for legal reform, or for a refiguring of the imaginary), something willed or desired might happen – new, potent and desirable images for women, if not actual legal reform. Thus, as Whitford herself has said:

> The problem with the creation of myths, however, is that it is an aleatory process. Who can tell in advance which reworking, which creation, is going to crystallize a potential shift in the collective vision and make a new configuration possible?[55]

Let us assume, for example, that Irigaray knows perfectly well that the legal declaration of a Bill of sexual rights would not necessarily lead to the culture of sexual difference she hopes for. Nevertheless, the claim is that she believes more realistically that to perform the declaration – for example, in her own published work – plays a useful role in contributing to the rhetorical conditions necessary for an eventual culture of sexual difference. In this case, again she is being naïvely instrumentalist, this time about her own rhetoric. In Nicola Lacey's words, 'the question of whether particular rhetorics *can* move us forward is a relevant question'. Lacey goes on to ask whether rhetorical strategies such as those used by Irigaray can 'dislodge the dominant conception'.[56]

Here, Lacey raises concerns about the performative status of Irigaray's work – what events does Irigaray seem to think might eventuate, (hypothetically) from the declaration of sexual rights, or (hypothetically) from a declaration of sexual rights understood to be a rhetorical gesture, or (actually) from her own declaration of sexual rights in her published work? Whichever is the status of the claim attributed to Irigaray, in each case the concern is what Irigaray seems to think might eventually result from her performance of declaration. This is why I think that Cornell's interpretation has been exceptional in its repeated interrogation of how Irigaray's discourse

---

54 *Op cit*, Whitford, fn 2, p 186.
55 *Op cit*, Whitford, fn 2, p 188.
56 *Op cit*, Lacey, 1998, fn 6, pp 246, 247.

could be thought of as 'acting now', instead of focusing only on what effects it might lead to in the future.

According to Cornell's early reading, Irigaray's discourse 'refigures' the feminine, rather than potentially leading to a cultural refiguring of the feminine. On Cornell's later reading, Irigaray's work *acts as a denial*: the denial that women should individually and diversely imagine the reform of sexual difference.

How, then, can we assess the performativity of Irigarayan sexuate rights? Thought of in performative terms, it could be said that Irigaray's very attempt to give women sexuate rights is infelicitous. The rights are not legally instituted. But this is to assume that the act whose success or failure we must assess is the legal or cultural institutionalisation of sexuate rights. What if, from another perspective, Irigaray does perform an act with her very declaration? It is Cornell who, in her earlier work, was one of the first to emphasise the importance of thinking of Irigaray's work in terms of performativity. Her approach did not restrict itself to a 'what might happen' or 'what the result might be' concept of performativity.

In some ways, Cornell's interpretation is a useful break from much of the literature which interprets Irigaray's work in terms of performativity, because it considers the extent to which, and the way in which, Irigaray's discourse works, rather than only considering what effects it might lead to. In other words, Cornell assess Irigaray's discourse in terms of its illocutionary, rather than its hypothetical perlocutionary, effects. Most commentators have asked, as Lacey does in the above example, what effects a legal or rhetorical declaration of speech acts might lead to (the perlocutive). Cornell asks what kind of an 'act' the declaration already is (the illocutive). So, it may be that Irigaray's declaration should be assessed not in terms of its possible effects, but in illocutionary terms. As such, for example, it could be seen as performing the 'why not' declaration for sexuate rights. It forces the reader to reflect, if fleetingly, on the 'why not' of sexuate rights. What, in our culture, prohibits their viability? Is an equality discourse more legitimate? More plausible or palatable? Why?

But this leaves us with the question of how stably we can determine the way in which a declaration acts. Cornell seems to agree that sexuate rights should be assessed in illocutionary terms. For her, however, the act is different from what Irigaray herself might acknowledge. According to Cornell, it acts as this declaration: 'I, Irigaray, declare that women shall not reimagine their sexual difference other than as I imagine it for them.' It may be, of course, that Cornell believes that Irigaray's discourse could have the causal (perlocutionary) effect of inhibiting women's freedom to reimagine their sexual difference. But I think that this is a less plausible interpretation. Whether or not Irigaray means to hinder women's freedom to reimagine their sexual difference (and let us assume that she does not), Cornell believes that the effect of her discourse is to declare a limitation of those possibilities. Let us assume that one reason for this is that Irigaray's discourse is too little informed, in Cornell's view, by plural ways in which women may wish to imagine that difference, generous engagement with and recognition of such differences. Because Irigaray's voice is monodiscursive in this regard, her discourse acts as a failure to affirm differences in how we reimagine sexual difference – irrespective of her best intentions.

There is no doubt that Irigaray's work opens itself to that risk. One doubt I have, however, and it is a doubt that one could direct at most of the literature which assesses Irigaray's work in terms of its performative effects, is its own commitment to fixing the question of how Irigaray's work does act in illocutionary terms. Let us assume that causal relationships are very hard to establish. It is, then, very hard to pose questions asked by Whitford and Lacey, such as whether rhetoric or, indeed, legal reform, are or would be sufficient to move us forward. But is it any easier to establish with certainty what the actual act of a speech act is – whether, for example, Irigaray's writing works as the act, 'I declare that women do not have the right to reshape their sexual imaginary', as opposed to the act, 'I declare that they do'?

As many commentators have written, the apparently self-present and instantaneous nature of the speech act, such as the promise or the marriage vow, is mediated by social factors, convention, context and the knowledge and expectations of the audience or participants in the speech act. This becomes apparent once we imagine the promise, or marriage, performed on a stage or cited. We can argue that Irigaray's rhetoric has multiple effects which actually occur. What we cannot do is fix or pin down exactly what those effects are, and for whom. Irigaray's discourse may well run the risk of acting as the declaration that women do not have the right to determine their own sexual imaginary. But they may also work as the declaration that women do have this right. A possibility that Cornell seems not to consider is that they also have the potential to work in both ways, in contradictory fashion, in a variety of different contexts, for multiple readers and even for the one reader.

For example, what if the condition of Irigaray attempting to give content to sexual difference is that she simultaneously declares that women have the right to give content to sexual difference (insofar as she is in the act of hypothesising such content) *and* that they do not – for example, insofar as her own act of definition simultaneously forecloses an affirmation of alternative sexual imaginaries – or, indeed, because the very failure and infelicity of Irigaray's 'imagining' amounts to a different kind of declaration (perhaps a lament) that women do not have the right?

What of the suggestion that the status of recognition in Irigaray's work may contribute to a rethinking of the politics of recognition? Many theorists agree that one of the insidious effects of colonial practices is the erosion of a colonised people's specific culture. Others argue that one of the problems with the logic of anti-colonialism is that it leads one to justify arguments about cultural specificity only in terms of the language of the proper, of identity, of the lost original. It might also be argued that colonialism's effects are worse, and more widespread, than the erosion of an original culture. It can lead to a failure of cultural and rhetorical space which will affirm positive differences, and in terms which will not reduce non-white Western cultures to the same as, the opposite of or the complement of the white.

If we return to Tully's concept of constitutional recognition, we see how few of these types of impoverishment of culture are captured by the question of whether legal institutions recognise actual differences. Legal institutions are needed, which need not be limited to an affirmation of differences designated as actual prior to legal change. What is needed instead is legal reform, which could create the conditions for inventing new cultural identities. Their legitimacy of recognition would not rely on their being original, proper, or on their existing 'before the law'. Many theorists debating the politics of recognition have subsumed feminism to similitude (or otherwise) to problems of recognition of cultural diversity. Instead, debates about the politics of recognition could turn their attention to more diverse models of difference negotiated in contemporary feminist contexts. One of the strengths of Irigaray's work is her position that our culture has excluded the possibility of sexual difference, and yet, that this does not render illegitimate a constitutional recognition of sexual difference. The performative work of this argument can be understood in multiple ways, as we have seen. Some critics debate the question of what real effects would arise from such a constitutional recognition, and whether Irigaray is overly optimistic in this regard. Some argue that the infelicity of the declaration is the very point of the work. Some argue that the work should be understood as a rhetorical, imaginary or poetic act. Nevertheless, some still ask what effects such an act might lead to. Others debate about how it works, now, instantly, as a rhetorical declaration. The debate itself might be seen as Irigarayan rhetoric 'working'. But the very debate requires that one departs from a view that constitutional recognition of cultural differences would be legitimate only from the point of establishing actual and sufficient evidence of significant differences waiting before the law.

CHAPTER 5

FEMINIST THEORY AND LAW: BEYOND THE POSSIBILITIES OF THE PRESENT?

Ralph Sandland

INTRODUCTION: UTOPIAN IMAGERY AND ITS (APPARENT) LIMITS

What is the nature of the Beyond? Does, or can, the Beyond figure in the writings of feminists and other critical theorists of gender as a *substantive* 'goal', or should it be understood only in terms of method? These questions are of the utmost importance for feminist theory generally, but they hold a particular resonance for lawyers. Law trades in both method and substance. Law gives results and, according to its own narratives, law can provide the 'last word'. In its own terms, law is closure; it has the power to guillotine discourse and to enforce outcomes. Of course, legal outcomes are deconstructable. But can the postmodern feminist engagement with law move beyond critique?

The strands of postmodern and poststructuralist discourse (both within and without feminist legal theory) with which I have most sympathy are informed by a utopian dynamic. This utopianism is now perhaps most closely associated, at least by legal scholars, with the work of Drucilla Cornell. In fact, Cornell's work is only one element within a broader feminist interest with the concept, and political purchase, of utopianism.[1] Despite the constancy of the gesture towards a utopian future, however, postmodernism is notoriously vague when it comes to *specifying* its *own* intended goals or outcomes.[2] Naffine and Owens, for example, arguing that a crucial part of this project is to 'sex' the legal subject, 'opt for discretion rather than valour [and] prefer to say that the nature of law after sexing is a tantalising prospect, but that it remains unknown to us'.[3] When a substantive outcome or goal *is* posited, it tends to be presented, as in the following extract, in self-deconstructing form:

> ... it is neither a man nor a woman who is coming, but something new, some odd kind of new being, a new step, an effect yet to be produced, some new sort of s/he or wo/man, something innumerable and unclassifiable, something

---

1   See, eg, Sarggisson, L, *Feminist Utopias*, 1996, London: Routledge.

2   Fegan, EV, '"Subjects" of regulation/resistance? Post-modern feminism and agency in abortion-decision-making' (1999) 7(3) FLS 241.

3   Naffine, N and Owens, RJ, 'Sexing law', in their *Sexing the Subject of Law*, 1997, London: Sweet & Maxwell, p 21.

unprogrammable, *the* impossible. Maybe what is coming is nothing as simple and unambiguous as an hermaphrodite or an androgyne, but something undecidably miscenated, something that has not happened yet, something singular, something possible, something impossible, something unimaginable and innumerable.[4]

Now, there are good reasons behind this postmodern orthodoxy – of the necessity constantly to attempt to straddle or transcend the opposition between the possible and the impossible, the imaginable and the unimaginable, and so on; to be vague and ambiguous about precisely who, or what, in this postmodern teleology, 'is coming'. Methodologically speaking, its purpose is to use 'deconstruction' to locate within the possibilities of the present the impossibilities of the future, as that which is presently excluded. This approach is aware that in the positing of the same or the similar is the trace of the other as that which is not posited. Otherwiseness is always already present and, as history tells us, present impossibilities can be future possibilities; even future realities. In more political (or ethical) terms, deconstruction has taught us that such future (im)possibilities will inevitably hold within themselves the trace of their own correlative impossibilities; for example, excluded subject-positions. Therefore, conceptual closure is to be resisted at all costs, as an ethical injunction, to 'do justice' to the 'other', by keeping open the space for otherwiseness.

In this project there can be no last word. Words are always open to interpretation. The author cannot authorise a particular meaning of his or her own text, because the concepts that animate it will always be susceptible to being revealed as violent, as hierarchical, as expressly or implicitly normative, as related to and dependent on other texts, pre-texts and contexts, which work outside or against the intentions of the author. In a very real sense, one is damned as soon as pen is put to paper. Of the various strands of 'postmodern' discourse, the particular contribution of deconstruction has been to reveal the inevitability of permanent instability; instability as a stable state, stability as an unstable state, in any discursive, historical or philosophical, context.[5] It is this instability of stability – in any (that is, every) context in which there is an inside and an outside – that has functioned as a generalised topography and cartography for much of recent critical studies. Postmodern feminism has learnt to live, albeit uncomfortably,[6] with the permanent danger or risk that to reach for the utopian future that it knows is logically (im)possible is to reinstitute the lines of force that constitute the tyranny of the present.

---

4   Caputo, JD, 'Dreaming of the innumerable: Derrida, Drucilla Cornell and the dance of gender', in Feder, EK, Rawlinson, MC and Zakin, E (eds), *Derrida and Feminism: Recasting the Question of Woman*, 1997, London: Routledge, p 157.

5   Deutscher, P, *Yielding Gender: Feminism, Deconstruction and the History of Philosophy*, 1997, London: Routledge.

6   Frug, MJ, *Postmodern Legal Feminism*, 1992, London: Routledge.

In the narratives of postmodern feminism, freedom and danger are not merely set in tension; rather, they imply each other, give form to the other, *depend on* each other. Therefore, to *specify* the intended outcome of any intervention, to attempt to give some definite form to that which is coming, is precisely to prevent its arrival. This, as Naffine and Owens have observed, is 'The conundrum at the heart of feminism'.[7] There is a sense in which the conundrum can never be unravelled: after all, the future can never truly arrive in the present. The closer we try to approach our utopian visions, the more they will recede. The version of utopia that circulates here, then, is in the form of an impossible aspiration. It is rather like attempting to reach the end of a rainbow: never properly achievable, but sometimes it may be possible to catch a glimpse of the possibility.

The essence of the point is that, in the acknowledgement of the validity of any given subject position, some will inevitably lose out; that to say that one way of living is good is very easily also to say another way is bad, and is to base that judgment on some, ultimately indefensible, version of the 'good life'. Hence, in the utopian version of the future, it will be for the subject to define the self, not the politician, legislator, police officer, religious leader or critical academic theorist. Indeed, in the very act of positing 'the subject' in his/her singularity, violence is done to other conceptions of human life as beginning from somewhere other than the 'I', that bounded individual who effaces the other, and to other ways of understanding our connectedness that do not begin on the assumption of the absolute bright line of the body as boundary of self. Thus, the last word is both radically unavailable and ethically unacceptable. And when the last word is 'justice' – when justice necessarily implies injustice, since justice can only be made manifest in the form of a rule,[8] and rules, as normative, are necessarily 'rules against' as well as 'rules for', when law functions programmatically yet what it called for is the unprogrammable – the difficulties of translating this approach into law are clear.

This is enough to explain the apparent lacuna in much of postmodern legal feminist and other critical writing. It is not oversight, but instead conscious political strategy. In part, it speaks of a politics of freedom, but in part also of a politics of opposition, which carries within it a critique of liberal humanism and its unified, self-contained, neutral, legal subject. Of course, the critique of the neutral subject of law posited by liberal humanism did not have to wait for the arrival of postmodern feminism in law schools. But the type of argument that emerges from postmodern feminism criticises, say, radical feminism, for assuming a unity to the elements of its conceptual apparatus

---

7   *Op cit*, Naffine and Owens, fn 3, p 21.
8   See Sandland, R, 'Seeing double? Or, why "to be or not to be" is (not) the question for feminist legal studies' (1998) 7(3) SLS 307, pp 330–35.

(concepts such as 'woman', 'man' and 'truth'), just as it criticises liberal humanism on, at root, the same grounds. As such, inherent in postmodern feminism is a claim to methodological, ethical, political and conceptual superiority, both over other forms of feminism and critical theory and over the liberal humanist theories that inform the legal construction of the subject.

This paper traces the intersection of these various points. I hope to show that the reluctance of postmodern feminist lawyers is unwarranted, as I believe that it is possible to argue for substantive outcomes within a legal context whilst remaining true to the utopian impulse. I want at the same time to consider more closely the nature of the Beyond, as it functions in postmodern feminist and other critical theories of gender. In doing this, I hope to show: first, that there is at the very least a qualitative element to the concept of 'Beyondness', and that to say that it is not possible to reach a pure Beyondness, some radically present utopia, does not mean that there is no element of 'more or less' than can be used to guide present interventions. Secondly, that the elision of this point in much postmodern feminist legal theory has given rise to a certain complacency, a certain lack of reflexivity, about the ethical defensibility of that theoretical school in its own terms, which threatens to undermine its project. Thirdly, but closely related, that a commitment to justice for women – the political basis of feminism – requires that the other be figured from the start, which is close to suggesting that the basis of feminism, as the construction of hierarchy, lacks ethical justification because it rests on the effacement of the other. The argument here is that it is not enough for feminism to use deconstruction or other postmodern mechanisms as a tool. For feminism to retain its relevance as a radical school of thought, it must self-deconstruct if it is to begin fully to comprehend the gravitational pull of the liberal humanist subject, coded male. Fourthly, these three points, taken together, are what allows, and should guide, the postmodern feminist engagement with law at the substantive level.

BEYOND THE PRESENT: UTOPIA OR LIBERALISM?

1 The separation of method and substance

The above remarks should not be thought of as a call for the abandonment or abolition of feminism, as a term, as a political movement, as a way of reading or writing, or in any other form. In negotiating this fine line, I have found it helpful to draw on a fruitful interchange of ideas between Katherine

O'Donovan[9] and Nicola Lacey.[10] Both are concerned here with the 'sexing project', which involves three elements: identifying the historical process by which the paradigm subject of liberal legal discourse, ostensibly neutral, has been constituted as explicitly or implicitly male; analysing the processes through which this process continues in the present; and attempting to intervene in that legal process to alter its axis and trajectory.[11] Both are concerned, too, with the question of how feminist engagement in this project is to avoid the trap of essentialism. O'Donovan criticises an argument that Lacey made in an earlier paper.[12] That earlier argument was directed against difference feminism, which Lacey chided for its assumption that the 'paradigm legal subject' is a male individual,[13] on the basis that to deploy such a construction is to make the error of equating masculinity with rationality.[14] Lacey's view is, in turn, criticised by O'Donovan to the extent that it contains an assumption that to deploy such a subject is *inevitably* to make truth claims, such that 'the sexed subject', so it would seem, *cannot* be deployed, even as a method of analysis. For O'Donovan, this is to fail to distinguish method and substance, when in fact 'Commitment to a mode of analysis as a deconstructive technique does not necessarily signify that the theorist proposes or accepts a substantive position'.[15] One can deploy 'the rational male' strategically, concede his existence, at least as a legal construct, for the purposes of deconstruction, without making any kind of substantive or 'truth' claim.

This helps to clarify the nature of the postmodern feminist project in law; substance (outcome) and method (means of achieving it) are interrelated, but strategically so, and different considerations pertain to each, such that, in a specific fact-situation, each may be relatively autonomous of the other. Method and substance must, therefore, be thought together yet separate. Naturally, this process also involves critique.[16] Critique, analysis or deconstruction is the basis of postmodern politics. In one formulation of the relation, it is from critique that commitment to specific substantive change is

---

9   O'Donovan, K, 'With sense, consent or just a con? Legal subjects in the discourse of autonomy', in *op cit*, Naffine and Owens, fn 3.

10   Lacey, N, 'On the subject of "sexing" the subject ...', in *op cit*, Naffine and Owens, fn 3.

11   *Ibid*, pp 67–69.

12   Lacey, N, 'Feminist legal theory beyond neutrality' (1995) 48(2) CLP 1.

13   *Ibid*, p 8.

14   This, of course, being precisely the assumption that liberal humanist law, coded male, wants us to accept as true.

15   *Ibid*, O'Donovan, p 50.

16   'A quick side-step is necessary in order to deny essentialism and stereotyping. Feminist critiques of the neutral figure of law must be accompanied by critiques of the construction of masculinity and femininity as binary opposites within a hierarchical system.' (*Ibid*, O'Donovan, p 49.)

derived. Method is the bridge, the domain of strategy, which is concerned with the most effective way to transform critique into substance. Hence, one way to understand the terminology here is that it refers to a separation of these three elements: of *substance* (outcome), the result of the transformation, by way of a critical *method* (strategy); of *theory* (critique) into practice. One might then be led to wonder how the third of these elements fits into O'Donovan's substance/method schema. However, in a different formulation of the relation, one more closely associated with postmodernism, there is a tendency to collapse theory and method into the latter term. This is, on the face of it at least, possible because the deconstructive method starts not from some theoretical set of assumptions (about what is right or wrong) that the reader may have (since to 'have' a 'theory' implies an affiliation to the 'master narrative' and the imperialistic mode of discourse), but instead with the text under consideration. Deconstruction, on one view, analyses texts for what they say; nothing more or less. Moreover, the refusal to articulate an opposition between theory and method can itself be seen as part of the deconstructive strategy of seeking the Beyond to the neat, but overpredictive, distinctions and divisions that structure conventional (legal) scholarship.[17]

But this is what has 'trapped' much of that scholarship at the level of critique, since how does one move beyond critique if one has no normative base from which to proceed? Moreover, how and why can, does or should postmodern legal feminism 'intervene' at all if not operating from some covert normative base? In short, utopianism *must* be thought of, in the context of *legal* method, as a *normative theory*. Anything else is both disingenuous (because all critique must have some normative base) and disempowering (because it has frequently panned out over recent decades as a refusal to engage with law other than in the form of critique). This does not mean that it is necessary to abandon the commitment to the Beyond in the name of normativity and closure. O'Donovan's distinction between substance and method implies, on the contrary, that, whilst there is no reason to limit, and very good reason not to limit, how utopia and its subject is conceptualised theoretically, there may be strategic reasons, on occasion, such as when a particular engagement with law is required, to posit a specific subject of law and to argue for a particular outcome. This is not to express a definitive conclusion, but is to make our best guess at the nature of utopia, based on the information available in the present. In turn, I would argue, this means that it is vital to distinguish *legal method* from *analytical method*. The former is concerned *solely* with the question of legal strategy. Analytical method (deconstruction) should be thought of as Derrida suggests, as the successor to critique based on some totalising theory

---

17 Derrida, J, *Positions*, 1981, Chicago: Chicago UP, p 3.

of the good life. These projects are mutually interpenetrative, but, for purposes of legal argument, it is vital that they be kept conceptually distinct.

I read this distinction in O'Donovan's essay. She argues that, as the binary oppositions (legal/illegal, male/female, etc) that form legal method are inherently deconstructable and unstable, there is the possibility of developing (legal) strategies which do more than reconstitute (the terms of) those oppositions; and that 'The trick is surely to uncouple legal subjectivity and traditional masculinity, whilst understanding the constitutive role of oppositions'.[18] It seems to me that, in the same way that I have suggested, O'Donovan sees these as two distinct projects, the former the domain of legal method, the latter the domain of analytical method, or deconstruction. And she glimpses utopia here, proceeding to argue, by way of an analysis of elements of family law and medical law, that the subversion of law's standard set of messages about the sexed nature of identity can 'open a space for subjectivities'.[19] But she does not engage in specifics. Instead, 'for me the "utopian moment" is indefinitely postponed'.[20] Ultimately, then, O'Donovan separates method from substance in order to endorse the current orthodoxy and *avoid making* substantive claims. Thus, even though we might see here significant elements of a blueprint by which to arrive at a better view of the Beyond, there is little in the way of information about the *nature* of the Beyond; rather, it is something that, at most, must be allowed to arrive. If we want any greater level of specificity, it is necessary that O'Donovan's insight be pushed further.

2   Thinking the distinctions reflexively

One way to make a start on this is to look at Nicola Lacey's response to O'Donovan. In essence, Lacey agrees with O'Donovan that method and substance can be separated in principle,[21] but is concerned that the subtleties of that distinction can easily be lost when introduced into a liberal humanist-constructed reality in which such ideas are deeply counter-intuitive:

> Law students, law teachers and practising lawyers alike tend to succumb to the sexually neutral self-conception of legal doctrine, and the effort to render visible that which has been so effectively repressed entails a constant struggle against the ideological grain of modern law ... As feminist writers, we need constantly to be aware of the rhetorical implications of our methods in the light of our likely audience and the current understandings of sexual difference which may inform their views. If those of us engaged in the 'sexing' project are

---

18   *Op cit*, O'Donovan, fn 9, p 52.
19   *Op cit*, O'Donovan, fn 9, p 64.
20   *Op cit*, O'Donovan, fn 9.
21   *Op cit*, Lacey, fn 10, p 69.

not merely to write for each other, we have to be aware of the fact that the contingency argument still fails to have a strong cultural hold: the idea of sex as construct, particularly in its more radical form,[22] is one whose reception is still tentative and fragile.[23]

Lacey suggests on this basis, as an example, that social constructionist arguments might enjoy greater purchase if grounded in the concept of gender rather than sex, since the malleability of gender is more readily acceptable by those towards whom academic debate is ultimately addressed than is the malleability of sex. Again, this is to underscore the separation of method and substance, and of the differential nature of the projects of critique and substantive (constructive, here legal) argument. I read Lacey's point to be that one might be committed to a methodology of critique which is informed by a theoretical analysis of sexed bodies as being socially constructed, and in some measure by law; and yet argue for a substantive position utilising a discourse grounded in the instability of gender, with full weight given to the risk that 'radical' constructionist arguments may alienate those that they try to persuade, either because the concepts deployed are too counter-intuitive, or because no tangible alternative to the neutral paradigm subject of law is offered by the writer. Moreover, inherent in Lacey's response to O'Donovan (as in O'Donovan's own position) is the assumption that the utopian moment *can* translate into legal terms and be given form in a legal context. For me, this is confirmation of the necessity of the task of thinking the nature of the Beyond that is a central concern of this paper, just as it points to the intimacy of the connection between that task and intervention in legal contexts.

As with O'Donovan, however, Lacey gives little firm indication of the nature of the Beyond. But she does conclude by suggesting that 'The future of feminism lies, I would argue, in the development and exploration of the links between feminist analysis and radical social critique more generally'.[24] This is the intersection of the various strands of my argument in this paper. A strategy that accepts, as I do, the need for a normative utopianism to guide engagement with law is, for the reasons explained earlier, a risky one. However, it may be that one way to minimise the risks is to think reflexively, not only about how strategy should be formulated, but also about the concepts (such as 'feminism') that underpin that project. In what follows, there

---

22 The 'radical form' of the sexing project holds that law actually constitutes real subjectivities, as opposed to the less radical critique, which holds that law constitutes a legal subject which can impede the quality of life of actual subjects, eg, by denying rights on grounds of legal status. Arguably, the logic of Lacey's position is that both options (really an oversimplifying binary opposition) are to be used strategically, with no *a priori* attachment to one or the other, even at a 'purely' theoretical level. This is the strategy adopted in this paper and, as such, Lacey's comments are particularly pertinent.

23 *Op cit*, Lacey, fn 10, pp 67, 72.

24 *Op cit*, Lacey, fn 10, p 76.

is inevitably a certain arbitrariness about the examples chosen, but I have chosen them carefully. I hope to be able to convey to the reader the sense of what might be called the *rhythm* of the postmodern feminist engagement with deconstruction, and to suggest that this must include a constant moving beyond the boundaries which that engagement encounters. As such, I start outside the central concerns of feminism, with the issue of gay rights. But, as Lacey suggests, and as I now hope to show, although 'gay rights' may at present be the stronghold of queer theory, with 'women's rights' being seen as the proper subject of feminist theory, these artificial and ghettoising distinctions between 'types' of critical theorists of gender are unhelpful by reason of what each 'type' of theorist leaves untheorised. This is perhaps a more psychologically than sociologically grounded jurisprudence, that investigates the self[25] as a locus for the *production* of oppression – and oppression, what's more, in liberal humanist form. Space must be allowed for introspection, the examination of the otherness within and the means by which it is constituted in order both to improve the quality and depth of our critiques and to bring the Beyond into the reality of law.

3 Utopianism, liberalism and the Beyond in critical legal theories of gender: an example from queer theory

I want to start by discussing an exemplary piece of critical legal scholarship, Les Moran's study of the background to the Sexual Offences Act 1967.[26] Moran shows how the 1967 Act, usually seen as a landmark towards the (still awaited) complete decriminalisation of male homosexual sexual activity in the UK, is nevertheless implicated in the enactment of a number of offences that, whilst 'neutral' on the face of it, were in fact targeted specifically at the gay male community. The 1967 Act came out of the activities of the Wolfenden Committee, the brief of which was to recommend reform of the law of obscenity in the wake of public concern about the high number of prosecutions for buggery, gross indecency and importuning a male person that had been brought in the early 1950s. Moran shows how, in the course of gathering evidence, the Wolfenden Committee marshalled 'technologies of examination, schemes of classification and projects of management and eradication',[27] the target of which was (the sexual practices of) 'gay men' (that is, as constructed in and by these discourses). However, Moran argues, not

---

25 I am using the concept of self here to refer both to each of us, as individuals, and to the various collective enterprises that we are engaged in. Hence, eg, insofar as there is a minimal shared consciousness underpinning the concept of 'feminist', feminism is posited here as having a self.

26 Moran, L, 'The homosexualization of English law', in Herman, D and Stychin, C (eds), *Legal Inversions: Lesbians, Gay Men and the Politics of Law*, 1995, Philadelphia: Temple UP.

27 *Ibid*, p 21.

only did these (medical and police) technologies often falter in the implementation, but also 'the Wolfenden Review was the inauguration of a new era that formally installed an incitement to put homosexuality into the discourse of English law'.[28] The 1967 Act opened a space that might be filled by exclusionary, negative, criminogenic (etc) constructions of male homosexuality, but also, as law now 'talked' (about) homosexuality, such space might alternatively be made to function as 'sites of contestation rather than exhaustible and stable expositions of the truth'.[29]

Thus, one finds at the close of Moran's paper a utopian moment, a possibility of otherwiseness, although its contours are not considered explicitly. How should one read Moran's goal? A reader familiar with Foucault might well recognise Foucauldian language and concepts running throughout Moran's argument. Moran shows how these regulatory discourses and their accompanying technologies and disciplinary strategies function on the underbelly of a law which is theoretically neutral, in the sense that there are no offences which apply only to homosexuals. That it might be possible to use law as a site in which to challenge these dominant constructions – turn law belly-up – implies an awareness of the Foucauldian argument concerning the relationship between power and resistance, as well as some version of the (problematic) Foucauldian opposition between law and 'discipline'.[30] Moreover, such a reading would also conceptualise the possibility of otherwiseness as other than that offered by legal liberalism, given Foucault's well known anti-humanist stance.

Yet none of this is said, and a different reader might cobble a liberal legal solution – formal legal equality of treatment – onto Moran's argument. Faced with the harsh realities of law, the strong gravitational pull of 'human rights' within a liberal legal context (not to mention its practical purchase, which

---

28 *Op cit*, Moran, fn 26, p 23.

29 *Op cit*, Moran, fn 26, p 23.

30 The relationship between law and discipline in Foucault's work is problematic in two ways. First, Foucault does not maintain a consistent view on the nature of that relationship. Secondly, to the extent that there *is* a dominant view of how Foucault understood that relationship, it is, in essence, one of succession. That is, law came first, in the 'Classical age', and has now been superseded by discipline. In modernity (Foucault's dates are always controversial but we can say that modernity began sometime around the late 18th or early 19th centuries), power operates not through legal rules and the 'prohibitory model', but through any number of 'micro-practices', such as psychiatry, medicine, architecture, etc, which do not prohibit behaviour but, rather, *construct* subject positions and behavioural possibilities. On this view, it can be said that power now operates at a place before, or in any case, away from, law. Law, with its talk of rights, is little more than a smokescreen that masks the true, and more subtle, operation of power through the various disciplinary strategies. Against this, some lawyers have argued, convincingly in my view, that any talk of an opposition between law and discipline is problematic, because modern law passes the test for inclusion as a disciplinary strategy, being concerned not merely to prohibit behaviour but to construct subject positions in Foucault's sense. See, eg, Smart, C, *Feminism and the Power of Law*, 1989, London: Routledge, Chapter 1; Hunt, A and Wickham, G, *Foucault and Law: Towards a Sociology of Governance*, 1994, London: Pluto.

postmodern feminism should not dismiss out of hand) and the extent to which the constructionist concepts that Moran deploys in his writing are, within the broader intellectual climate, counter-intuitive, it is perhaps not unrealistic to accept that this is the 'default' reading of such texts. Lacey's concern in this regard has been referred to above. The point here is that it is not enough to use new words. As David Halpern observes:

> New critical vocabularies are helplessly overwhelmed and reabsorbed ... by older and more familiar ones, while prior epistemologies and methodologies continually resurface within the intellectual framework of even the most radical innovations ... That tendency produces a kind of terminological drift whereby the vocabulary coined to articulate conceptual advances is gradually resignified until it comes to designate the very concepts that it was invented to displace.[31]

Merely to designate a given site as one of potential contest leaves open the question of the mission of that contest, and, without that focus, the risk of deradicalisation increases. At best, the reader is left to vacillate between vague utopianism and deeply problematic and conservative liberalism, which has tended to attach 'equal rights' to gender rather than sexuality, marginalising homosexuality in the process.[32] My first main point against Moran, then, is that, in order to move closer to utopia, it is not enough to call its name; it must also be given some form. It is a point about substance, and the need for it.

My second point is more concerned with method and the set of concepts that Moran uses to inform his critical methodology. To put the argument at its strongest, it is that Moran's utopianism is *founded on the exclusion of the feminine*. In his study, he cites evidence given by the Admiralty to the Wolfenden Committee regarding the technologies employed in the Navy for the detection of homosexuality amongst sailors. The list details a whole set of practices of examination – of the suspected man, his genitalia and anus, his clothing and 'other suspicious objects' – but the first point on the list contains the advice: 'Note the general appearance. Look for feminine gestures, nature

---

31 Halpern, D, 'Historicizing the subject of desire: sexual preferences and erotic identities in the pseudo-Lucianic *Erotes*', in Goldstein, J (ed), *Foucault and the Writing of History*, 1994, Oxford: Blackwell, pp 19–20.

32 The methodological import of this latter point is that it is not merely concepts of 'sex' and 'gender' that should be kept in our toolbag, as Lacey, thinking like a feminist, seemed to suggest (see above, fn 25 and accompanying text), but also concepts of 'sexuality'. In the case of 'gay rights', arguments grounded in the malleability of 'gender' carry a greater risk of counter-productivity than arguments grounded in the malleability of sexuality. It is perhaps the most important reason for the conceptual boundary that is created by the construction of 'feminism' and 'queer theory' as separate and distinct entities, that the former inclines towards the replacement of sex with gender, and the latter to its replacement by sexuality. But, once the question of whether to deploy gender or sexuality is seen as practical or empirical, above all strategic – an issue that goes to the question of method rather than substance – then the methodological distinction that is created by the opposition of feminism and queer theory is surely brought into question. I will return to this issue below.

of the clothing and the use of cosmetics, etc.'[33] Moran fails to follow through on this. In his study of the construction of male homosexuality in law as a deviant subject-position, there is no mention of the function of 'the feminine' as a means of categorising males. Yet homosexual males are, at some level at least, understood by the technologies that produce them, as the above citation makes clear, as being less than 'real men' by reason of being in some way infected with femininity. Moran's glimpse of utopia is at the expense of what it submerged in his argument; that which he places beyond his discursive horizon.

I have suggested above that Moran's failure to follow through the implications of his analysis of the 1967 Act risks the deradicalisation of that analysis in its subsequent interpretation. The claim now is somewhat stronger: that Moran's failure to consider the function of the feminine within the technologies of male homosexuality that he discusses profoundly deradicalises his position, in and of itself, irrespective of the risk of a liberal humanist interpretation. This is because it repeats the traditional Western philosophical phallocentric gesture of 'othering' femininity, just as femininity (in this instance) is relied on as the sign for otherness within the hierarchy of masculinities. Thus, Moran's utopianism (incidentally, much like that of Foucault) rests on a certain sexism, for want of a better word, which is not only politically (methodologically) unacceptable as a basis or a manifesto for critical (especially feminist) engagement with law, but which, by reinforcing gender as the main frame of social hierarchy, is also strategically problematic if the aim is to go in some sense 'beyond' the traditional frame of reference and categorisation. This is because it leaves unexplored the paradox which 'the feminine' performs within phallocentric discourse: as the sign for object yet also as blemished subject; as the sign for outsideness that nevertheless functions on the inside of that discourse; as both inside and outside; and, hence, as a fissure in the border that discourse attempts to erect. In the particular context, the effect is that the distinctions between masculinities – distinctions that Moran wishes to see exhibiting ever greater diversity – are always in danger of collapsing back into themselves when set against the foil, the historical (etc) reality, of the male/female distinction. If the goal of critical intervention is to wrest some of the power to define reality from straight white men, in societies in which straight white men have historically had most of the power to define reality and so have defined it in their own interests, then a strategy which risks erasing distinctions between men through the mechanism of the repudiation of the feminine (this being the strategy which straight white men have tended historically to prefer) is obviously a poor one.

It is crucial to understand the qualitative distinction between the two criticisms of Moran that I have laid out. The first criticises Moran for the lack

---

33 PRO HO 345/7 CHP/21, cited in *op cit*, Moran, fn 26, p 17.

of *substance* in his utopian vision; the second is concerned exclusively with his *analytical method*, or the theory that he is using to inform his argument. This is an example of the importance of O'Donovan's insistence on that distinction. What it boils down to here is this.

First, to criticise on the grounds of a failure to deploy an analytical method to interrogate its own exclusionary processes does not mean that a *substantive* argument for 'gay rights', in whatever forms that might take, must be *a priori* rejected as a possible legal goal. In England, the House of Lords recently decided the case of *Fitzpatrick v Sterling Housing Association*.[34] The point at issue was whether the gay partner of the tenant of rented accommodation could inherit the tenancy on his death. In order to be so able, Sched 1 to the Housing Act 1977 required that he could be defined, *inter alia*, as a member of the tenant's 'family'. The House of Lords, by a majority, held that he could. It may be that, had the dissenting judgment of Ward LJ in the Court of Appeal (in which he held that gay partners could be defined as 'husband and wife', as spouses, not merely as members of each other's family) been adopted, the legal subject would have moved further still. The construction of a gay partner as an (indeterminate) 'family member' is effectively to desexualise gay men in the act of, purportedly, bestowing 'equal rights' on them.[35] But that is not the point here. Add as many caveats as you like, but surely it is unarguable that this decision moves the legal construction of the subject *closer* to *any* version of utopia? Is it not possible to commit to a strong substantive concept of Identity in this instance, even if that means utilising as *legal method*, as rhetoric, the neutral subject of law that has been subjected to so many devastating theoretical critiques? And is that not *still* the case, *here*, even if we agree with one or more of those critical theoretical positions, and even if our enthusiasm for 'equal rights' to succeed to a tenancy is misread by our students, colleagues and practitioners as evidence of a 'belief' in the general validity of the neutral legal subject? Does it matter, *here*, if our distinctions are too subtle for their audience?

Secondly, thinking reflexively about the decision in *Fitzpatrick*, it seems equally unarguable that the House of Lords would not have been able to take the step that it did, had feminism not provided the groundwork by having

---

34 [1999] 4 All ER 705, and see Sandland, R, 'The Housing Association, the judges, the tenant, and his lover' (2000) 8(2) FLS 227.

35 It is worth pointing out that here is an example of the strategy of attaching 'equal rights' to gender rather than sexuality, in order to deny those rights to a sexual minority, as discussed above, fn 32. On the other hand, and to make the point that there is no once and for all answer, the desexualisation of gay identity in law is not always a bad thing. Thus, in the context of the 1967 Act, it could be argued that it is precisely the sexualisation of gay men by law (at least that particular construction) that is the problem. The same is true of the debate over 'gays in the military', in which allegations of uncontrollable homosexual urges and their likely negative effects on military discipline, morale and control are what fund both an outright ban and the fudge of 'don't ask, don't tell' that is, bizarrely but apparently, policy in the US forces.

already moved the legal definition of the family away from the married heterosexual couple over the preceding decades,[36] through campaigns around domestic violence, for example, as well as around issues such as entitlement to housing and other services. Yet, in the House of Lords' narrative, the ground for the decision in *Fitzpatrick* was cleared by (male) judges responding to changes in 'society'; the role of feminism, and of women more generally, is effectively effaced. Hence, both Moran's position and that of the House of Lords function through the erasure of 'the feminine'. This suggests that neither is too far from the liberal humanist norm, and hence points to a necessity that queer theory attend to feminist insight. In other words, 'feminist theory' is in some sense 'the Beyond' to 'queer theory' at this methodological level (the opposite is also true); and, therefore, any conceptual distinction between feminism and queer theory should be dismantled if it is to be possible to decentre the implicit reference to the normative liberal humanist subject. That reference is made because, by marking both 'the feminine' and 'the queer' as distinct deviations from that norm, such an approach remains complicit in the positing of differential deviation, and hence of the norm. We divide ourselves and allow the historically entrenched paradigm male subject of law to rule.

Finally, it is worth reflecting on the fact that these forces circulate in Moran's work outside of and against the intention of the author. Rather, here is an example of how the text can follow its own trajectories, of the depth and perniciousness of the patriarchal context, its invisible structuring of our thoughts and arguments.

4 Utopianism, liberalism and the Beyond in critical legal theories of gender: an example from feminist theory

One legal scholar who has given sustained consideration to the way in which identity is formulated through the exclusion of otherness; to the possibilities for the attainment of a position somehow 'beyond' this present reality; and to the role that law can or should take in this process of transformation, is Drucilla Cornell. I have discussed Cornell's work elsewhere,[37] but I have quite specific reasons for returning again to Cornell at this point. First, her work anticipates the criticism that I have made of Moran's analytical methodology. As Caputo notes, femininity and homosexuality 'are always treated together'[38] by Cornell. Secondly, Cornell has always emphasised the

---

36 I am grateful to Joanne Conaghan for underscoring the importance of this point to me.

37 See Sandland, R, 'The mirror and the veil: reading the imaginary domain' (1998) 6(1) FLS 33; *op cit,* Sandland, fn 8, especially pp 311–17, 327–30.

38 *Op cit,* Caputo, fn 4, p 146.

difference that race makes, and I want to introduce the relevance of race to this discussion, because it is my contention that, just as some claims for 'gay rights' can rest on the repudiation of femininity, so, too, can claims grounded in gender rest on the expulsion of race. Thirdly, the following discussion of Cornell's work can also be read as providing a second example of how radical and utopian arguments can transmogrify (at the level of method) into something much more orthodox, both in the sense of drifting back into liberalism and in the sense of being subject to textual forces and buried normative assumptions which act to reconstitute the boundaries and reinstate the hierarchies which, at the level of authorial intention, the text attempts to transcend, redefine or question.

Let me start by very briefly outlining Cornell's position, which is a distinctive variant on the themes of instability and utopianism, which draws from jurisprudence, philosophy and psychoanalytic theory. For Cornell, personhood is, by definition, the realisation of selfhood as sexed and sexual. Sex, or gender, is a psychoanalytic category precisely because sex/gender and sexuality are the ordering principles of the passage into individuality. These qualities are the fundaments of Identity. However, the boundaries of these categories cannot be fixed; rather, as textual entities, they are deconstructable. Each one of us, although to a degree 'trapped' by our self-image as gendered, as being with sexuality, is nevertheless able to rework our performances, to explore and develop our potential, to move closer to the realisation of our dreams. Cornell sees this as *the* basic human right, and the only limitation that should be imposed on our ability to explore what she terms 'the imaginary domain' is when such self-created selves impinge on or 'degrade' the imaginary domain of others. This 'degradation prohibition' applies equally to law – law must not privilege any one version of the 'good life'. Instead, 'the separation of the right from the good is crucial for the recognition of our equal personhood precisely because our own deeply held convictions about what is good for us sexually may push us in the direction of thinking that our way is the only way'.[39] Therefore, law:

> ... can give us the right to represent our sexuate being, and can protect the imaginary domain as the space we need to contest, imagine, and engage with the meanings given to gender, sex and sexuality. But it cannot give us a substantive definition of what constitutes actual freedom for any individual person, because to do so would violate her right to self-representation of her sexuate being.[40]

Hence, for Cornell, it is legal-political liberalism that can help to establish the conditions precedent for maximum personal freedom and the nearest approximation to a utopian society. In this version of the story of the road to

---

39 Cornell, D, *At the Heart of Freedom: Feminism, Sex and Equality*, 1998, Chichester: Princeton UP, p 176.

40 *Ibid*, p 24.

utopia, the neutral subject of law turns out not to be our sworn enemy but our indispensable ally.

I want to make two points here. First, rather than seeing the relationship between liberalism and utopianism as the facilitation of the one by the other, as Cornell suggests, I think that it is more accurate to argue that Cornell's liberalism in fact *displaces* her utopianism, and this is precisely because it is too 'across the board'; paradoxically, too apolitical. For instance, in *At the Heart of Freedom,* she argues that the right to the imaginary domain includes the right to found a family irrespective of sexuality, to live openly as what we are without fear of intimidation, and any number of similar rights with which I have no problem. This, as she repeatedly emphasises, is not merely the right to be left alone.[41] Rather, the State and the law have a responsibility not so much to protect as to *facilitate* the exploration of the imaginary domain by all of the citizenry, which means, for example, access to reproductive technology or to child care services, and to protection from the degradation of the imaginary domain by others. However, I have rather more trouble with some of Cornell's other examples, which include, for instance, the equal right to the imaginary domain of consumers of pornography and of workers in the sex industries. There might, in some future utopia, be an argument for this,[42] but, at the moment, the truth is that pornography overwhelmingly peddles male fantasies that depend on the construction of Woman as object. Cornell does agonise over these issues rather more,[43] but nevertheless concludes that the principle that 'law must not choose' (her 'insistence on abstraction')[44] is more important than the need to offer protection through legal prohibition or regulation, as it were, at the margins of degradation. And, in any case, how can one human being judge the moral choices of another, given the fundamental otherness and unknowability that we represent to each other? Similarly, Cornell argues against what she calls the 'conscription' of fathers into families through the censure of 'deadbeat dads', since this is to degrade the imaginary domain of such men. As one final example, she argues that the US Supreme Court should have declined jurisdiction in the case of *Hurley v Irish-American Gay, Lesbian and Bisexual Group of Boston,*[15] and 'the conflict should be left in the street, not taken to court'.[46]

---

41 See, eg, *op cit,* Cornell, fn 39, p 40.

42 The arguments around pornography, both outside and within feminism, are complex and have been made more so by the emergence of gay pornography, which has brought into question many of the assumptions that underpinned the hostility that many feminists (and others) have long felt, and continue to feel, towards pornography. It is not my intention here to enter into discussion of these debates. See, eg, Jackson, E, 'The problem with pornography: a critical survey of the current debate' (1995) 3(1) FLS 49.

43 *Op cit,* Cornell, fn 39, pp 45–58.

44 *Op cit,* Cornell, fn 39, p 53.

45 115 S Ct 2338 (1995). See, also, Stychin, C, 'The nation's rights and national rites', in Stychin, C and Phelan, S (eds), *A Nation by Rights,* 1998, Philadelphia: Temple UP.

46 *Op cit,* Cornell, fn 39, p 61.

My objection to this is that Cornell's refusal to adjudicate in societies where inequalities are structural is to side with the status quo.[47] I understand that, for Cornell, as for many others (myself included), law is seen as a marginal component to the project of social transformation; but, nevertheless, as a matter of legal analysis, Cornell's liberalism effaces her utopianism, since it re-enacts the radically neutral (but historically male) subject of legal discourse. In the context of current legal systems, it acts as a conservative force. This approach is problematic (some would say out of touch with reality), to posit even the possibility of law as somehow the pure presence of neutrality, totally transparent, totally without substantive symbolic value, ring-fenced from the political. To the best of my knowledge, there has never been such a legal (or indeed other human) system that has even approximated this; but, of course, this is *precisely* the claim which, historically, liberal humanist law has made for itself. As a theoretical or methodological framework, it might be that Cornell's position has much to commend it, but as an argument about substance, about legal outcomes, it fails the reflexivity test. We might know that utopia is unknowable, but we do know that it is not more of the same. It is not enough to demand our own space. For me, at least, we need to be involved in the politics of the signification of space; to see that, as law plays a significant part in the definition of identity or social space, whether we like it or not, there is a need for theories and strategies that try to engage with law at that substantive level of definition and adjudication.

My disagreement with Cornell can be highlighted by returning to *Hurley*. My reading of the required strategy in that case is straightforward. It entails the deconstruction of the opposition that the organisers of the St Patrick's Day Parade attempted to construct between 'Irishness' and 'Gayness'. Heterosexuality has no *a priori* exclusive claim on any national or cultural identity: being straight is not a pre-requisite to being Irish, Irish-American or, indeed, a member of any national group. Indeed, insofar as such a claim is made, it carries with it, as a central element in its conditions of possibility, the trace of gay Irishness. The role of the court in this case was, I would suggest, plain. It was to affirm the imaginary domain of those for whom sexual and national identity are intimately connected, whatever that sexual identity be. It was not the claim of the gay community in Boston that heterosexuality was incompatible with Irishness. There was no attempt here to degrade the imaginary domain of the march organisers. Yet the denial of the expression of identity was precisely the intention of the march organisers. It was incumbent in the Supreme Court to prevent this. To suggest, instead, that 'the conflict be

---

47 Cornell knows this, and deploys this argument against others, as when she argues that sexuality is a political statement and, 'even if the person wants to avoid politics, the expression of sexuate being demands that one be allowed to associate with any others, *a choice which can involve political stances*' (*op cit*, fn 39, p 41, emphasis in original), but fails to interrogate her own position from this point of view.

left on the streets' is to fail to undertake an analysis of the political and social history that constituted the exclusion of homosexuality that was at issue in this case. Much the same point could be made in relation to the other examples that Cornell gives. The responsibility of heeding the utopian call requires more than Cornell is prepared for law to offer. I would rather align myself with Penelope Deutscher,[48] who argues that:

> What is needed is legal institutions not just limited to an affirmation of differences designated actual prior to legal change. What is needed instead is legal reform which could create the conditions for inventing new cultural identities whose legitimacy of recognition did not rely on their being original, proper, nor in their lying 'before the law'.

The affirmation of the possibility of gay Irishness by law would not satisfy this utopian requirement, but, surely, it would be a step towards it? This, of course, as in the discussion of *Fitzpatrick* above, is an argument about substance and legal strategy, which says nothing about method and the *analytical* project.

Interestingly, and this is the second main point that I wish to make against Cornell (shifting now in my analysis from substance to analytical method), the only occasion in *At the Heart of Freedom* that Cornell is prepared to abandon her insistence on abstraction is when she discusses female circumcision or genital mutilation. She explains that, although she is told by Third World women that, 'as a Western woman, I just don't get it ... I have not changed my mind'.[49] This statement is to be found in one of the many places in Cornell's work where she discusses race. Cornell has consistently maintained that, as we are marked by gender, sex and sexuality, so are we marked by race, and that a substantively prescriptive feminism or gender politics must be avoided if the importance of race to the formation of identity and, hence, to the exploration of the imaginary domain is not to be elided. Yet it is notable that, in Cornell's texts, race is synonymous with other than white women. Race appears as the sign for otherness when Cornell wishes to give some specific shape to the other woman. When Cornell's primary concern is questions of sex and sexuality *per se*, race is not generally an issue.[50]

I have argued elsewhere that this is a consequence of the primacy given by Cornell to sexual difference by her dependence on a Lacanian frame of reference.[51] But perhaps there is more to it than this. Perhaps Cornell's alliance with Lacan – to be sure, the alliance of a woman who demands equivalent value from her man – who forms her alliance with him on her own terms – should be put in the context of her alliance with Derridean deconstruction,

---

48 Chapter 3, in this volume.

49 *Op cit*, Cornell, fn 39, p 170.

50 This is a difficult point to provide examples of, since it is a reference to an absence in Cornell's texts, and so is a point that I must ask readers to verify for themselves.

51 See *op cit*, Sandland, fn 8.

now latent[52] (although her work continues to be profoundly marked by it, as it is by her engagement with Levinas, Nagel and others); in the context of her more recent alliance with Rawls and Kant. Perhaps, in other words, Cornell's repeated 'turning to' iconographic figures amongst masculine, Western scholarship can be read as a trope for her work as a whole; which is to say that it moves (as its method) within a certain economy of sameness, that its turn to whiteness and masculinity is achieved by the repudiation of the *racial* quality of *whiteness* – that is, a repudiation of otherness in racial terms; and one which works against the intentions of the author. Perhaps, in the same way that Moran's argument for gay rights turns unwittingly on the expulsion of the feminine, Cornell's argument for the right to the imaginary domain turns unwittingly on the expulsion of racial otherness, by making 'race' (non-whiteness) the sign for 'other' in her work.

It might be thought[53] that the pluralisation of the concept of origin offered by Judith Butler is the mechanism by which to displace the primacy of sexual difference. Certainly, Ellen T Armour has recently argued that 'The fullest realisation of the promise that whitefeminism's turn to a multiple feminist subject or to the body will yield more substantial attention to race occurs in Judith Butler's work'.[54] Butler has argued, for example, against Irigaray,[55] that to foreclose around sexual difference as the primary site for the differentiation and performance of selves is an act of violence perpetrated against those other loci of social differentiation. Instead, for Butler, the self is created in the interrelationship of any number of different vectors of identification. It is not just sex and sexuality that are there from the beginning, that frame our assumption of personhood, but race, class and a host of other, perhaps more personal and less easily shorthanded, normative matrices. For Butler, sexual difference is racially marked, racial difference is sexually marked (etc), and the self is never singular. Cornell is equally attentive, at the level of surface politics, to the differences that race, etc, makes. She argues, as does Butler, that these differences are in themselves unstable, without essential meaning, and political. But what distinguishes Butler's approach from that of Cornell is that Butler provides a methodological framework for analysis, a way to think about the subject, which offers at least the potential to resist the temptation to elide these differences. That is, this can be seen as a way to transcend 'race' as boundary at the level of analytical method and yet respect racial difference at the level of substance and legal method. Substantively, the political context and history of racial difference in law has established race as a sign for

---

52 Cornell has not mentioned Derrida in her last two books.

53 *Op cit*, Sandland, fn 37, pp 322–25.

54 Armour, ET, *Deconstruction, Feminist Theology and the Problem of Difference*, 1999, Chicago: Chicago UP, pp 31–32.

55 Butler, J, *Bodies that Matter: On the Discursive Limits of 'Sex'*, 1993, London: Routledge, pp 36–49.

hierarchy, and this political and social reality cannot be ignored by law or lawyers. To dismantle this hierarchy is, at least, a necessary precondition, again, I would say, of *any* version of utopia. Sometimes, this will entail arguing the relevance of racial difference, and, on other occasions, its irrelevance. Sometimes, it will be apposite to deploy a 'neutral' legal subject, and sometimes to deploy the subject as differential, socially marked, as a matter of *legal* method.

Different considerations, however, apply at the level of critique, of analytical method or deconstruction. Here, it is important not to confuse 'transcend' with 'erase'. The methodological transcendence of the racially marked body must continually reflect on the political reality of the racially marked body; and, importantly, on how that political reality rests on an ability to dissimulate the colour of whiteness. Hence, methodological transcendence, in the realm of critique or analysis, does not mean, at least cannot *yet* mean, a refusal to acknowledge race as boundary; rather, it means a refusal to interrogate its constitution. Thus, one should seek to collapse the opposition between 'feminism' and 'critical race theory', since that opposition constitutes each as 'the Beyond' to the other. Butler's frame, I would argue, is an important contribution to the possibility of thinking in this way.

5 Liberalism, utopianism and the Beyond: an example from critical race theory

Despite her praise for Butler, however, Armour argues that the patterns detectable in Cornell's work can also be found in Butler's: '... in essays where blackness is not an issue, whiteness is never raised.'[56] And I would argue that this continues to be the case in Butler's more recent output. In *Excitable Speech*,[57] for example, race only figures, on the surface of the text, when Butler discusses racism, but there is otherwise no consideration of how the text is figured by race at a more general level. For Armour, this analytical lacuna is not confined to the work of Cornell and Butler. Indeed, she argues that these two writers have done more than most to attend to questions of race alongside questions of sex and sexuality. And that their work can nevertheless be located within a specular economy of Sameness – the terms of which are set by whiteness, heterosexuality, masculinity, etc – again, as was the case in the discussion of Moran, above, shows the extent to which that economy prefigures at some deep level our thoughts and our politics.[58] It is Armour's

---

56 *Op cit*, Armour, fn 54, p 36.
57 Butler, J, *Excitable Speech: A Politics of the Performative*, 1997, London: Routledge.
58 See, eg, *op cit*, Armour, fn 54, p 39.

thesis, developed at some length and with scrupulous attention to detail, that this tendency is endemic in, to use her term, 'whitefeminism'.[59]

Much of the spadework for Armour's position has been performed by Irigaray, who in her work has shown repeatedly that, under patriarchy, Woman/women is/are trapped within this specular economy of sameness, subsisting within it only as male invention. The feminine circulates here only as the sign for otherness and can be put to work by either sex.[60] Women, meanwhile, that is, those women who are (not) the invention of men, are excluded (included) as the sign for other. Irigaray has sought to show the instability of this schema, to make difference rather than sameness her organising principle, to make a space in her work for difference to operate, to occupy, to subvert – to move beyond simply the reversal of the terms of – this economy. Yet, for Armour, this new logic of difference fails to escape the dominant economy, since Irigaray, too, fails to consider the racial markings of both that sameness and that difference. She argues that 'Whiteness remains in a position of mastery over Irigaray's differing and deferring woman'.[61] It appears that the debate over whether Irigaray can be charged with essentialism has obscured the fact that, for both her attackers and defenders, essentialism has been understood overwhelmingly as meaning sexed, or biological, essentialism; and in this there is a prior assumption, itself essentialist.

For Armour, 'white woman' is a political-historical construct that is produced, *inter alia*, in opposition to racial otherness. White woman in this taxonomy *is* 'Woman', deconstructed or not. Black woman is black and, hence, is not woman at all. This point should be read through the substance/method distinction. It is, however, a point relevant to both. Thus, to deploy the category 'woman', even pluralised, without the constant and simultaneous deployment (in some shape or form) of race reinvents (white) Woman/women as raced, but invisibly so:

> Race and woman, then, stand in supplemental relationship to one another and to the specular economy that figures them. Each is called to the scene by lack, by desire for plenitude and fullness. As sites of lack, race and woman reassure man of his assumed plenitude and fullness.[62]

This situation is neither stable nor inevitable, however, because, 'As figures of man's boundaries, sites that lie just beyond his reach, they fissure his plenitude and fullness'.[63] But, as supplemental to each other, part of the

---

59 For Armour, 'whitefeminism constitutes a specular reflection of the text of Western metaphysics and its inscription by race' (*op cit*, fn 54, p 151).

60 See Richardson, Chapter 6, in this volume.

61 *Op cit*, Armour, fn 54, p 130.

62 *Op cit*, Armour, fn 54, p 165.

63 *Op cit*, Armour, fn 54.

conditions of possibility of each other, as well as of masculinity, race and gender must be figured together, otherwise:

> Whichever supplement is left unchallenged goes underground but continues its silent and invisible inscription of the text or context in question.[64]

Hence, the failure of whitefeminism to come to terms with the conditions of possibility of its own existence as racially marked simultaneously marks its failure to move beyond Western metaphysics, and liberal humanism (the art and science of man-as-himself) in particular; hence the necessity of the dynamic of moving Beyond, first at the level of analytical method and, consequently, as the substantive form that, wherever possible, intervention in law must take.

But how does Armour propose to move beyond the current situation? It is on this question that I find her work to be of problematic usefulness. I do not claim to do justice to the richness of Armour's argument here, but her basic strategy is, first, to reaffirm that, in Irigarayan difference and deferral, it is possible to glimpse women otherwise. However, and secondly, as Irigaray fails to challenge the specularisation of race within the phallocentric economy, her work is in need of supplementation, which Armour attempts through a reading of Derrida on race (just as, earlier in the book, she had used Irigaray's work to supplement that of Derrida, by showing that the economy of difference that Derrida describes has sexual difference as (it turns out, one of) its organising principle(s)). The aim is to work simultaneously along two axes, to show the limit of Man, of his claim to universality, through his *colonisation* of sex and race, his need to render otherness in sexual and racial terms as the Same, yet his concession of those differences in the process. It is Man who has built the great walls of history, but it has never been clear whether those walls are intended to keep civilisation in or keep barbarity and otherness out. The wall, the border, has always marked the end (in all its various meanings) of empire, both its success, its reach, and its failure to colonise, its limit. Reading race and sex together is not to show two borders, but rather to show the interspersal of these two tropes along and as that border, even as they follow their own trajectories.

How, though, to read sex and race together? Here, as a third move, Armour turns to Heidegger and, in particular, to his concepts of *Dasein* and *Geschlect*.[65] Not Heidegger as he wanted to be, but Heidegger deconstructed:

---

64 *Op cit*, Armour, fn 54, p 166.

65 That these terms are problematic and marked by *difference* is the starting point of Derrida's dual reading of Heidegger, but, for the sake of maintaining the momentum of my argument, I will translate them as an existentially conceived 'beingthereness' (the fact of human existence) and 'genre' or 'dispersibility' (the different ways there are of 'being human') respectively.

Heidegger after Derrida.[66] Heidegger's aim in the deployment of these concepts was to attempt to locate a place before the humanist subject. This place, he claimed, is *Dasein*, a place 'more primordial than the man to whom a proper or properties can belong',[67] which is before difference, an essence that is no more than the fact of human existence. However, even pure human existence must have a form if it is to be human, and, for Heidegger, what marks the humanity of human essence is handedness, the physical ability to use one's hands as instruments of creation and expression. Thus, *Dasein*, that place before human form, is in fact marked by the cut between humans and other animals. From here it is a short jump to the proposition that the other is sub-human. This, Armour suggests, shows first that racism is in fact in at the start of Man, and hence Heidegger fails in his attempt to find some place before that closure, since his attempt merely gives a new name to that place where the subject of Western metaphysics ('Man') is constituted. Similarly, Heidegger had argued that *Dasein* is a place before sexual difference, but, as Derrida points out, in making that claim, Heidegger is in fact using sexual difference as the limit of *Dasein*, which means that *Dasein* is marked by this cut also: sexual difference was also there, at and as the beginning of Man. Armour concedes this, but argues that, even so, this is not to say *how* difference is figured; it is to insist that what is 'dispersed' *is* difference (since difference is the mark of the origin), and difference can always be dispersed differently. Here, then, Armour finds her route to utopia through Heidegger; destabilised maybe, since his borders, marked only as requiring difference, are permeable, are both opening and closure, but through Heidegger nonetheless.

This is Armour's logic (and it is in many ways a parallel of Cornell's position): if difference was there at the start, then difference must be neutral. Why? Because *Dasein* is neutral. This is not, she claims, essentialism (although it looks a lot like it):

> If sexual difference resides at *Dasein*'s level, and if *Geschlect* is its bearer, then perhaps race, too, resides at that level. Let me be clear here. I am *not* claiming that 'black' and 'white' or 'man' and 'woman' are ontological categories. Rather, I am claiming that these current divisions are funded by *Dasein*'s dispersibility as borne by *Geschlect*. Humanity has not always divided itself into races and into sexes/genders (at least not in the same way it has recently come to do).[68]

---

66 See Derrida, J, '*Geschlecht*: sexual difference, ontological difference' (1983) 13 Research in Phenomenology 65; Derrida, J, '*Geschlecht II*: Heidegger's hand', in Sallis, J (ed), *Deconstruction and Philosophy: The Texts of Jacques Derrida*, 1987, Chicago: Chicago UP.

67 *Op cit*, Armour, fn 54, p 159.

68 *Op cit*, Armour, fn 54, pp 161–62. For discussion of times and places in which human existence has been 'dispersed differently', see Laqueur, T, *Making Sex: Body and Gender from the Greeks to Freud*, 1990, Cambridge, Mass: Harvard UP; Synnott, A, 'Tomb, temple, machine and self: the social construction of the body' (1992) 43(1) Br J Soc 79; Asher-Greve, JM, 'The essential body: Mesopotamian conceptions of the gendered body' (1997) 9(1) Gender and History 432.

Brilliant though I believe Armour's work to be, I find this route to a *methodology* of Beyondness to be deeply problematic. First, her use of the concept of 'supplement' seems to imply that the supplement is a mere addition, as that which makes whole that which is lacking. For Armour, an analysis of race as difference can simply be attached to an analysis of sex as difference.[69] Here, she suppresses its (always already present) alternative meaning, as that which *replaces* the thing that is supplemented. What does it mean to bring race and sex together in a process of mutual and constant supplementation and resupplementation? I do not know the answer to that question, but it may be that recasting this relation as one of *difference* (which it surely is) would add to the productivity of the process. That is, I am suggesting that Armour's thesis may be valuable at this level, although her text seems to attempt (maybe of its own volition, since this seems to threaten the (in any case always already unstable) linearity of the book?) to play down the potential of this endless play of resignification and alinearity.

If this point is corrective, my second criticism is rather more fundamental. The turn to Heidegger strikes me as odd. *Geschlect*, dispersibility, Armour claims, can found a non-originary origin for difference, what she calls a 'nonfoundational foundation'.[70] But, in Armour's scheme, *Geschlect* has its own origin, in *Dasein*, and 'Access to *Dasein's* differential structure comes through repeating the neutralizing gestures with which metaphysical humanism dismisses differences'.[71] That is, it is *only* through the *failure* of those gestures (to neutralise) that difference can be glimpsed.[72] This is *Dasein* functioning in a context in which the economy of sameness that it enacts is put in the broader context of the economies of *difference* that, in turn, fund it. But *Dasein* deconstructed is still posited by Armour as 'being there': essence still exists, even if we understand the instability of its existence. But why accept this as a matter of analytical method?

If this point is read through the distinctions between substance and method, and between legal and analytical method, that I made earlier in this essay, my argument becomes clearer. At the substantive legal level, and in terms of *legal* method, the problem of essence, although crucial, is nevertheless less relevant than it is at the level of *analytical* method, where any invocation of essence is absolutely to be resisted. Substantive intervention, I would argue, *should be* with the intention of disrupting 'essence' as a legal-ontological category, and so, perhaps, at this level it may be indicated that arguments be framed in terms of the dispersibility of essence, which in more simple

---

69   See, eg, *op cit*, Armour, fn 54, pp 163, 165, 166.

70   *Op cit*, Armour, fn 54, p 163.

71   *Op cit*, Armour, fn 54.

72   *Op cit*, Armour, fn 54.

language might mean, for example, an argument that the legal categories of sex, gender, race, sexuality and nationality should be inclusive in spirit; that, to be specific, law should recognise that different women (etc) have different interests, passions, aspirations, and so on. But Armour concedes the existence of essence as an *a priori analytical* 'given' as well. For her, this is an inevitability that *theory*, and not just *strategy*, must accept. Why? Can't we have dispersibility without essence? What is the effect on her conception of *Geschlect* as the nonfoundational foundation to point to its own origin? This is the point at which Butler's work, despite its (conceded) latent attachment to the specular economy of Sameness, nevertheless points beyond Armour to a concept of origin as plurality without essence; that has no particular site or origin in time or space; that will not be tied to debilitating concepts like *Dasein*, concepts that are given *proper names*, that claim the origin in the name of that which is not one, when it must surely follow, to the contrary, that that which is not one can have no one name, not even the name of 'nonfoundational foundation'?

The specular economy of Sameness that Armour critiques leaves its mark on her own writing, in this name, this act of naming, which is surely one of appropriation. Her concern is race, the race of gender. Her text is marked by only two races, however: white and African-American. To be fair, Armour makes clear that she is talking only about her own 'current American context'[73] and calls for further research to investigate the European roots of discourse on race and sex, but, even so, there are more than two races in America. Yet Armour implies at least that it is sufficient to work within the frame of the binary opposition. The novelty of her argument is to cast the binarism of gender and the binarism of race within the specular context of each other, but the failure to move beyond binarism – the simplified and simplifying matrix of Western metaphysics – *at the level of analytical method* raises the question of the degree to which she has heeded her own call. She does violence, funded by some sort of dream of the subject, to racial (hence sexual, etc) diversity, to her own utopian vision, the 'multiply figured subject'.[74] In the end, she returns to liberal humanism as end, in the sense of goal, and in the sense of closure.

CONCLUDING COMMENTS

The desire to give priority to the means by which one's own identity is implicated in one's own oppression is an understandable one. But there is something fundamentally depressing about the fact that the current range of

---

73 *Op cit*, Armour, fn 54, p 179.
74 *Op cit*, Armour, fn 54, p 156.

critical theories of identity – feminism, queer theory, critical race theory, even masculinity studies – replicate so exactly the taxonomy of the norm and its deviations. In this paper I have attempted to show that these boundaries tend to function conservatively, divisively, hierarchically. If it is to be possible to glimpse more than a very parochial, self-centred conception of Beyondness, the deconstruction of these self-imposed boundaries is a necessary pre-condition. As my criticism of Armour's work underscores, however, this is not, of itself, sufficient. There is also a need for a more broadly based reflexivity about the practice of analytical methodology. It is not enough to consider race, sex, sexuality, gender, nationality (etc) together. It is also necessary to be alive to the temptation to fall back into binarism, of which these categories are merely sub-sets. Utopia may be unreachable, but the commonality of all these various critical positions is that it is somewhere Beyond the binary discourse of the norm and his deviants.

I have also argued in this paper that this analytical project must be conceptualised as separate from the project of intervention in law, which does not allow the luxury or the safety of the indefinite postponement of the utopian moment. Rather, in the legal arena, utopia must be given some definite, normative form. This – the distinction between analytical and legal method – might seem to itself rely on the very binary logic that I have argued must necessarily be transcended. But I would argue against such an interpretation. First, because, insofar as this border exists, it should be figured as deconstructable. Secondly, the focus of this paper has been on the application of this methodology in a legal context, but it is of course the case that deconstruction functions in any number of contexts – intervenes in any number of modernist paradigms – and so, the logic of this approach is that of the innumerable, not of binarism. Indeed, part of my argument is, necessarily, that law itself is a plurality of contexts, so that, even in terms of legal intervention, postmodern feminism should be thought of as being Beyond binarism. Thirdly, I would argue that there is a fundamental opposition between the postmodern conception of the subject of plural and fluid and modernist conceptions of the subject as a unity. Engagement with law, therefore, necessitates some sort of 'modernisation' of the postmodern position as a strategic concession; but the articulation for this purpose of a normative utopianism is only justifiable if it allows the possibility that law can be pushed further towards that impossible possibility of a utopian society without borders, without norms. Foucault has suggested that:

> Political analysis and critique, for the most part, have to be invented – but so do strategies that will allow both modifying these relations of force and coordinating them in such a way that this modification will be possible and register in reality. That is to say that the problem is not really defining a political 'position' ... but to imagine and to bring out new schemas of politicization. If 'to politicize' means going back to standard choices, to pre-

existing organisations, all these relations of force and these mechanisms of power that analysis mobilizes, then it's not worth it. The great new techniques of power ... must be opposed by new forms of politicization.[75]

It may not be the function of the critical lawyer to be at the forefront of this process. Law as context limits the possibilities for the articulation of new forms of politicisation. But perhaps this is not inevitable. Perhaps the current form of law – its constructions, its methodology, its rules of evidence, its search for Truth, and so on – is historically contingent. Maybe, in utopia, law would be less about self-righteousness and more about humility and respect for the other. But, in the meantime, the task of critical lawyers must be to do our best to live up to Foucault's injunction, which means, in sum, to heed the responsibility, the necessity, to concede some definite shape to our respect for the other, to remember the lived reality of injustice while we continue our search for the impossible future Beyond the realities of the present.

---

75 Foucault, M, 'Power affects the body', in Lotringer, S (ed), *Foucault Live: Collected Interviews 1961–84*, Hochroth, L and Johnston, J (trans), 1989, New York: Semiotex[e], p 211.

PART II

LEGAL SUBJECTIVITY: THE PERSON, SELF AND OTHER

CHAPTER 6

A REFRAIN: FEMINIST
METAPHYSICS AND LAW

Janice Richardson[1]

This chapter draws upon the work of two contemporary feminist philosophers, Drucilla Cornell and Christine Battersby, to question what it means to be a person, and the relationship between this image of being a person and law. I use the term 'metaphysics' to delineate an area of thought that raises questions about what it means to be a 'person'; to have, or to be, a 'self', and the relationship between this self and others. In the law school, 'law' is considered in a number of ways: constitutional law; debates about citizenship; and in terms of legal subject areas such as family, contract, tort, crime, etc. Whilst feminism may be taught in law schools, it is not always the case that the way in which subjects are defined is useful to feminism. For example, within constitutional law it is easy to assume that law must be seen as operating in a 'top-down' manner; that the legislature passes the law to tell us what we can and cannot do.

Whereas the Ancient Greeks were concerned that law should facilitate the citizen's ability to live a good life, the question in modernity has become one of legitimation. The question is asked: under what circumstances, if any, should law be obeyed? Does law represent the will of the people? The problem with this framework is that the debate easily assumes that power is something that only affects us from above. As feminists were quick to point out, 'the personal is political'. In other words, power also operates at local levels, in struggles between husband and wife, employer and employee, for example. The effects of law at this level can only be understood by going beyond an analysis of court cases – and even beyond wider considerations of what goes on in solicitors' offices – to consider its more diffuse effects upon day to day power struggles. In other words, law's effects must be understood at these practical levels. The area of metaphysics I want to discuss is focused upon such 'personal issues', without making the reverse assumption that the only type of analysis worth considering can be limited to a local level.

Further, within the law school, assumptions are made regarding a public/private divide; that is, that there are certain areas of life, such as domestic life, which should be outside the reach of the State. The way in which feminists have fought to have the issue of wife beating viewed as a

---

1   My thanks to Christine Battersby for her helpful comments and suggestions on a draft of this chapter.

political, rather than simply a 'personal/private issue', illustrates this divide. Sometimes, even the definition of public law and private law can obscure the different positions of men and women within the private sphere. 'Public law' is defined as that which involves the State, whereas 'private law' is defined as involving the relationship between individuals. To categorise law in this way effectively masks the domestic sphere by subsuming both family law and commercial law within the term 'private'.

I want to start from a different position, by examining the question: who are these 'persons' who are subject to law? The meaning of the term 'person' has a legal, as well as a philosophical, history. Women were not classified as persons until the 'Persons case': *Edwards v AG of Canada* (1930),[2] in which Lord Sankey said:

> The word ['person'] is ambiguous and in its original meaning would undoubtedly embrace members of either sex. On the other hand, supposing that, in an Act of Parliament several centuries ago, it had been enacted that any person should be entitled to be elected to a particular office, it would have been understood that the word only referred to males, but the cause of this was not because the word 'person' could not include females but because at common law a woman was incapable of serving a public office.[3]

This was viewed as a breakthrough, as, previously, women had not been viewed as persons.[4] In a now classic feminist analysis of this case, Sachs and Wilson[5] describe how the newspapers actually congratulated women on the progress they were making in becoming persons! This assumption, that law simply reflects social change, will not really surprise lawyers. It is common for judges to talk as if no case had ever been wrongly decided. Within their inverted world, if the courts had previously thought that women were not classifiable as persons, then, by definition, they were not persons. This position resonates with that of Hegel,[6] for whom recognition by the law represented recognition by the community itself. Given that the courts had changed their opinion, then, by definition, women had attained personhood. This approach takes seriously the claims that 'law' makes for itself: to be able to dictate reality.

---

2   [1930] AC 124, p 128. For extracts and discussion of the case, see Bridgeman, J and Mills, S, *Feminist Perspectives on Law: Law's Engagement with the Female Body*, 1998, London: Sweet & Maxwell, p 18.

3   *Ibid, Edwards*, p 128. Emphasis added.

4   See, eg, *Bebb v Law Society* [1914] 1 Ch 286 (despite legislation referring to 'person', a woman was refused permission to sit Law Society preliminary examinations on the ground that she would not be allowed to practice as a solicitor later); *Jex-Blake v Senatus of Edinburgh University* (1873) 11 M 784; *Chorlton v Lingus* (1886) 4 CP 374.

5   Sachs, A and Wilson, JH, *Sexism and the Law*, 1978, Oxford: Martin Robertson.

6   Hegel, GW, *Hegel's Philosophy of Right*, Knox, TM (trans), 1967, Oxford: OUP.

The first theorist whose work I want to discuss, Drucilla Cornell, also takes seriously law's claim to dictate reality in ways that relate to personhood – but, this time, with a feminist aim. Cornell wants to draw upon the assumption that, at this point in time in the West, we see ourselves as being born with legal rights. In other words, what it means to be a person now includes an ability to go to law to claim rights. There is, therefore, much at stake in her work. According to this framework, it is possible to create a just society by formulating the right legal tests. (She has even gone so far as to make the difficult claim that capitalism could be undermined by the use of these rights.) Her project is, therefore, aimed at fully extending these rights to women by thinking about ways in which the law can give expression to practical feminist concerns, such as rights to abortion and protection from sexual harassment, through to rethinking adoption laws and the image of the family itself. This is the central framework that has been developed within her last two books, *The Imaginary Domain*[7] and *At the Heart of Freedom*.[8] Her work is ambitious and imaginative, in that it starts with an image of what it means to be a person and links together a philosophical system with a practical legal principle.

This works by concentrating upon the idea of freedom. She wants to keep in play the question, 'Would free and equal persons agree to this decision?'. This is to act as a broad legal principle. She proposes that this question should be asked whenever legislation is passed or a judicial decision made. The image of what it means (or could mean) to be a person is therefore central to her work.

I have much sympathy with the aims of Cornell's project and think that there is merit in any pragmatic use of law.[9] However, Cornell's work moves beyond a pragmatic position to embrace the view that we really are constituted as subjects with rights. She argues:

> Perhaps in the end I am Hegelian enough to think that we are actually constituted in modernity as subjects of right and so, in a sense we cannot step outside this sphere of law.[10]

---

7 Cornell, D, *The Imaginary Domain: Abortion, Pornography and Sexual Harassment*, 1995, London: Routledge.

8 Cornell, D, *At the Heart of Freedom: Feminism, Sex and Equality*, 1998, Chichester: Princeton UP.

9 I have argued that there are pragmatic problems with this approach to a legal test. Not only can it subtly be easily misinterpreted by judges, it ignores the practical considerations, such as the length of even employment tribunal proceedings, the endless documentation and cross-examination, that make applicants feel like victims – even whilst they simply claim 'personhood'. I want to leave this objection aside to explore the broader implications of Cornell's view of personhood for a model of social change. (See Richardson, J, 'A burglar in the house of philosophy: Theodor Adorno, Drucilla Cornell and hate speech' (1999) 7 FLS 3.)

10 Florence, P and Cornell, D, 'Towards the domain of freedom' (1997) 17 WPR 8.

She assumes that human sociability, and the recognition that we give each other, must now be attributed to (or at least channelled through) the law. Cornell's approach provides an interesting response to the *Persons* case. To explain this, the implications of the case need to be outlined. As discussed above, women were initially deemed not to be classifiable as 'persons'. This was changed as a result of the *Persons* case, thereby paving the way for allowing women to have some of the same rights as men. This scenario raises the well worn debate about whether women should be classified, in law, as 'just like men' in order to obtain the same rights as men, or whether particular rights should pertain to women *as women*. Other chapters of this book deal with Irigarayan (and other arguments) that women cannot be simply defined with respect to men – as being either 'like men' or 'not like men'. They raise the question, how did men become the *neutral* measure?

This debate can be illustrated by considering an area of law that has historically suffered from an assumption that men are the norm, against which women should be judged. Section 1 of the Sex Discrimination Act 1975 states that it is unlawful to treat a woman 'less favourably than a man' (and vice versa). It was, therefore, argued in the courts[11] that the Act could not be used to prevent discrimination against a pregnant woman because she could not show that a comparable pregnant man would not have been dismissed. As the Act could only operate by comparing women with men, the courts then decided to compare the employer's treatment of pregnant women with their treatment of sick men. (The European Court of Justice later effectively overruled this approach, to argue that dismissal on the grounds of pregnancy constituted direct sex discrimination.)[12] The earlier approach makes perfect sense if you are focused upon the question of how an employee who is not at work is to be treated. The problem is that women's ability to give birth is seen as an aberration, rather than a norm, within this frame of reference.

An important move within feminist philosophy – as well as law – is to show how, within certain belief structures, the position of women cannot simply be added into models without disrupting the whole framework. It therefore becomes difficult to argue that the position of women in the framework is a marginal issue. It can become a fault line that undermines the legal or theoretical structure from within. So, in this practical, legal example, a focus on sexual difference asks: what falls out of our analysis when workers are viewed purely in terms of their ability to work? This example opens up broader questions of social organisation, including our attitudes to birth and to work.

Cornell's conception of what it means to be a person responds to the debate as to whether women should be viewed as having particular rights *as*

11 *Haynes v Malleable Working Men's Club* [1985] ICR 705 (EAT).
12 *Dekker v Stichting Vormingscentrum Voor Jonge Volwassen (VJV- Centrum) Plus* Case C-177/88 [1991] IRLR 27 (ECJ).

women. She argues that women should be 'added in' (viewed as subject to legal rights) *as persons* (not as women). So, rights are to be viewed as attaching to the idea of being a person. However, she aims to avoid the problem of women simply being subsumed within a neutral term, 'person' – who is really viewed as having a male body and traditional lifestyle – by her unusual definition of the term 'person'. This can be illustrated by the way she talks about 'the project of becoming a person':

> What we think of as 'individuality' and 'the person' are not assumed as a given but respected as part of a project, one that must be open to each one of us on an equivalent basis.[13]

There is an image of overcoming what you have been – or rejecting stereotypes – in an act of personal transformation, which is protected by law. She describes this in terms of 'going beyond the limit'. Cornell's view of the person is not solipsistic. In other words, she does not envisage that we change individually, through an act of will, but that there is a collective, transformation, an 'acting out' of different ways of living, facilitated by the law. In order that we should have any hope of being successful in this 'project of becoming a person', Cornell cites three conditions that should be protected by law:

> ... (1) bodily integrity; (2) access to symbolic forms sufficient to achieve linguistic skills permitting the differentiation of oneself from others; and (3) the protection of the imaginary domain.[14]

In this context, it is important to note that her concern that we should be able to 'differentiate ourselves from others' is intimately linked with Cornell's 'project of becoming a person'. Although there is reference to bodily integrity in condition (1), differentiation from others is to be safeguarded by allowing access to symbolic forms and linguistic skills. Presumably, she has in mind an ability to define oneself – rather than to view oneself as, for example, only a wife/partner/mother, etc – with respect to others. This could be contrasted with a position in which 'differentiation from others' involved being able to throw them out of your house. Her emphasis upon ideas is in keeping with Cornell's whole system. Her model prioritises the imagination. It is this collective imaginary (both conscious and unconscious) that she refers to by the term 'imaginary domain'. Again, this is to be protected by law. She proposes that the protection of the 'imaginary domain' should operate as a very broad legal principle. For example, a transvestite cannot be prevented from wearing drag in public because it forms a part of 'who' he imagines himself to be. A woman who is subject to sexual harassment is to make a legal claim that the harassment interferes with her self-image – and, hence, her project of becoming a person.

---

13 *Op cit*, Cornell, fn 7, p 4.
14 *Op cit*, Cornell, fn 7, p 4.

Cornell is rightly concerned about the way in which those claiming sexual harassment are viewed as victims appealing to law for protection. She argues that the claim to be able to protect one's imaginary domain means that one is set up, not as a victim, but as claiming personhood. This ties in with her argument that, whenever a legal decision is made, then the question addressed by the judges should be, 'Would free and equal persons agree to this?'. Given the choice, persons would not agree to a legal decision that would undermine their imaginary image of themselves.

For Cornell, the project of becoming a person involves being able to act out our sexual identity that derives from 'how we imagine ourselves to be'. The stress on the imagination means that her model appears to conceive of social change as occurring as a result of our ability to *think* about ourselves differently. It is possible to reverse her model, so that it is the collective acting out of identity that becomes the impetus for changes in self-image. However, generally, her stress is upon a 'top-down' change. This is emphasised by her plea that we try to 'create psychic maps from outer space',[15] to encourage the rejection of stereotypes. This is illustrated by her description of the imaginary domain in *Heart of Freedom*:

> The imaginary domain is the space of the 'as if' in which we imagine who we might be if we made ourselves our own end and claimed ourselves as our own person.[16]

I sympathise with Cornell's aims but am worried by this abstraction. We cannot remove ourselves from the way in which we are treated in our everyday lives, but that does not prevent social change. For example, it may be that a legal secretary can have an interesting social life, in which she acts out her identity in any number of different ways. When she is treated as an emotional punch ball and as having low status on a repeated daily basis, it is difficult to sustain this fantasy – and, indeed, it remains a fantasy. Cornell's argument would be that, by a collective process of imagining the world differently, she, with others, could change – her job, the attitudes of law firms and, possibly, society at a broader level. However, it is the daily *ambiguities*, for example, as to what is a reasonable request at work, and how this is negotiated (without necessarily being thought through), that is an important part of common experience.

I want to compare Cornell's image of the person and social change to that of Battersby, to be discussed below. By considering these two theorists together, Battersby's work can be used to bring into sharper relief the main problem with Cornell's approach and to point in the direction of a different approach to 'the law'. Whilst also arguing for the need to change minds and

---

15 *Op cit*, Florence and Cornell, fn 10, p 20.

16 *Op cit*, Cornell, fn 8, p 8. The reference to the idea of taking ourselves as our own end, in contrast with the idea of ourselves as something to be used for a purpose, is Kantian. Kant's view of personhood will be outlined and discussed below.

challenging accepted interpretations of history, Battersby's image of ourselves and relations to others is more 'bottom-up' than that of Cornell. It relies less upon an imaginary realm. There is also an emphasis upon the mundane, repeated tasks and habits; the negotiation of power differences; and ambiguity as to what constitutes abuse. The aspect of Battersby's work that I most want to explore, in the next section, is her different model of identity, which emerges like a pattern out of these habits and echoes of past experiences, rather by than leaps of the imaginary.

Cornell makes an analogous 'top-down' move in relation to the role of law. Law is posited as acting down upon the person, facilitating his/her 'project of becoming a person' – just as social change is understood to occur as a result of changes in the imagination. In both cases, there is a realm that works from above to alter something else. In Cornell's system, there is a closer link between these 'realms' of the 'imaginary domain' and of law than is contained within this analogy. The law is called upon to protect our collective imagination ('the imaginary domain'), and yet the law is actually a creation of the imaginary domain itself. In other words, Cornell's argument that we are subjects with rights relies upon the argument that, in modernity, we *imagine* ourselves to be subjects with rights. She is an astute political campaigner and is not naïve about the conservatism of actual court decisions, but, understandably, she wants to make women's rights permanent. She wants to think of a time when the fight, for example, for the right to abortion, is won, which, I think, leads her to take too seriously law's claim to dictate reality. She wants to give us scope to define ourselves, rather than offering a definition of what it is to be a person, so that her model emphasises transcendence of our current position and the possibility of collective change. However, the one thing that is already defined is that being a person means being subject to law. This not only undercuts her emphasis upon our ability to define ourselves; it makes law integral to our self-definition from the start.

Cornell's position is complex with regard to the relationship between theory and practice. There appear to be two Cornells. One proposes the imaginary domain within a liberal framework, and the other is the radical socialist feminist activist. I suspect that what lies behind this is a commitment to radical politics that views her theoretical position as a practical engagement with liberals. To put it into their language, she is saying to them, 'If you buy the arguments of Dworkin and Rawls, then you must accept this feminist analysis'. Although she is clearly convinced by her arguments – they are not adopted just for pragmatic purposes – it is tempting to try to account for her more radical activism by viewing her theoretical work as strategic. This paradox can be accounted for by considering her Hegelian position. Just as Adorno was concerned to analyse the work of his contemporaries as an indication of 'where we are now', so Cornell deals practically with the US liberals. It is not merely a strategy, but neither is it the last word that can be said about her theoretical position. This would account for her eclectic use of contemporary theorists. The problem then becomes: if her stress is upon practical reason, then does her suggestion work? Below, I want to argue that her engagement with the liberals undermines the more radical aims of her project. Central to this problem is her image of the person.

When different persons, with rights, compete for the courts' acknowledgment, this is too easily assimilated into a model suggested by the right wing in the US. The right wing view of a person is as an enterprise. You gain personal 'capital' by doing a law degree, just as you would buy a record. It implies an 'instrumental' approach to life.[17] In other words, you gather up any life experience that may help to improve the quality and quantity of your life as if you are in a supermarket, gathering up goods. Aspects of your life and experience are treated like commodities, presumably with the idea that you finally lie down on your death bed and ask whether you had your money's worth out of life. Cornell does not share this approach; her socialist and feminist agenda is clear. However, my concern is that her conception of the 'project of becoming a person' can be too easily co-opted by this right wing agenda. In both cases, the courts are set up as neutral arbitrators between competing individuals.

I now want to compare Cornell's understanding of what it is to be a 'person' with that of Kant, in order to discuss how Christine Battersby reworks Kant's framework. As Battersby[18] illustrates, for Kant, the term 'person' has a specific, technical meaning that differs from the term 'human being'. Whereas both men and women could be classified as 'human beings', Kant is much more ambivalent about the classification of women as 'persons'.[19] At stake is a meaning of 'person' that is intimately linked with morality and rationality. For Kant, a rational decision is one that has been made irrespective of that individual's circumstances and desires. It is a decision that any person would make (as it is unaffected by particular circumstances). Central to this is an abstract view of freedom. Kant assumes that freedom involves making a decision that is unaffected by the material world in which decisions are made. This image of a person is therefore rational, autonomous and – unlike other aspects of Kant's views of the self, to

---

17 For a detailed argument about the use of instrumental rationality, see Adorno, TW and Horkheimer, M, *Dialectic of Enlightenment*, 1973, London: Verso. For arguments relating to this image of the US courts, see Gordon, C, 'Governmental rationality: an introduction', in Burchell, G *et al*, *The Foucault Effect: Studies in Governmentality*, 1991, Exeter: Harvester Wheatsheaf.

18 Battersby, C, *The Phenomenal Woman: Metaphysics and the Patterns of Identity*, 1998a, Cambridge: Polity, pp 63–67, 78; Battersby, C, 'Stages on Kant's way: aesthetics, morality and the gendered sublime', in Zack, N, Shrage, L and Sartwell, C (eds), *Race, Class, Gender and Sexuality: The Big Questions*, 1998b, Oxford: Blackwell, pp 227–44 .

19 Battersby cites a number of instances within Kant's work in which there is ambiguity as to whether women can be persons (see below): *ibid*, Battersby, 1998a, pp 63–66.

be discussed – involves abstracting from the particular aspects of the embodied self.

Curiously, this 'person' may not exist. Kant split the world into two, by arguing that there is the 'phenomenal' world – made up of appearances of things, that is, the way in which they appear to us. The world of appearances is comprised of everything that appears to us in space and time. Secondly, there are (or, rather, there might also be) things as they are in themselves – what an object 'really is' irrespective of the way in which it appears to us in the spacio-temporal frame. By definition, we cannot be aware of things as they are in themselves (which he refers to as corresponding to the 'noumenal' realm). When this is applied to what is meant by a 'person', then his analysis becomes even more complicated. Within this system, the 'person' is a technical term which refers to the noumenal self (that is, the self as it is 'in itself', rather than the self as we perceive it). We do not know anything about this 'person' because we only know how we *appear*, in space and time. If the person did exist then he would be able to make rational decisions, unaffected by desire or external influence. These rational decisions are automatically viewed as moral because they would be decisions that anyone would make, and, therefore, it would be contradictory to cause others pain. To be moral, we have to treat each other as if we were 'persons'. As we cannot know that we are 'persons', then we must be guided by the moral law: 'I should never act except in such a way that I can also will that my maxim should become a universal law.'[20]

Before turning to Battersby's work in detail, it is useful to consider Cornell's reworking of this aspect of Kant. In keeping with her own project, Cornell argues that Kant's central theme is one of freedom. He asks the question, 'What do we have to be in order to be free?', and answers that we need to make decisions which are uninfluenced by all external influences and internal desires. This then leads him to argue for the moral law as a guide to how a person would react if it were possible to remove himself in this way. In a move derived from Foucault's 'What is Enlightenment?'[21], she reverses this question to ask, as a legal and moral test, discussed above, 'What is not necessary for us to be free?'. The Foucauldian answer, on which she relies, is that to be free we need to avoid any pre-existing definition of who we are and what we can become; we should try to go beyond the limit of what we are. For Cornell, this collective act of transcendence is to be protected by law. Above, I have argued that the openness of the imaginary domain is undermined by the definition of persons as legal subjects.

---

20 Kant, I, *Grounding for the Metaphysics of Morals: On a Supposed Right to Lie Because of Philanthropic Concerns*, 1993, Indiana: Hackett, p 14.

21 Foucault, M, 'What is Enlightenment?', in Rabnow, P (ed), *The Foucault Reader*, 1991, London: Penguin, pp 32–50.

Battersby points out that, although Kant defines Enlightenment in terms of independence of opinion and speech, which is appropriate to autonomous and rational persons in his essay, 'What is Enlightenment?', it is clear that this does not apply to women. In the *Anthropology*,[22] Kant argues that, within the public sphere, husbands (or other men) should speak for women. Further, in the *Observations on the Feeling of the Beautiful and Sublime*,[23] Kant denies that women have the capacity for duty-based action and autonomous choice that is central to his definition of personhood. Similarly, in *The Metaphysics of Morals*,[24] women are refused personhood when Kant classifies them as passive citizens, lacking civil personality, along with domestic servants, minors, apprentices and hairdressers!

Battersby's response to Kant results in a total reworking – and undermining – of his system from within. She asks what emerges if the historical position of women – along with women's bodies – were to be treated as the norm (rather than as an aberration, within philosophical systems, which assume men as the norm). There is insufficient room to do justice to this project, and so, I want to illustrate her work by drawing upon only a few central themes and to contrast these with Cornell's position.

PERSON AND TRANSCENDENTAL SELF

Whereas Cornell reworks Kant's view of personhood so as to include women within a broadened definition of the term, Battersby concentrates mainly upon a different aspect of Kant's view of the self, the 'transcendental self'. This requires some explanation. In Kant's model, the aspect of the self that maintains itself as stable in opposition to nature (or the material world of objects) is termed the 'transcendental self'. This transcendental self imposes order on nature such that nature appears to exist in space and time. In other words, Kant uses the term 'transcendental self' to describe an aspect of the self that he infers from the way in which we are said to order the world. It is not viewed as embodied but is inferred as a counterpart of nature – viewed as dead, disorganised matter. The transcendental self is that which orders nature/matter and we only infer the existence of the transcendental self in opposition to nature/matter.

---

22 Kant, I, *Anthropology from a Pragmatic Point of View*, Gregor, M (trans), 1974, The Hague: Martinus Nijhoff, pp 79–80, cited in *op cit*, Battersby, 1998a, fn 18, p 64.

23 Kant, I, *Observations on the Feeling of the Beautiful and Sublime*, Goldthwaite, JT (trans), 1960, California: California UP, cited in *op cit*, Battersby, 1998a, fn 18, p 65.

24 Kant, I, *The Metaphysics of Morals*, Gregor, M (ed and trans), 1996, Cambridge: CUP, p 92, cited in *op cit*, Battersby, 1998a, fn 18, p 64.

By a detailed reading of Kant, Battersby illustrates how he aligns this aspect of the self as male and nature/matter/other as female.[25] The difficulty with his position is clear if the position of woman is viewed as the norm, rather than as an aberration. Battersby illustrates how it is impossible to think birth, in which the self cannot be defined by what is not-self (or 'other'), within the Kantian system. In birth, otherness emerges gradually out of the embodied, fleshy self. This argument illustrates the way in which birth is being thought philosophically, which – for those of us who are squeamish about this point – in no way depends upon an assumption that women should have children (or sentimentalises birth). It recognises the need to account for the possibility of birth within a philosophical system that aims to say something about 'who we are'. With regard to the Kantian system, the failure to be able to think birth provides a weak point. Battersby goes beyond illustrating this weakness to construct an alternative image of the self.

Battersby's model envisages a self that emerges gradually from patterns of movement or becoming. This model can be understood as making sense of birth against a philosophical tradition that has failed to consider the normality of bodies that can become two. Birth is understood as the emergence of a self by thinking of matter that is living and able to transform itself to become two bodies from one. This is not possible within the Kantian system, in which the (transcendental) self imposes its framework on matter in order to perceive it within space and time. In Kant's model, matter (or bodies) appear as only passive or dead. There is an analogy between this description, which tries to think the possibility of birth as normal, and the *emergence* of a self through repeated acts and interaction with others. In Battersby's model, unlike that of Kant, there is no clear self/other divide; the self is not made stable by the rejection of what is not-self. Temporary stability of the self occurs through 'habit, repetition and temporary equilibrium of force fields',[26] like water running through a sieve that has reached a stable level because of the water pressure. There is a stable amount of water in the sieve when there is a temporary, *dynamic* equilibrium.

It is important that Battersby's model is not confused with Carol Gilligan's[27] image of women, who are described as adopting an ethic of care, in which they empathise and 'open up' to others. Battersby rejects this conservative model. In Battersby's model, there is no pre-existing self to be empathetic. Battersby envisages a self that emerges out of difference through patterns. There is a gradual emergence of 'who we are' through patterns of

25 She argues that this Kantian move has been repeated within contemporary psychoanalysis – in which the stable (male) self is defined as against the mother/other.

26 This image of 'force fields' draws from a Foucauldian view of power as forming ever present, intersecting force fields from which identity emerges. See *op cit*, Battersby, 1998a, fn 18, p 206.

27 Gilligan, C, *In a Different Voice: Psychological Theory and Women's Development*, 1982, Cambridge, Mass: Harvard UP.

behaviour, which includes both the imaginary and physical action. Battersby has illustrated that there is nothing new or radical about the image of the caring woman and the reasonable man – both are detailed by Kant, whose *Observations on the Feeling of the Beautiful and Sublime*[28] would have graced the pages of any women's magazine.

Having briefly outlined the models of self (and person) of both Cornell and Battersby, I want to consider their implications for issues of personal change (and, given that both, in different ways, emphasise relationality, this necessarily involves social change), along with the role of law. I have already indicated both my sympathy with the more radical aims of Cornell's project and concern about the way in which she envisages change. Her stress is upon our ability to imagine ourselves differently. It is this collective imaginary, or 'imaginary domain', that is to be protected by law. Law itself is central to her definition of 'who we are today', because – as part of our collective imaginary – we view ourselves as subjects with rights. Having benefited from the legal struggles of earlier generations of women, I have nothing against the pragmatic use of law. However, as illustrated by the *Persons* case, I am suspicious of the way in which law is allowed to be so central to our definition of ourselves.

Further, Cornell's is a top-down framework, in which law is called upon to protect not only the imaginary domain and bodily integrity, but also:

> ... access to symbolic forms sufficient to achieve linguistic skills permitting the differentiation of oneself from others.[29]

This is a very different model of self and otherness from Battersby's model, in which self and otherness emerge through patterns of relationality that do not assume a pre-existing self. However, there are some similarities. Cornell's 'project of becoming a person' does envisage a transition, an emergence of the self. Although she calls for the law to protect the possibility of differentiating one's self from others, her system does not imply the Kantian move that the self is made stable by being *defined against* the other. Additionally, Cornell's image of what it is to be a person is embodied and does take seriously sexual difference. Like Battersby's model, it also takes seriously racial, sexual and other differences between women. My concern is with the top-down way in which the imaginary is the driving force for social change and the way in which this impacts upon her conception of law.

---

28 Kant, I, 'Of the distinction of the beautiful and sublime in the interrelations of the two sexes', in *op cit*, Kant, fn 23, pp 76–96.

29 *Op cit*, Cornell, fn 7, p 4.

Battersby reworks the history of art and philosophy to allow the work of women artists to emerge – in a manner that falls outside our frame of reference if male bodies and traditional lifestyles are taken as norm. This is illustrated by her work on, for example, Karoline von Günderode,[30] whose reworking of the sublime reflected women's socialised ambivalence to a move in which the self is defined as against otherness. Drawing from Adorno, Battersby argues that historical changes now help us to see/appreciate the work of these artists/poets. Seeing and understanding their work also affects us in terms of allowing us to envisage another kind of self/imagination/ embodiment/model of change.

I briefly outlined a small part Battersby's work to try to illustrate her broader project of thinking through the implications for metaphysics of taking female bodies and subject positions as the norm. This results in a model of the self that is much more 'bottom-up' than that of Cornell. There is no stress upon an imagination that can create personal/social change. Instead, there is a greater emphasis upon embodiment – of matter that can think and change itself without being ordered from above. I want to expand upon this image of change and its implications for law. Before doing so, it is useful to consider the place of the imaginary in Battersby's model, and the extent to which she can incorporate Cornell. Despite the fact that Cornell's image of a person is embodied (and not defined as against matter or otherness), the emphasis upon imagination still evokes an image of a self that orders the world from above by employing imagination. Against this, Battersby wants to think of matter that is active.

Neither Battersby nor Cornell has written about the other's work. However, Battersby does discuss Judith Butler – a feminist philosopher who, like Cornell, is greatly influenced by Hegel. Without going into Battersby's detailed argument with Butler's position (which differs from that of Cornell), it is interesting to note Battersby's argument that:

> ... it is necessary to posit identity as emerging not through 'symbolic' codes traced on matter (women's bodies) that remains inactive, passively traced from outside and above. Instead, we need to think identities emerging through non-dialectical contact between forces, in which 'self' and 'other' are not antagonistic categories. Thinking the female body that is normatively not simply 'penetrable' but also fleshy and 'wombed' allows us to register 'otherness' that can exist within the self itself.[31]

When Cornell calls upon the law to defend 'access to symbolic forms sufficient to achieve linguistic skills permitting the differentiation of oneself from

---

30 Battersby, C, 'Unblocking the oedipal: Karoline von Günderode and the female sublime', in Ledger, S et al, *Political Gender: Texts and Contexts*, 1994, London: Harvester Wheatsheaf, pp 129–43.

31 *Op cit*, Battersby, 1998a, fn 18, pp 122–23.

others',[32] Battersby can account for this move. It envisages an image of matter that is structured in a top-down manner by the imagination.[33]

Central to Cornell's reworking of law are the ideals of freedom and equality. Her legal principle is based upon a refrain, the repetition of the question: 'Would free and equal persons agree to this (legal decision)?' Battersby's project of thinking identity in a way that takes the female as norm immediately runs counter to Cornell's legal principle in her treatment of both freedom and equality. She describes women's lives as traditionally involving relationships of dependency – from dependency of the foetus to the dependency of children upon their mother. She states:

> Indeed, when we continue to treat individuals as ideally independent and equal, we continue to take the (idealized) male subject as norm.[34]

Similarly, in drawing from Kierkegaard, she argues that:

> Political agency is possible; but the agent has to live with radical ambiguities ...; with power discrepancies; and with relational dependence on others.[35]

Interpreting Battersby with respect to law, Cornell could argue that most people in the West have some notion of the idea of formal equality under the law – even if Battersby is right to say that this is not reflected in our daily lives. I might not expect to be appointed a partner in a solicitors firm if I am pregnant, but I would not expect anyone to give that as the reason for the rejection – even if it appeared to be unlikely that I would take part in the litigation lottery. However, I have taken Battersby's comments out of context. A distinction can be drawn between Battersby's statement that there are normally power discrepancies in relationships – and that, therefore, the ethical task is to decide which of these constitute abuse – and the use of this to attack (rather than build upon) formal equality in law at a pragmatic level.

Battersby's recognition of inequality can usefully be considered in the context of, for example, the 19th century case law that held that employees could not sue for workplace injury.[36] Sadly, this is an instance of Cornell's test (almost) being applied, albeit in the wrong way. Judges, keen on *laissez faire* economics, argued that the workers, as free and equal[37] persons, had chosen

---

32 *Op cit*, Cornell, fn 7, p 4.

33 This is similar to Marx's response to Hegel: that our understanding of the world derives from what we do on a daily basis to survive. However, this parallel breaks down. This is not only because Marx's image of 'what we do to survive' focused upon the economic realm, but also because this involved a different image of the person from that being described by Battersby.

34 *Op cit*, Battersby, 1998a, fn 18, p 205

35 *Op cit*, Battersby, 1998a, fn 18, p 197.

36 This was overturned by *Smith v Baker & Sons* [1891] AC 325.

37 Workers were, by now, formally equal in law. As a result of the abolition of the master and servant legislation in 1875, it was no longer an offence to refuse to work for the master.

to work in unsafe conditions and, therefore, took on the risk of injury. Ignoring the interdependency and inequality involved in this instance meant ignoring the fact that the only other choice on offer involved destitution.

To explain how political agency is envisaged, it is worth considering Battersby's view of identity in more depth. Although Battersby rejects the abstract freedom and autonomy of the Kantian person, this does not mean that it is impossible to think agency within her model:

> The subject that I will posit is neither free nor autonomous but is also not simply passive. It is both marked – 'scored' – into specificity by its relationship with 'otherness', and yet is itself also capable of agency and of resisting modes of domination. This self is not only shaped by 'the other', it is also self-shaping as potentiality is transformed into actuality via echo and the feedback loops of memory.[38]

This is quoted out of context and needs to be unpacked. The reference to 'scoring' evokes an image of repetition, of identity being 'carved out', but, more accurately, it is a musical analogy. We are not passively carved out by our past. Our past is also understood through our present – in the same way as a refrain in a song is only recognised retrospectively as a refrain when it has been repeated. This, along with references to the echo and feedback loops, undermines the Kantian image of a self that constructs his world in space and time. Kant's model is disrupted by Battersby's emphasis upon hearing. The refrain is never simply a repetition of the same. Subtle changes can then be perceived upon further hearing.[39] Hearing also involves bringing otherness inside oneself – we have to listen to everything and make sense of it retrospectively. In other words, by emphasising vision, as Kant does, the self appears to be more in control. We are able to orientate our vision in order to categorise the external world of objects. If we want to shield ourselves from any objects, then we can close our eyes. Kant's emphasis upon vision therefore stresses a sense of division between the self and that which is viewed as external (or 'other') to it.

By considering hearing, Battersby problematises such a split between self and other. Just as the possibility of birth (that there exist bodies that can become two) cannot be understood in terms of a model that defines self as against otherness, it is difficult to think of hearing within these terms. We cannot easily cut ourselves off from what is heard. It is taken into the self and retrospectively understood as patterns emerge over time. These are not metaphors for the self but are actually important aspects of the human condition that must not be rendered incoherent by any philosophical model that purports to say something about what it is to be, or to have, a self. In making this move, Battersby draws upon the work of Irigaray, who uses an

---

38   *Op cit*, Battersby, 1998a, fn 18, p 12.
39   Thanks to Rachel Jones for this point.

analysis of senses other than sight, particularly the sense of touch in *Speculum*,[40] to trouble masculinist models of identity.[41]

This is *not* a view of social change as occurring dialectically between the social structure (including law) and a self. It should also be emphasised that there is no pre-formed self within this model. The system is dynamic, but without being based upon the notion of dialectical change. Again, this can be compared with Cornell's model. It is curious that Cornell wants to use her image of law to fix rights permanently. Within her system, the imaginary domain is open to change, so that, when we start to think differently about what it is to be a person, this may impact upon how we think about law. This includes the possibility of questioning the form of, or even necessity for, law. Battersby's model offers the possibility of viewing law differently. Law, rather than being central to our self-definition – as in Cornell's model, becomes one of the forces that may contribute (by varying degrees) to the production of this dynamic self. As it is not central to the definition of the self, its tactical use must be assessed by a consideration of its daily impact on lives. Without embracing the idea that only local analysis should be considered, it focuses attention on the practical impact of 'law'. This includes not only a concern with the stereotypes of women that are perpetuated and challenged in our collective imaginations, but also an emphasis upon the material circumstances from which these arise and are challenged. This leads towards an analysis of the way in which law impacts upon (but does not dictate) the ambiguity of daily negotiations, in which power is rarely equal.

---

40   Irigaray, L, *Speculum of the Other Woman*, Gill, G (trans), 1985, Ithaca: Cornell UP.

41   For an analysis of the move away from an emphasis upon vision as the main sense upon which philosophy is based, see, also, Jay, M, *Downcast Eyes: The Denigration of Vision in Twentieth Century French Thought*, 1993, California: California UP.

CHAPTER 7

EQUALITY IN THE LAW AND IRIGARAY'S DIFFERENT UNIVERSALS

Ewan Porter

There is an assumption at the heart of any legal system that considers itself to be liberal. This is that all citizens should be treated as equal in the eyes of the law. Any challenge to this assumption is immediately in danger of being labelled as one, or more, of those things that such liberal systems despise (fascist, élitist, oppressive, etc). In this paper, I will be looking at this 'given of equality'. It may seem that the idea that there might be something wrong with the idea of equality is so alien to our culture that it verges on the ridiculous, if not the dangerous. However, we need only to ask such a simple question as 'whose equality?' to start down the road to what I hope will be a fruitful examination of this concept, upon which so much of our legal theory is dependent. This critique will be presented as an exposition of the work of the French philosopher, Luce Irigaray. I will be endeavouring to show that she is able to give a convincing answer to the question, 'Whose equality?' and that her answer troubles this notion so much that it also demands a completely different foundation for the law – a foundation in difference.

We can begin by asking, 'Who (or what) is it that is equal in the eyes of the law?'. Whether we respond with the answer, 'Citizens', 'Subjects' or 'Persons', we will always have to resort to an abstract universal notion. Those individuals who come under the law will be treated as equal to any other individual. As such, they will be designated to accord with a model of a universal legal subject. The answer to the question of 'Who is equal?' is 'Everyone', which would not seem to be a very enlightening or useful answer. What might take us a little further is to ask: 'What is everyone equal to?' The answer to this will be, 'The universal legal subject'. Universal, not just because it is an abstracted general notion, but because it is one that should apply to absolutely everyone. It is this notion of a universal subject that Irigaray criticises. So, my assessment of her critique of equality will be based on an examination of her critique of the universal subject. Before I do this, I will need to give a brief sketch of how Irigaray considers this universal subject to have been represented in theory.

The easiest way to convey her assessment of the theoretical constructions of the subject is simply to quote the title of one of the chapters of her book, *Speculum of the Other Woman*: 'Any theory of the "subject" has always been appropriated by the "masculine".'[1] From this title, we can derive a fair

---

1   Irigaray, L, *Speculum of the Other Woman*, Gill, G (trans), 1985, Ithaca: Cornell UP.

assessment of her evaluation of the history of Western philosophy, as well as the social, cultural and legal systems that are based on its theoretical constructions. Although we could criticise Irigaray here for her tendency to represent the whole of Western philosophy as a phallocentric enterprise, what is at issue here is not whether there have been exceptions to this monolithic misogyny, but how this appropriation of the subject has worked. Even if we reduce her exaggerated claim (and there are stylistic reasons (which we shall come back to later) as to why this exaggeration takes place) to the suggestion that those theories of the subject that have been most influential have always been appropriated by the masculine, we still need to understand how and why this takes place, and what the results of her critique might produce.

Although Irigaray is concerned primarily with psychoanalytic theories of the subject, in this chapter I shall be reading her work as applicable to philosophical theories, such as that of Kant, on which many accounts of the legal subject are based. My justification of this is again to draw attention to her own title: 'Any theory of the "subject" has always been appropriated by the "Masculine".' What would bring all these theories together, for Irigaray, would be to adopt the position that, as theories, they all participate in the symbolic order. The 'Symbolic' is a Lacanian psychoanalytic term, which refers to the ability of the subject to participate in language.[2] Here, language does not only refer to words, vocabulary and grammatical rules, but, as Joan W Scott explains:

> ... it is, rather, a meaning constituting system; that is, any system – strictly verbal or otherwise – through which meaning is constructed and cultural practices are organised and by which, accordingly, people represent and understand their world, including who they are and how they relate to others.[3]

Theories are not only products of language users – they can also be historical interventions into or influences on the way we use, think about and construct language. Irigaray's point is that the symbolic, of which these theories are necessarily and inextricably a part, is itself a gendered system. In *Speculum*, she traces the masculinisation of the symbolic and of all theories from Plato through to Lacan. With regard to Plato, she executes a lengthy reading of his myth of the cave, in which she is able to give a convincing account of how it is a foundational move of philosophy to exclude women.[4] In trying to sum up this book, we could (rather brutally) say that the whole of our culture is based

---

2   For a full and accessible account of Lacan's system and theory, see Grosz, E, *Jacques Lacan: A Feminist Introduction*, 1990, London: Routledge.

3   Scott, JW, 'Deconstructing equality-versus-difference; or, the uses of poststructuralist theory for feminism' (1988) 14(1) FS 34.

4   See *op cit*, Irigaray, fn 1, pp 243–365. I will not try to present a synopsis of her ingenious deconstruction of Plato here, but will merely hint at the associations she makes between the shape of the cave, the womb and Plato's privileging of the movement of philosophers away from this '*Hystera*', towards the sun.

on the exclusion of women. A theme that occurs again and again throughout her texts is that this exclusion is more than just a privileging of the male or masculine position – it is not just a crude attempt to enable men to reach and maintain positions of symbolic power – it is also necessary to the whole functioning and maintenance of the system. In the final note of the book, she puts it thus:

> ... in relation to the working of theory, the/a woman fulfils a twofold function –
> as the mute outside that sustains all systematicity; as a maternal and still silent
> ground that nourishes all foundations ...[5]

If the symbolic is really a male or masculine symbolic that depends on the exclusion of women, and if theory is automatically implicated in this exclusion, the problem then becomes one of trying to find a place or method by which women can enter into language. Part of the reason that Irigaray's writing is so impenetrable and strange is that she is attempting to use a language which she does not consider to be her own – it is not her mother tongue, we might say – to express and create a symbolic that would include the female and feminine. She can only do this with the resources available to her, and therefore uses a strategy of mimicry to unfaithfully repeat, distort and, therefore, subvert the symbolic that is attempting to exclude her. She writes:

> That place may only emerge if the feminine is granted its own 'specificity' in its
> relation to language. Which implies a logic other than the one imposed by
> discursive coherence. I have attempted to practice that other 'logic' in the
> writing of *Speculum* ...[6]

So, to a certain extent, I am misrepresenting Irigaray here by attempting to sum up her thought and writing in more familiar theoretical terms. Rather than presuming that this chapter represents a faithful representation of Irigaray's thought, it would be more accurate to think of it as an interpretation of just some of the associations and suggestions that emerge from her writing. In this spirit, I would like to concentrate on some of the differences and distinctions that Irigaray draws attention to and challenges. She considers the masculinisation of the symbolic and, therefore, Western culture as a whole to be so successfully hegemonic that it even effects the representations of a female/feminine imaginary.

The 'Imaginary' is another Lacanian psychoanalytic term, which describes the stage in the formation of the ego in which an infant can recognise himself or herself as 'whole'. Because this stage precedes the symbolic and full entry into language, it has often been used by feminist theorists to try to construct a

---

5   *Op cit*, Irigaray, fn 1, p 365.
6   Irigaray, L, *This Sex Which Is Not One*, Porter, C (trans), 1985, Ithaca: Cornell UP, p 153.

moment that might be described as more authentically feminine.[7] The recognition takes place in a mirror, but, for Irigaray, the (Lacanian) theory behind this already denies a woman's 'specificity of her own relationship to the imaginary',[8] because it is constructed according to what the male gaze would see in a flat mirror. In Irigaray's words, it 'reflects the greater part of women's sexual organs only as a hole'.[9]

So, Irigaray's task is not only to try to disrupt the symbolic sufficiently to create a place for a female/feminine symbolic; it is also an attempt to refigure the imaginary in such a way that it would allow her to see her own specificity in her relationship to it. She repeatedly mimics the positions that she considers culture and theory to have attributed to women in order to undermine those cultures and theories. By drawing attention to oppositions such as subject and object, and sun and earth, she is able to emphasise how deeply embedded these positions are in the male/female opposition. By taking her position as the one that is already given to her in the symbolic, she shows how woman is actually the ground (the earth) upon which man has built his theoretical abstractions.

IRIGARAY'S CRITIQUE OF THE UNIVERSAL SUBJECT

The standard of the universal subject is only able to set itself up as a standard if it has (as a subject) an appropriate and compliant object to reflect its self-image. Irigaray plays with the idea of woman as the mirror in which man sees an inferior copy of himself. In fact, rather than thinking of the universal subject as the standard by which other subjects are measured, she suggests that this abstract standard can only exist because woman is 'a benchmark that is ultimately more crucial than the subject, for he can sustain himself only by bouncing back off some objectiveness, some objective'.[10] These theories of the subject make her into a flat, static mirror or object in order to be able to erect their subjectivity. If she is allowed to move, or to curve, or to show herself as she really might be in her own subjectivity, then his erections collapse.

It is Kant's transcendental self that Irigaray takes as a prime example of a construction of the universal subject. The transcendental self, in Kant's system, is what needs to be presupposed in order to bring all the elements of

---

7　Examples of very different uses of the imaginary in feminist theory include Le Doeuff, M, *The Philosophical Imaginary*, Gordon, C (trans), 1989, London: Athlone; Gatens, M, *Imaginary Bodies: Ethics, Power and Corporeality*, 1996, London: Routledge; Cornell, D, *The Imaginary Domain: Abortion, Pornography and Sexual Harassment*, 1995, London: Routledge.

8　*Op cit*, Irigaray, fn 1, p 133.

9　*Op cit*, Irigaray, fn 1, p 89.

10　*Op cit*, Irigaray, fn 1, p 133.

experience together into an understandable whole. It does this by applying the categories and forms that are the basic framework and structure of our thinking, to our perceptions. This not only brings our experience together into a coherent whole; it also makes the 'I' (that is experiencing) into a single, coherent self. However, for Irigaray, it is the transcendental nature of this self that is another symptom of the theoretical forgetting of woman and of the mother. Because it is transcendental, it stands out from, or above, the material world that it both projects and perceives:

> Rising to a perspective that would dominate the totality, to the vantage point of greatest power, he thus cuts himself off from the bedrock, from his empirical relationship with the matrix that he claims to survey.[11]

The reference to the matrix is part of a continuing play between matter, *mater* and matrix, which again is mimicking the positioning of woman as nature, earth or ground. So, Kant's transcendental subject, and any theory of the subject, according to Irigaray, distances him from the earth/woman/mother. By doing so, he distances himself from the *sine qua non* of his existence, subjectivity and life itself. It is these movements of theoretical abstraction that Irigaray reads as having used woman as a ground or foundation on which to build higher and more ethereal structures and systems which can then forget about the bedrock of their abstracted being. From Plato's attempts to move towards the sun and the heavenly world of forms, through the universalisation of the Kantian transcendental self, to the self-reflexive Lacanian subject, these theories can all be seen to function on the exclusion of woman.

What is required, then, is a re-evaluation of what all these theorists and universalists are trying to reach or create, as well as what it is that they are trying to move away from, forget or destroy. As far as Irigaray is concerned, we could say that without the Mother there would be no life; without the concrete there would be no abstract; and without the particular there would be no universal. She would like a closer examination and non-misogynistic evaluation of the particular, if that is to be the position that woman is assigned. This would call for an attentiveness to the specificity of each woman's *hic et nunc* and the radical difference, not just between men, and their death driven futurity and finitude, and women, but also between women themselves.

Not only is woman positioned as object, matter and ground, etc, but this ground must be formed out of inert matter if it is to provide the stable foundation of a bedrock for his erections. This inertia is not only a lack of movement or change; it is also a way of making woman silent and unrepresentable within the theory and culture. Taking the Kantian transcendental subject as paradigmatic, Irigaray reinterprets its powers of

---

11 *Op cit*, Irigaray, fn 1, pp 133–34.

projection. The Kantian subject projects and represents the object or objective world through its framework of space and time, the categories and the schemata of the imagination. But this is much more than a neutral attempt to make sense of the chaos. Irigaray states that 'he projects a something to absorb, to take, to see, to possess ... as well as a patch of ground to stand upon, a mirror to catch his reflection'.[12]

Irigaray sees something like a reversal of roles here. Where she would consider the truth of the matter to be that woman is already there and, as mother, creates and sustains the subject, Kant's view of the object is that it is merely a projection and construction of the subject. He recognises the necessity of the object for the formation of the subject, but refuses to allow it/her to have its/her own voice or representation. To allow the object to speak would be to upset the unity and coherence of the subject, who needed this myth of projection and inertia to become the transcendental subject:

> The silent allegiance of the one guarantees the auto-sufficiency, the autonomy of the other as long as no questioning of this mutism as a symptom – of historical repression – is required. But what if the object started to speak?[13]

What, indeed? This seemingly mad question lies at the very heart of Irigaray's early writing. It can be interpreted in any number of ways. I shall put forward a few paraphrases of it here to try to suggest how it might be useful when considering the legal subject. She could be asking what would happen if the object took on some of the qualities of the subject, the qualities that enable it to participate in culture or to enter speech through the symbolic. But Irigaray is not asking 'what if the object became a subject?' In doing so, she is, therefore, leaving open space for the kind of speech or language that would be proper to woman as she is in herself. By maintaining the position of object, she is not tied to repeating the moves that have made language the domain of the universal, the abstract and the masculine. To bring objects into speech would be to make the particular, the concrete and the feminine articulate the uniqueness of their being and experience.

Irigaray takes up the position of the object in order to maintain a radical difference from the universal subject, as he has been constructed by theory. But this does not mean that she wants to accept passively the role that has been given to her by a phallocentric culture. The inertia and silence of the object is only the inertia and silence given to it by the theories that require these qualities in order to create and maintain their positions. The possibility of the object starting to speak is only mad when viewed from the position of these masculine theories. Woman and the object only appear to be silent because theory and culture refuse to listen properly or be sensitive to her movements and presence. What would enable us to hear woman and the

---

12 *Op cit*, Irigaray, fn 1, p 134.
13 *Op cit*, Irigaray, fn 1, p 135.

object, as well as feel her presence and movement, would be a completely different theory of subject and object. It would be one in which the dichotomy of subject and object would no longer be dependent on the object simply being an inert reflection of the subject, a theory in which the object would be granted existence in her own right.

Irigaray tries to express a theory of radical difference which would move beyond the fixed poles of sameness and difference. She does not just take up difference as the opposite of sameness or equality; she tries to develop a notion of difference that is no longer allied to the sense that it is still just one term, or pole, of a binary opposition. With reference to sexual difference, in particular she suggests that male/masculine and female/feminine:

> ... are terms that cannot fittingly be designated by the number 'two' and the adjective 'different', if only because they are not susceptible to comparison. To use such terms serves only to reiterate a movement begun long since, that is, the movement to speak of the 'other' in a language already systematised by/for the same.[14]

The difference at stake here is no longer to be thought of as that which is different from the same. To be different in the prevailing phallocentric symbolic is simply to be different from the same, to be the object of the subject or to be the imperfect copy. What she would like us to recognise is a radical alterity that she calls the 'other of the other' that escapes being represented as the 'other of the same'. These terms are, again, responses to Lacanian theory, which explicitly refused the thought of the other of the other. The only other possible was to be the other of the masculine same. The other of the other would be an otherness that is not derivative of, and does not refer to, the same old masculinised theory.

This radical difference would also have ramifications for legal theory, in that the term 'difference' is not only treated as the opposite and accompanying pole of sameness; it is also the opposite and accompanying pole of equality. So, if equality is what is at stake in our analysis of the presuppositions of liberal legal theory, the kind of difference that might emerge as a useful alternative is not difference as the simple opposite of equality. To allow Irigaray's kind of difference to work in a legal theory or system would be to open a space that would allow the representation of anything that was not premised on a masculine model. But, in the very act of doing this, it would also have to undo the system of sameness which had excluded it. It would have to usher in a new kind of seeing and listening that would be able to recognise and cherish the radical alterity already present in all those others of others that are still excluded from recognition as whole and proper persons in their own right.

---

14   *Op cit*, Irigaray, fn 1, p 139.

Equality and difference become transformed when considered in the light of Irigaray's writing, because they both become resonant with the historical investments and exclusions that have formed them as the concepts that we know. They are no longer simply abstract, ahistorical terms that have absolute and definitive meanings. Instead, we see difference begin to undermine equality's pretensions by showing how it has actually privileged the male model of subjectivity. According to Irigaray's theory, if we are to still hold on to a principle of equality under the law, it must be an equality that recognises its own implication in the exclusions that have been carried out by the theories and cultures which have produced and adhered to it as a principle. Irigaray suggests that it is time to institute a principle of difference that is able to assess the specificity of every individual in their own particular situation, rather than try to make them fit an abstracted universal model of subjectivity or personhood (one which approximately half of those individuals are already set up to fail to achieve).

One danger that would need to be avoided in this reconstruction of theory would be to turn difference into another ideal. If we concentrate purely on these theoretical implications, difference could very easily turn into a philosopheme in its own right, which would still avoid the practical implications that led to its interrogation in the first place – the attempt to address legal issues in the specificity of women's actual lives. Simply to propose a switch from a formal equality in the law to a formal difference would be a move that would still be in danger of forgetting about the concrete content which fills these formal structures in all sorts of different ways. This is not to say that Irigaray completely rejects a theoretical/philosophical reconstruction of these concepts in favour of purely practical interventions, but that the theoretical exposure of the supposedly neutral model of the universal subject and equality should make a significant difference to women's lives. Indeed, although it might be tempting to reject the notion of a universal altogether, she refuses to do so; instead, she again tries to subvert its use in order to produce a more historically responsive and responsible concept that would mediate, rather that legislate or determine.

DIFFERENT UNIVERSALS

In later works, such as *Sexes and Genealogies*,[15] Irigaray engages directly with the law and with the notion of the universal that she sees at work in it. In the lecture entitled 'The universal as mediation', she undertakes a critique of Hegel's analysis of the law. She examines the implications of Hegel's

---

15 Irigaray, L, *Sexes and Genealogies*, Gill, G (trans), 1993, New York: Columbia UP.

distinction between *Moralität*, which is concerned with a morality that is considered to be more subjective, immediate and individual, and *Sittlichkeit*, which is more objective, mediated and concerned with the community or nation. She also sees two types of law at work: the law of estates; and the law of social customs, which she also describes as religious law. But she is particularly concerned here with how these should come together in the family. The problem for her is that, even though these two realms of law can come together in the family, the only realm that civic, or State, law recognises is the law of estates, which is based on property and, therefore, concentrates on money. She seems to take a view of the family which endows it with the possibility of bringing together the public and private, *Moralität* and *Sittlichkeit*, and subjective and objective. This mediation does not take place in the wider culture as a whole. She laments the fact that 'our discourse is incapable of rethinking a universal as mediation and not as truth resulting from arbitrary forms'.[16]

What she is very concerned with is that mediation should take place between the father and the mother in the family. She wants to institute what she calls an 'ethics of the couple'.[17] It is here that she can be read as starting to move away from her earlier work, such as *Speculum*. She is now basing her model on a firmly heterosexual couple, whereas, in *Speculum* and *This Sex Which Is Not One*, she was more concerned with an economy of women among or between themselves. But, more than this, she now seems to be suggesting that, when she uses the word 'nature', she 'means earth, water, fire, wind, plants and living bodies, which precede any definition or fabrication that tear them away from roots and origins that exist independently of man's transforming activity'.[18]

The style of Irigaray's writing now seems to be moving away from the mimicry employed in, for example, *Speculum*. She appears to be positing her own truths when she presents a version of history that assumes the transition from pre-historic gynocracy to a patriarchal and sacrificial culture as unequivocal fact. This creates a tension within her *oeuvre* as a whole, between the earlier Irigaray who exposed the cultural and historical construction of concepts and histories and the later one who posits cultural facts. However, it is not necessary to read her as presenting an eternal truth here; it can more usefully be read as another tactical intervention in her attempt to usher in an ethics of sexual difference.

Irigaray still retains an emphasis on the here and now, and on the gendered specificity of individuals, in her later work. Her analysis of Hegel again leads her to the conclusion that the specificity of each person within a

---

16 *Op cit*, Irigaray, fn 15, p 128.
17 *Op cit*, Irigaray, fn 15, p 132.
18 *Op cit*, Irigaray, fn 15, p 129.

family unit is sacrificed to that unit. According to Hegel, the only right that each member of the family has in-themselves is the right to life. But, because he considers each person within this unit to be only a stage in his dialectical process, his or her own life becomes subordinated to that of the family, and the State in turn. As history develops, so Irigaray sees the gendered roles within the family becoming more demarcated. The father becomes associated with the name and property, while the mother becomes associated with the earth, as a guardian of substance and a reproductive body. As far as Irigaray is concerned, the patriarchal 'exclusive emphasis on the woman's role as mother has gone in step with a lack of respect for the natural order'.[19] Indeed, the mother is subordinated and often (literally) sacrificed for the maintenance of the male genealogy. The law reflects this only too well for Irigaray, in that:

> No right protects the woman's life against violence in the home, against unwanted pregnancies. A right that should be guaranteed and protected by society and the State is instead a barely tolerated claim, sometimes partially heeded but always at the mercy of decisions made by specific individuals: this doctor, this judge, this expert will consult their consciences and decide on a woman's right, within a context that allows no generalisations. The process has to be started from scratch and pursued in isolation by each woman in turn since there is no legal recourse that is specific to woman.[20]

Here, Irigaray herself appears to be moving closer to the universal. But this universal will be very different from the universals that she has been so critical of – universals of the same. Any universals she will produce will be universals of difference. She is still insisting on a universalised right to life, although this will be a very restricted universal, in that it will also need to take into account 'gender as one constituent of the human race, not only in reproduction but also in culture, spirit'.[21] In other words, even if we are to universalise the right to life, we also need to be open to the gendered aspects of the history of that concept. For example, we could pay attention to the patriarchal assumption that the child's right to life somehow trumps the mother's. Irigaray suggests that this supposedly natural judgment has only arisen because the child carries on the father's name, blood and law.

Irigaray holds the view that women have become more associated with nature, while men have held control over the cultural and spiritual development of nations. She cites a long list of Greek myths to support her reading of this ancient divorce of nature from culture and spirit and its basis in the murder, exile or burial of women.[22] While she wants there to be a 'right to natural and spiritual life for both men and women',[23] she also suggests that

---

19   *Op cit*, Irigaray, fn 15, p 131.
20   *Op cit*, Irigaray, fn 15, p 132.
21   *Op cit*, Irigaray, fn 15, p 132. Emphasis in original.
22   *Op cit*, Irigaray, fn 15, p 134.
23   *Op cit*, Irigaray, fn 15, p 132.

there is an 'irreducibility of sexual difference'. This assertion of the irreducibility of differences has often lead to accusations of essentialism – whether this is seen as biological, psychological or social. But to assert that differences are irreducible does not have to be the same as asserting the essences of two different sexes. Irigaray claims that these differences are the result of historical or cultural practices; and, even where she asserts them in morphological terms, they can still be interpreted as open to negotiation and evolution over time.[24]

However, the trouble with my description of this as involving historical transition is that the history at stake still belongs to the patriarchal order. As Irigaray would put it, the maternal-feminine is that which is hidden in 'the nation', and it is this idea of the nation which 'allows the articulation of spirit, of time, of history'. So, the maternal-feminine is what 'invisibly continues its work of underpinning the existence of the whole social body'.[25] And it is this invisibility that needs to be challenged. 'Women must become socially visible in their sexed singleness. *Otherwise the social body splits off from the natural body* (civil law from natural law).[26]

So, the universal, for Irigaray, will be a universal of mediation, which will also evolve over time. Irigaray even suggests that Hegel, who could be described as a philosopher of the most absolute of universals, had a conception that was limited by the fact that 'He was a male, he lived between the 18th and 19th centuries [and] he was mortal'.[27]

She denies the possibility of a *'neuter* universal',[28] because, as we have seen, its neutrality will always have been based on a theoretical model that has been appropriated by the masculine – it will be a male neuter. It is the gender blindness of this male neutrality that perpetuates the forgetting of nature and the social exclusion of women. Of course, this perpetuation also continues within the male neutrality of the law. The right to life, which would be a natural right, rather than a cultural or spiritual right, has been lost in civil law.

> A kind of pseudo-objectivity claims to lay down the law today. It lays claim to a whole range of rights without protecting that most elementary right: the right to life. Thus the laws on private property that place no limits on the deleterious effects of a consumer society are nothing more than an abstract idea guaranteed by civil society ...[29]

---

24 For useful discussion of essentialism with regard to Irigaray's writing, see Fuss, DJ, '"Essentially speaking": Luce Irigaray's language of essence', in Fraser, N and Bartky, S, *Revaluing French Feminism*, 1992, Bloomington: Indiana UP; Schor, N, 'This essentialism which is not one: coming to grips with Irigaray', in Burke, C, Schor N and Whitford, M, *Engaging With Irigaray*, 1994, New York: Columbia UP.

25 *Op cit*, Irigaray, fn 15, p 134.

26 *Op cit*, Irigaray, fn 15, p 140.

27 *Op cit*, Irigaray, fn 15, p 138.

28 *Op cit*, Irigaray, fn 15, p 140. Emphasis in original.

29 *Op cit*, Irigaray, fn 15, p 142.

So, for Irigaray, the rights protected by civil or State law are based on the law of estates and patrimony. The State is not concerned with what she sees as the universal of mediation that would lead to the creation of rights that would be appropriate for women alongside those which already exist for men. Its primary concern is for money, an abstract and empty grounding for law.

Her analysis repeatedly draws attention to the fact that the universal has its own historicity: that it 'changes from century to century' and that its status 'is to be a mediation'.[30] She also sets out, quite categorically, what this universal might look like when she states that:

> Without doubt, the most appropriate content for the universal is sexual difference. Indeed, this content is both real and universal. Sexual difference is an immediate natural given and it is a real and irreducible component of the universal. The whole of human kind is composed of women and men and of nothing else. The problem of race is, in fact, a secondary problem ...[31]

This statement presents us with a difficult tension that is both convincing and disturbing. Although I shall try to show the tactical reasons for making such a bold pronouncement, I would also like to draw attention to the possible dangers that could be attributed to statements such as this. It is fair to say that the world is made up of women and men. But to suppose that is an 'immediate natural given' is coming dangerously close to an essentialist position.[32] For someone who is usually so attentive to exclusion, she must be aware of the power of her 'and nothing else', which would seem to exclude children from humankind, unless they are to be thought of as little men and little women. What is most disturbing about this statement, though, is its hierarchisation of differences. Relegation of racial and other differences to a secondary position is the kind of statement that white Western feminists have long been accused of.[33] But, for Irigaray, the question of sexual difference is definitely the question of our age that needs, at the very least, to be taken into account when considering any ethical, legal or political question. Indeed, she states that 'Sexual difference probably represents the most universal question we can address'.[34]

As we have seen above, Irigaray is concerned to make an intervention in the symbolic order – an intervention in and through language – and, as such,

---

30 *Op cit*, Irigaray, fn 15, p 147.

31 Irigaray, L, *I Love To You*, Martin, A (trans), 1996, London: Routledge, p 47.

32 The assumption that sex is a natural given has been challenged recently by many thinkers. See, eg, Butler, J, *Bodies That Matter*, 1993, London: Routledge; Foucault, M, English Introduction to *Herculine Barbin: Being the Recently Discovered Memoirs of a Nineteenth Century French Hermaphrodite*, McDougall, R (trans), 1980, London: Harvester; Laqueur, T, *Making Sex: Body and Gender from the Greeks to Freud*, 1990, Cambridge, Mass: Harvard UP.

33 Most famously by bell hooks in *Ain't I a Woman: Black Women and Feminism*, 1982, London: Pluto.

34 *Ibid*, Irigaray, p 47.

the positing of sexual difference as universal can be interpreted as a tactical gesture to instigate a use of language that would give equal significance to the two genders. It is because the gendering of language is not as obvious in English as it is in the original French that this intervention is in danger of being interpreted as an essentialising move.

The question of how faithful Irigaray's mimicry of the traditional philosophers has become may also arise here. We could read this as an example of her own desire to institute the universal, and could argue that this later work shows all the hallmarks of a philosophy that is likely to exclude other others. This would occur in the same way as women were excluded as the other of the same, as diagnosed in her earlier work. But, again, if we interpret this as being primarily concerned with the symbolic, and language in particular, then the institution of a universal of sexual difference becomes an inclusive, rather than an exclusive, concept. In other words, if we see her delimitation of the human race to women and men, and nothing else, as a rhetorical strategy to help elevate the status of sexual difference to that of a universal in the symbolic order, rather that just a particular characteristic of each individual, then it might aid the recognition of sexual difference, other differences (such as racial differences) and other others.

So, we could describe Irigaray as both belonging to and subverting the tradition of philosophers of the universal. To understand this, we need to be clear of what this means for her and how it differs from what it has meant in the past. What was wrong with the universal for Irigaray was that it was not universal. It related only to the male subject and, as such, was more concerned with either civic or spiritual affairs than with nature. What this also meant for Irigaray was that it followed the trajectory of Western philosophy being concerned with what transcended, or was outside of, life. As far as she is concerned, the universal has traditionally been about death. Again, she takes Hegel to be the paradigmatic example of this philosophical death drive. If there is to be a universal, Irigaray would have it play its part in the daily workings of everyday life and of relationships:

> The universal – if this word can still be used here – consists in the fulfilment of life and not in submission to death, as Hegel would have it.[35]

EQUALITY AND EQUIVALENCE

To return to the notion of equality, Irigaray links the abstract universals of the likes of Hegel to a dangerous and fatal equality. If we were not to transform the universal into a mediating one, then, in her words:

---

35 *Op cit*, Irigaray, fn 31, p 24.

... claiming to be equal to a man is a serious ethical mistake because by so doing woman contributes to the erasure of natural and spiritual reality in an abstract universal that serves only one master: death.[36]

So, it seems that equality in the law is not even an appropriate tactical measure that could be used to try to gain a position of power sufficient to produce the desired differential rights. She argues that, because 'women's exploitation is based upon sexual difference, its solution will come only through sexual difference'.[37] She writes this under a sub-heading of 'Women: equal or different?' and states, without any trace of strategic mimicry at all, that:

> The human species is divided into *two genders* which ensure its production and reproduction. To wish to get rid of sexual difference is to call for a genocide more radical than any form of destruction there has ever been in History.[38]

Although we can circumvent the problem of essentialism that might be discerned in this passage by redescribing Irigaray's description of sexual difference as a natural given as a rhetorical strategy, we must, nevertheless, engage with her claims about genocide. In trying to read this sympathetically, we could say that the desire for a neutral equality, if it is still based on the concept of neutrality and equality that has been appropriated by masculinist theory, is the desire for all individuals to measure up to one gendered standard – the masculine. What she means by 'genocide' here is probably the elimination of a race and culture – more specifically, the final elimination of a female/feminine race and culture. Again, it is a question of language and the symbolic results of the loss of a genus (the female/feminine) through cultural or legal blindness, rather than through an orchestrated campaign of murder.

However, having dismissed equality as an 'ethical mistake', and having suggested that a neutral quality would amount to genocide, Irigaray does, in fact, go on to try to construct a differential equality. Indeed, she even advocates equality as a legitimate strategy in certain cases. Such a struggle for equal rights would only be 'in order to make the differences between women and men apparent',[39] but this strategy is not enough if it only leads to a visibility of the differences. These differences then need to be acted upon, not to overcome them, but to allow them the social recognition that they deserve. If equality is attained without using the position attained to change the culture, then women are still only participating in an alien environment. Irigaray uses the example of equal pay, which she considers to be a legitimate

---

36 *Op cit*, Irigaray, fn 31, p 27.

37 Irigaray, L, *je, tu, nous: Toward a Culture of Difference*, Martin, A (trans), 1993, London: Routledge, p 12.

38 *Ibid*.

39 *Ibid*, p 84.

right to fight for. But she sees no point in stopping the struggle once this right has been granted, because the working culture, its jobs and its environment have been developed to suit the needs of a male workforce.

Irigaray's proposed solution is to institute different laws for each sex. What is of great importance to her is that these laws are written. As written laws, they would then be public representations of sexual difference. In fact, the way that she puts this suggests that she thinks that these different laws exist already, but they require the further step of the social representation that their legal encoding would provide:

> All these misunderstandings could be resolved by the recognition that different laws exist for each sex and that equivalent social status can only be established after these laws have been encoded by civil society's elected representatives.[40]

What is at stake for Irigaray here is not whether the laws exist pre-discursively or not, but the representation and recognition that the writing of such laws would allow. This representation and recognition is described in terms of social equivalence, which is not the same as equality; although this equivalence is sometimes still expressed as equality, even though it is an equality that needs to be based on difference. For example, she states that:

> Equality between men and women cannot be achieved without a *theory of gender as sexed* and a rewriting of the rights and obligations of each sex, *qua different*, in social rights and obligations.[41]

The issue of representation is very central to her attempts to set out the specific women's rights that she would like to be written into the law. She is concerned with both the social and the religious representation of sexual difference and how this can be enforced through legal rights.[42] In an interview, she lists these rights and, although some of them are linked to the universalisation of mediation and sexual difference that she is advocating, others are particularly relevant to the position of women in Italy, where she was actively involved with the women's movement at the time. The list includes: the right to human dignity, which includes control of images and representations of women and the exploitation of motherhood; and the right to human identity, which involves the legal encodification of 'virginity' and 'motherhood'. Virginity here means 'physical and moral integrity',[43] a right which would help create and maintain a woman's identity. Motherhood is

---

40   *Op cit*, Irigaray, fn 37, pp 85–86.

41   *Op cit*, Irigaray, fn 37, p 13. Emphasis in original.

42   In this chapter I am only addressing issues of social representation, which leaves out a great deal of Irigaray's work which is concerned with religious representation. For readers interested in the religious aspect of her work, I would recommend Ainley, A, 'Divine spirit and feminine space: Luce Irigaray and the ethics of alterity', in Blond, P (ed), *Post-Secular Philosophy*, 1998, London: Routledge.

43   *Op cit*, Irigaray, fn 37, p 86.

described as 'a component (not a priority) of female identity'[44] in order to give women a right to choose about pregnancy.

Irigaray does point out that virginity and motherhood have been valued and commodified by patriarchal exchange systems, and so, it is understandable why she would want to reclaim them for women. But, although she carefully redefines them so as to avoid their traditional associations, she is still in danger of being read as repeating a patriarchal evaluation of women in terms of virginity and motherhood. The trouble with identifying only these two characteristics of a woman's identity is that she is in danger of limiting other possibilities at the same time. By writing them into separate laws, there is also the possibility that they would be treated as a table of reference, used to define what might be a suitable role for a woman. If these protective rights are to function properly in aiding women to flourish, they must not only increase women's social visibility, but also contribute to the change in vision that would enable them to be seen in a new light as different but of an equivalent value.

Irigaray's list of women's rights also includes a legal definition of the 'mutual obligations of mothers-children'; the right of women to defend their life, space, traditions and religion 'against all unilateral decisions emanating from male law'; financial protection for celibacy; equal family benefit for each child; media broadcasts to be equally targeted for women and men; equivalence in systems of exchange, including linguistic exchange; and equal representation in civil and religious decision making bodies.[45]

The last three assertions reinforce the view that Irigaray is attempting to produce some sort of equality between the sexes; an equality in difference that recognises and values those differences. Perhaps this would be better expressed as equivalent social visibility and status. Gail Schwab also reads Irigaray as proposing a principle of equivalence, suggesting that it 'moves beyond the sameness implicit in the concept of equality, and recognises the importance of multiplicity and variety in human experience and life in general'.[46] This is a useful reading, in that it is able to take into account Irigaray's insistence on the maintenance of sexual difference as a necessary component of any legal reform. It is just such a concentration on multiplicity and difference that has always contributed to Irigaray's theoretical innovation and appeal. Schwab is also right in pointing out that theorists such as Drucilla Cornell draw on Irigaray's work in order to posit a system of equivalent rights that would affirm sexual difference.

---

44 *Op cit*, Irigaray, fn 37, p 88.
45 *Op cit*, Irigaray, fn 37, pp 88–99.
46 Schwab, G, 'Women and the law in Irigarayan theory' (1996) 27 Metaphilosophy 152.

However, Schwab also fails to take account of Irigaray's most extreme anti-egalitarian moments, such as the invocation of genocide cited above. Nor does she consider the possibility of institutional inequality that might arise from such a rigid division of the sexes in law. It is in order to avoid such possibilities that Cornell returns to the notion of equality. Cornell's claim that 'We need a vision of equality if we are to protect equivalent rights from degenerating into a new defence of separate but equal'[47] seems like a necessary supplement to Irigaray's proposals.

Cornell suggests the introduction of a programme of equivalence rights which would also be transformative, for the reason that they would not only be in place to enable women to participate in the male world; rather, they would be designed to 'enable women to value the choices [they] make about [their] lives and work without the shame of [their] "sex", even if such choices do not fit into the pre-established social world'.[48]

The advantage of a principle or vision of equivalence would be that it would be able to retain difference as the foundation for law. It would also be able to keep open the legislative boundaries while, at the same time, enabling practical and practicable legislation to take place. Indeed, I would like to suggest that equivalence could act as the universal of mediation that Irigaray has mobilised for. As a principle, it could mediate between equality and difference, opening up the desired space of communication and recognition.

In this chapter, I have attempted to draw attention to the shift in focus from the 'philosophical terrorism' of utopian impossibility in the earlier work to the more constructive, programmatic pronouncements of her later writing. While the later writing is obviously an attempt to build on the spaces opened up by the de(con)structive demolitions of *Speculum* and *This Sex*, they can sometimes appear to be working against her early exhortation to:

> ... never give ourselves orders, commands or prohibitions. Let our imperatives be only appeals to move, to be moved, together. Let's never lay down the law to each other ...[49]

It is the form or style of these later constructions that also differs from her earlier work. Although Irigaray is explicitly attempting to institute different formal constructions through the universal of mediation, she no longer appears to be practising the other logic of *Speculum*.[50] This would leave us with the question of what another kind of law would look like if it was to be constructed according to that other logic. What would be involved in this

---

47   Cornell, D, *Transformations*, 1993, London: Routledge, p 155.

48   *Ibid*, p 141.

49   *Op cit*, Irigaray, fn 6, p 217.

50   See Deutscher, Chapter 4, in this volume for a different reading of Irigaray's later writing, where it is interpreted as more closely linked to the project and style of the earlier writing.

would also bring us back to an elaboration of what it would mean if the object started to speak. It is impossible to answer such a question here, but we can try to imagine some of the consequences of such a fundamental change in the imaginary and the symbolic. We can agree with the later Irigaray that there is an urgent need for legal representations of and for the female/feminine; that rights specific to women can help to provide some of the social recognition required to obtain socio-economic justice; and that the writing of these rights into the law will also help to protect and affirm their identity. But this does not seem to fulfil the radical potential held out by her early writing. The proposals outlined above would only go part of the way to the full institution of a law that would recognise and valorise woman and women. What is still at stake is what these female/feminine identities that are in need of recognition, protection and affirmation might look like, as well as what exactly it would mean to recognise, protect and affirm these individuals.

Irigaray's early critique of the universal subject has so successfully opened up the question of subjectivity and identity that legal subjects would now need to be thought of in much more fluid and relational terms.[51] According to Irigaray, the legal subject could no longer be thought of as 'one' or singular. This multiplication must also count for the law itself and its institutions, because the law should now be able to recognise each other as other (of the other). By so doing, it would also transfigure itself so completely as to become unrecognisable as the law as we know it. Its bodies and institutions would become more fluid and dynamic as they learned how to relate to the specificities of its multiple subjects. Although the later Irigaray is explicitly mitigating for a change in the content of the law, she can also still be read as implicitly advocating these changes in its form, although the form of her later writing tends to draw attention away from this radical destabilisation, tending towards a more reformist construction.

---

51 See Battersby, C, *The Phenomenal Woman: Metaphysics and the Patterns of Identity*, 1998, London: Polity for a metaphysical interpretation of female subjects and identities formed as relational and emerging from patterning. Richardson, Chapter 6, in this volume presents an interpretation of this theory and its application to legal theory.

CHAPTER 8

COMMON HUMAN NATURE: AN EMPTY CONCEPT?

Alison Assiter

In the classical social contract story, the individual political subject, the classical liberal individual, is the bearer of rights and duties. The most significant moral ideal in this tradition is the preservation of the freedom of this individual. In the modern world, in this tradition, not only are individuals assumed to be 'persons' in this classical liberal sense; we are also rational utility maximisers – much social scientific theory operates on the assumption that this is what we all are.

For some communitarians, the classical liberal conception of the person is too formal and empty. Instead, as Sandel has put it, personhood presupposes, as Hegel recognised, a 'narrative' through which we live out our lives.[1] Recently, communitarian liberals have accepted this kind of point and have argued that there are certain characteristics of persons – our gender, our race, our sexuality – which are formative of our identities, and without which it is not possible for any of us to make choices. Citizenship, for some of these thinkers, provides one such narrative – for the civic republican tradition, we can be persons only if we are also citizens – citizenship involves a commitment to one's fellow citizens, and service to the public.

For the classical liberal, the person or the self was literally disembodied. This disembodied individual of classical liberal theory is reinforced in Christianity, and especially in the early Protestant tradition. Early Protestant reformers made nature suspect, robbing it of its previous status as a source of religious inspiration. Protestantism was connected with attacks on magic, superstition and witchcraft.[2]

On the other hand, some communitarians suggest very particular examples of the sorts of collective body with which we must identify. Many characterise such collective entities by example – the nation, the family, one's sexual orientation. The idea that we might simply identify with our fellow human beings is regarded with the same sort of horror with which early communitarian critics viewed the classical liberal self – it is subject, it is said, to the same kind of emptiness.[3] Whereas early communitarian critics of

---

1   See Sandel, M, *Liberalism and the Limit of Justice*, 1982, Cambridge: CUP.

2   See Turner, B, *The Body and Society*, 1984, Oxford: Blackwell.

3   See Young, IM, 'Two concepts of self-determination', conference presentation, University of Bristol, September 1999.

liberalism suggested that the classical liberal self was incoherent[4] – that is, that it could not provide a basis for choice, these critics of the idea that we might identify with the whole of humanity dismiss it with a cry of 'Oh well, if that is all you mean ...'. Alternatively, they will say that any attempt to characterise qualities of the whole of humanity will degenerate into something less – into a description of white men in the 17th century, or of white Europeans, or of heterosexuals.

HUMAN BEINGS: ARE WE EMPTY?

I would like, in this paper, to attempt to describe some common qualities of human beings. I begin from the premise that individuals are necessarily part of social arrangements; that there is no such individual as the isolated, autonomous, desiring being that is assumed by some versions of liberalism. I start from the assumption that feminists, Foucauldians, Althusserians and communitarians are right to emphasise the embeddedness of individuals in social and political communities. On the other hand, I believe that the communitarians and the others go too far in their emphasis upon the necessary embeddedness of individuals in particular 'constitutive' communities. The identity and the values of individuals are never wholly determined by their families, nations or workplaces or by the particular 'discursive practices' of the societies in which they find themselves. Elsewhere, I have looked at some of the dangers consequent upon going too far with this view, in that it discourages individuals from questioning the values of constitutive communities when, intuitively, in some cases, it is perfectly clear from the consequences of adherence to those values that they cannot be all there is to morality.[5]

However, whilst I would question the view that identities and values are derived from communities like nations and families, I would go along with the communitarian that there is an objective and substantive picture of 'the good'. I strongly disagree with those liberals who suggest that there can be as many competing conceptions of what it is to lead a good life as there are individuals.[6] What I would like to do here is to defend the idea of a common humanity with which we must all identify by outlining and defending a notion of objective human need.

---

4   See, eg, *op cit*, Sandel, fn 1.

5   See Assiter, A, 'Communitarianism and obedience', in Brecher, B *et al*, *Nationalism and Racism in the Liberal Order*, 1998, Avebury: Ashgate.

6   For some spelling out of this argument, see Assiter, A, 'Why pluralism?', in Calder, C (ed), *Liberalism and the Limits of Justice*, 2000, Aldershot: Avebury.

In the first part of the paper, I would like to look at some of the arguments that have been put against the notion of objective human need. I will consider four such arguments. Most of these are not original to me.

First of all, there is the argument that there is no distinction between needs and wants, since both are brought into being by the social arrangements in which we find ourselves. One version of this argument was proposed some time ago by Althusser, and I have argued against him[7] in another context. I set out Althusser's argument as follows: needs exist only as effective demand; effective demand is either individual or productive; productive consumption is directly dependent upon the production process; individual consumption depends upon the level of income available and on the nature of the products that one can buy; production takes place in relations and uses forces; forces and relations occur only here. Hence, the existence of needs depends on production. I then suggested that the terms used in this argument, as it is set out by Althusser, refer only to the capitalist mode of production, but I argued that more general expressions could be used that did not have this connotation. I also suggested that the relevant class of needs should be restricted to needs for material or physical objects of some kind.

Having developed, in this fashion, a strong argument against Althusser, I criticised it in the following way. First, there are some needs that a person might have, but, because he or she cannot afford to buy items to satisfy him or herself, they do not get expressed as part of effective demand. Secondly, some individual might fail to recognise the existence of a need that he or she might have – someone who is starving might not be in a state to be aware of what his or her needs really are.

One of the responses offered to the argument attributed to Althusser here brings me to the second of the arguments that have been put against the concept of objective human need. This is that the assumption that there are objective needs is both metaphysical (and, hence, the supposition might be, unproveable) and paternalistic, in that it involves someone else in outlining the nature of a person's needs. Stephen Lukes, for example, has described the assumption of objective needs as a 'paternalist licence for tyranny'.[8] In other words, the assumption that needs are different from expressed preferences or wants allows for the manipulation of individual wants in the interests of some powerful group or person. It is argued by liberals that the assumption of non-expressed needs is incompatible with individual liberty. I shall have more to say about this argument in a moment.

---

7   Assiter, A, *Althusser and Feminism*, 1990, London: Pluto.
8   Lukes, S, *Power: A Radical View*, 1976, London: Macmillan, quoted in Benton, T, 'Realism, power and objective interests', in Graham, K (ed), *Contemporary Political Philosophy*, 1982, Cambridge: CUP, p 8.

Thirdly, it is said that it is impossible to define needs. Kate Soper[9] quotes Aristotle with approval: 'When life or existence are impossible ... without certain conditions, these conditions are "necessary" and this course is itself a kind of necessity.' She says:

> ... rather than condemn the circularity of his definition, we should accept it as a salutary reminder that in all attempts to argue for or against certain conditions as needs ... we are already involved in judgments about what constitutes 'life' or 'the good' for human beings.'[10]

She argues that needs are always relative to ends; ends are necessarily value-laden. Therefore, definition is impossible.

Fourthly, and following on from this, it is argued that need claims are normative.[11] Statements of need take the form 'A needs X in order to Y.' All necessities are conditional. If all need statements imply that a need is relative to a particular end, and ends vary enormously, then it is not possible to provide an objective definition of a need. Ted Benton,[12] for example, whilst being sympathetic to the realist position, continues to have reservations about it. He argues that, in existing social arrangements, and in deploying scientific practices that comply with those existing social arrangements, it is impossible to discover whether or not there are any 'real interests' that underlie those that are discoverable using felt preferences. This kind of point leads him to express reservations about research that can do no more than reveal expressed preferences. Such research does not register unarticulated wants, potential aspirations, which might have been formed were it not for the persistent relationships and practices that shape wants within that society. In other words, those liberals who advocate freedom as a primary value in order to allow the multiplicity of felt desires to flourish are assuming that autonomy consists of the ability to express the wants that one believes one has. But these beliefs may be false or tainted or in conflict with one's 'true' interests.

Yet, Benton argues, it is difficult, without describing 'real' needs as the needs that individuals would express under conditions of genuine autonomy, to escape the tyranny argument. If the agent is allowed to have non-expressed needs, then someone other than this person has to determine which are the 'objective' needs of that individual. He concludes, along with earlier critics, that statements of need are irreducibly value dependent. However, the difficulty of establishing what a need might be in certain circumstances should not detract from the claim that needs exist and are objectively present. Someone who has to spend all day searching for water, for example, has a need for water, whatever their 'felt preferences'. Someone who has lived

---

9   Soper, K, *On Human Needs*, 1981, Brighton: Harvester, p 11.

10   *Ibid.*

11   See Benn, SI and Peters, RS, *Social Principles and the Democratic State*, 1959, London: Allen & Unwin.

12   *Op cit*, Benton, fn 8.

through a severe hurricane, a war or a tornado and who has had his or her home destroyed needs shelter, whatever their preferences. What sort of water they need, and what sort of home, should be for the person him or herself to decide. However, to say that the needs in these cases are descriptions of 'values' is true only in the sense that the description of any basic need involves reference to some value. The values in question, however, are quite unlike those that have been stressed in arguments about the irreducible plurality of value. In the case of abortion, for example, or *sati*, or adherence to the Muslim faith, there is clear room for disagreement about values. In the case of values that underlie the expression of the kinds of basic human need outlined above, the scope for disagreement is not present in the same way. This argument, as I wrote previously, will be further spelt out below.

CATEGORIES OF NEED

I should like to argue, in the next section of the paper, that there are different categories of need claim. David Miller[13] has identified them as follows:

(a) instrumental needs: for example, Fred needs a bow in order to play the cello;

(b) functional needs: for example, a tennis player needs a racquet;

(c) intrinsic needs: for example, a starving peasant needs food.

In the first case, the need is a means towards achieving an end. The second type of need is where the need is a requirement of the carrying out of a certain function. The third simply appears to be the statement of a need *per se*. Marx described 'natural needs' in such a way that they appeared to fall into the third category. They are simply needs of the individual as a natural being. 'Physically,' he says, 'man lives only on those products of nature whether they appear only in the form of food, heating, clothes, a dwelling, etc.'[14] Brian Barry[15] gives the example, 'A needs physical health' as an example of a need statement that is not elliptical. It could be spelt out as 'A needs physical health in order to survive', but the 'in order to' appears to be redundant. A different way of putting this point is that survival is a necessary condition of pursuing any ends that a person might have (with certain exceptions, for example, Antigone). Survival and physical and mental health could be argued, following Gewirth,[16] to be necessary conditions of acting in any way at all.

---

13   Miller, D, *Social Justice*, 1976, Oxford: Clarendon.
14   Marx, K, *Grundrisse*, 1973, Harmondsworth: Penguin, p 528.
15   Barry, B, *Political Argument*, 1976, Atlantic Highlands: New Jersey Humanities.
16   Gewirth, A, 'Is cultural pluralism relevant to moral knowledge?' (1994) 11 SPP 22.

Natural needs, then, will be needs that individuals have as natural beings. These needs may take different forms, depending upon the social arrangements in which they are manifested, but the needs, nonetheless, remain invariant; although it is true, as Marx put it, that 'Hunger is hunger; but the hunger that is satisfied by cooked meat eaten by knife and fork differs from hunger that devours raw meat with the help of hands nails and teeth'.[17] It appears that the presence of the knife and fork alters not just the mode of satisfaction of the hunger, but the hunger itself. However, both kinds of hunger are, nonetheless, hunger. What remains constant is the need for food. We can empirically discover what survival and health needs are from facts about biological and physiological constituents in social contexts.

Natural needs could be said to be 'real', then, insofar as they exist independently of any particular social interpretation of their mode of satisfaction. They are independent, further, of any particular epistemology about their mode of manifestation. Biological science can be used to make discoveries about them, and medical science will provide evidence of the destructive effects of their non-satisfaction. But they exist independently of any of these discourses, and they relate to the objective goals of survival and health. These goals are universally important. If these statements are value laden, then so be it.

Some needs are basic to the human race as a whole. For example, if members of the human species could survive without using their sex drive, then this need would cease to be basic. There would still, however, be a basic need for something that allows for procreation. What about ceasing to need to eat? So long as human beings continue to need some form of sustenance, they have a basic need for this. Basic needs could not disappear altogether without human beings ceasing to be.

Far from the existence of 'objective', non-expressed needs being incompatible with individual liberty, then, on the contrary, the satisfaction of basic needs is a precondition of anyone being free to do anything at all. The argument could be put in the following way:

(a) all human beings have basic needs which must be satisfied, if they are to act in any way at all;

(b) these needs, therefore, ought to be satisfied, and this is a universally valid 'ought'.

It is a basic principle of rationality, because a contradiction ensues if (a) is affirmed and (b) denied. We might alternatively argue along the following lines: we will, as a matter of fact, converge on certain universal claims, deriving from the fact of our common humanity: starvation is wrong; lack of

---

17 Marx, K, *Selected Works in One Volume*, 1971, London: Lawrence & Wishart, p 197.

shelter is wrong. As it stands, this claim tells us nothing about what these basic needs are; neither does it tell us anything about the social conditions necessary for their satisfaction.

Even so, there are three ways in which these kinds of argument might be criticised, and I shall mention each. First, it could be argued that this basic moral claim is too broad, in that it covers other animals as well. Secondly, it might be said that it is too narrow, in that it tells us very little about any one human being. And, finally, it will be said that the claim is not really universal, but, as with the liberal argument, it purports to be universal when in fact it only refers to a limited group of people. I shall attempt briefly to respond to each of these critical points in turn.

First of all, I will consider the argument that the claim is too broad because it encompasses other animals. In a provocative recent article, Mary Midgley asks: Is a Dolphin a Person?[18] The question, she points out, actually came up during the trial of two people who, in May 1977, set free two bottlenosed dolphins used for experimental purposes by the University of Hawaii's Institute for Marine Biology. If the possession of Cartesian rationality in the deductive sense were necessary for being a person, then the dolphin is clearly not. But, there are people – young children and people with certain kinds of special needs – who may not possess minimal Cartesian rationality or, indeed, the more extended type of Cartesian rationality. It seems, then, that the possession of Cartesian rationality is neither necessary nor sufficient for being a person. The question of how human beings are distinguished from animals is a very large one, which I shall not go into here. An important point for the argument, though, is that, if we are to ensure the satisfaction of the basic needs of future generations, then we may need to think more broadly than in terms of satisfying the needs of human beings. In order to satisfy the basic moral claim, we may need to include the needs of other animals and indeed those of the environment. A contemporary of Descartes, a woman philosopher, was much more sympathetic than Descartes to non-human animals. Anne Conway, writing in the 17th century, suggested that:

> There are only three species of thing 'God, Christ and the Creatures' ... there is no fourth kind of being. Beings are not to be multiplied without necessity ... Let us take an Horse, which is a Creature induced with divers degrees of perfection by his Creator, as not only strength of Body, but (as I may so say) a certain kind of knowledge, and love, fear, courage, memory and divers other qualities which are also in man: which also we may observe in a Dog ...[19]

---

18 Midgley, M, *Utopias, Dolphins and Computers: Problems of Philosophical Plumbing*, 1996, London: Routledge.

19 Conway, A, 'The principles of the most ancient and modern philosophy', in Warnock, M (ed), *Women Philosophers*, 1996, London: Everyman.

The appropriate response to the first argument, therefore, may be that it does not matter that the minimal claim includes other animals as well as human beings.

On the second counter-argument, that referring to a common human nature is not saying very much, I would briefly say the following: the reference to a common humanity and to common human needs is a very basic claim. However, today, some 800 million people are starving across the globe and, each day, some 34,000 children die for want of food and medical care. (Some of these children are in one of the world's richest countries: the US.) This, therefore, underscores the importance of the basic universal moral claim.

The third objection denies that there is any universal human nature or that there are any universal values at all. Several writers have argued that ethical beliefs are necessarily plural. This plurality is said to reflect the diversity of humanity. For some people, ethics has historically been the product of whichever group has monopolised political right: for example, Greek male citizens or the liberal, male, white individual. Some of their needs and desires are then identified with rationally grounded principles and are thus converted in to rights and duties. For others, there is simply a plurality of values, within which it is not possible to talk of a human nature or any universally applicable values.

This plurality argument has been expressed in many different ways, and it has recently been enormously influential. The assertion of difference has become, for many, the principal dynamic of contemporary society. New social movements – environmental movements, gay and lesbian, black and disability groupings – assert a politics of difference that challenges universalising voices.

One might ask, however, is the 'cultural imaginary' necessarily or only contingently plural? Are values plural only in today's postmodern world, or is pluralism a characteristic of all possible worlds? Is the universalising voice ruled out *a priori*, or is it only culturally inappropriate in the world of today? It surely cannot be ruled out as either necessarily impossible or as *a priori* impossible, because that would be a move analogous to the liberal view being rejected: it would involve ruling out one possible, coherent and widely accepted view of the world as impossible or incoherent. If it is only contingently ruled out, then that opens up the possibility that it might re-emerge as an important world view. Might it not re-emerge in a possible non-racist, non-sexist Mars?

It is only possible to articulate the position that reality is irreducibly plural or dual from a perspective that allows conversations between the outlooks. If it allows conversations, then does it not allow commonalities? I can only recognise that a 19th century American history which is written from the perspective of white women, or of black slaves, differs from one which is written by an American white male, who excluded the former from seats of learning on condition that I, a white, professional woman, can converse with descendants of black slavery, as well as with descendants of American colonisers. Recognition of plural voices surely strengthens the notion of a common humanity with a common voice.

The cultural theorist, Paul Gilroy, asks us to rethink Hegel's master/slave relation in favour of the position of the slave.[20] In Hegel's version of the master/slave dialectic, the master achieves self-consciousness through the suppression of the slave. Against Descartes, Hegel recognised the need for an 'other' if a subject is to gain consciousness of itself as a self-reflective, rational self. But he reinforced the role of the slave. Gilroy reverses this role and suggests that, for the slave, death is in act (and was chosen by several black slaves in the US) preferable to subordination. For such people, of course, the argument about needs is inapplicable. But for whom is death preferable? For those who no longer live? As a symbol to others that they, too, can resist slavery in this way? But death is a tragic and drastic solution for these others. As a symbol for the emancipation of slaves, no doubt it is valuable, but is it not, again, the perspective of the universalising voice (purged of its explicit non recognition of Cartesian others) that allows us to see 'death' as a symbol of emancipation? Is it not the perspective of universal humanity that produces this recognition?

I am arguing, then, as Descartes claimed in the 17th century, that there must be scope today for the universalising voice, based partially on the recognition of a common humanity. There must also be a place for the voices of particular groups: women, black Africans, refugees, indeed university staff, and many more. Moreover, some of the designators of these groupings belong to them by necessity. It is much more difficult for me to change my race or my sex than it is for me to change my designation as member of the staff of the University of the West of England. There will be some practical and moral consequences that follow from this.

The difference between descriptions being only contingently true of me and, therefore, amenable to alteration, and those that are more necessarily true of me is played on by Woody Allen in his film *Bananas*, in which the hero, played by Allen, bemoans the fact that he dropped out of college. 'What would you have been if you'd finished school?' he is asked. 'I don't know,' sighs Allen, 'I was in the black studies programme. By now I could have been black.'

If there are objective needs of human beings as a group that must be met before anyone can do anything else, it follows that we each have reciprocal material and moral obligations to each other to ensure that these needs are satisfied.

---

20   Gilroy, P, *The Black Atlantic, Modernity and Double Consciousness*, 1993, London: Verso.

WOMEN'S NATURE?

One thing that follows from this is that representing any grouping as lying outside the human order is an extreme form of oppression that should be regarded as objectively wrong. As a matter of fact, historically, women have been used, symbolically, to represent the natural and non-human order. But to describe women in this way is to fail to recognise their membership of a common humanity with common needs. Braidotti has spoken of the 'unacknowledged and camouflaged sexual distinction at the very heart of philosophy'.[21] Like me, Descartes argued that the central characteristic of human beings is equivalent in all of us, women included.

In her work on Descartes, Genevieve Lloyd[22] writes that the Cartesian method is supposed to be open to all. Indeed, Descartes was at pains to point out, in the first Discourse, that 'his mind' was in no way out of the ordinary.[23] Reason or good sense, he claimed, is complete and entire in each one of us, women included.[24] Yet, Lloyd points out, it is in fact unlikely that this method applies to both sexes in the same way. First, the development of the Cartesian method (as, indeed, is the case with the practice of the sciences today) requires certain conditions to be met. Descartes himself made sure, before he began applying his method, that 'my mind is free from all cares' and that he had obtained for himself 'assured leisure in peaceful solitude',[25] in order to apply himself seriously to the destruction of all his former opinions.

Lloyd points to a letter from Elizabeth – the noblewoman with whom Descartes corresponded – where she said:

> ... the life I am constrained to lead does not allow me enough free time to acquire a habit of meditation in accordance with your rules. Sometimes the interests of my household, which I must not neglect, sometimes conversations I cannot eschew, so thoroughly deject this weak mind with annoyances or boredom that it remains, for a long time afterward, useless for anything else.[26]

Lloyd suggests that the lives of women, despite their theoretically equivalent reasoning powers, prevented them from any significant involvement in the collective interests of science. She further argues, however, and more importantly for the context of this paper, that it was not just the 'dailiness of life' that militated against sexual equality.

---

21 Braidotti, R, *Patterns of Dissonance*, 1991, Cambridge: Polity, p 193.

22 Lloyd, G, *The Man of Reason: Male and Female in Western Philosophy*, 1984, London: Methuen.

23 Anscombe, E and Geach, P (ed and trans), *Descartes' Philosophical Writings*, 1972, London: Nelson.

24 *Ibid*.

25 *Ibid*, p 95.

26 *Ibid*, p 49.

It was also the association that reason took on, for Descartes, with pure thought. Reason, for him, provided the foundation for science. Descartes sharply separated the requirements of truth seeking and knowledge gathering from the practical affairs of everyday life. Lloyd argues that this reinforced already existing distinctions and associations: masculinity with reason; femininity with nature and the body. It paved the way for Rousseau's explicit differentiation between the roles of men and women, and for the clear association between women and disorder. 'Never,' Rousseau said, 'has a people perished from an excess of wine; all perish from the disorder of women.'[27] Women are also, for Rousseau, through their closeness to nature, objects of adulation and an inspiration to virtue. The sexes require different education: it is the role of women to be educated to be pleasing to men.

Descartes, then, was right to see women and men to be equivalent in their possession of a common humanity. Yet, his account of the nature of this humanity was wrong. The view of reason that Descartes described is not equivalently possessed by men and women. To outline the nature of this humanity in the way that Descartes and other liberals have done is to describe an attenuated humanity – it is to describe, as many feminists have argued, the characteristics of certain educated, white men, and these white men are effectively disembodied. The notion of reason deployed by Descartes, and subsequently by many liberals, was, as many feminists have argued, one that did not apply to everyone. The 'free and equal' reasoning being turns out to be a disembodied version of the white, educated male. However, if one is instead to describe humanity in terms of its material nature; its material needs, a different picture emerges. As beings with natural needs, we are all caught up in a system of obligations to one another – obligations to one another to satisfy our various material needs. Depicting anyone or any grouping as lying outside this system of reciprocal obligation is an extreme form of discrimination that fails to recognise the humanity of that grouping.

In fact, throughout history, many groupings have been so represented. For example, black Africans have been, at various historical moments, represented as 'lacking in civic or moral virtue'.[28] Effectively, they have been depicted as subhuman. This representation of certain groupings as subhuman can be used, as Philip Lawrence has argued,[29] to justify their extermination. Colonisers of the US used depictions of Amerinindians as subhuman savages to justify the total annihilation of a population. There were similar representations, in American popular culture during the Second World War, of Japanese people. In the Gulf War, as Said put it, 'Arabs are only an attenuated

---

27   *Op cit*, Lloyd, fn 22, p 63.

28   Lawrence, P, 'War and exclusion: the aesthetics of modernist violence' (1998) 12(1) Global Society 103.

29   *Ibid*.

recent example of Others who have incurred the wrath of a stern White Man'.[30] In Britain, whilst recent colonial policies have not usually gone quite so far as these, they have involved representing colonial peoples as 'inferior'.[31]

I have argued in this paper that there are objective needs of human beings as a group, and these objective needs describe the material nature of all of us, women included. There is a common humanity, as Descartes recognised, but this common humanity is not as he described it.

Just as there are needs of human beings as a whole, so there may be objective and natural needs of women as a group. A while ago, it was anathema for feminists to express a view like this, since it was the assertion of biological differences between men and women that led to such objectionable policies as women being refused access to education (on the ground that it would divert energies from childbearing). Nowadays, when the absurdity of denying any common biological characteristics is recognised, the time may be ripe for considering whether or not there are biological needs of women as a group that are significant, not only for women, but for the species as a whole. It may be, for example, that the childbearing role of women, which at the moment is necessary for the species as a whole and which leads to specific biological needs of women, should be retained, on moral grounds, and that sex-specific natural needs are significant for the survival of humanity.

---

30 Said, E, *The Culture of Imperialism*, 1992, London: Chatto and Windus.
31 Zubaida, S (ed), *Race and Racialism*, 1970, London: Tavistock.

PART III

'MINORITARIAN POLITICS'

CHAPTER 9

SEXUAL CITIZENSHIP: LAW, THEORY AND POLITICS

David Bell and Jon Binnie

The notion of sexual citizenship is attracting increasing attention from academics and activists alike – spurred on by the currency of the language of citizenship (conceived as a bundle of rights matched by a bundle of responsibilities) in political and legal discourse more broadly, and by current reorientations of the terrain of sexual politics. The central questions circulating around the notion, however, remain: is the concept of citizenship the best way to mobilise sexual politics? Who is a sexual citizen? How can we use the notion to begin to interrogate the intersections of law, politics and identity?

The background to the debates on sexual citizenship is critical work on the notion of citizenship itself. Particularly important here are feminist and postmodern revisionings of citizenship, which work to critique the universalising tendencies of citizenship discourse and rights discourse. The first part of our chapter, therefore, introduces very briefly those elements of critical approaches to citizenship which have resonances for sexual citizenship. We follow that with a short, critical appraisal of two recent attempts to define the terrain of sexual citizenship, by Jeffrey Weeks[1] and Diane Richardson.[2] In the light of their distinct formulations, we then move on to explore competing readings of attempts to mobilise citizenship discourse in the context of sexual politics.

CITIZENSHIP

The concept of citizenship has both excited and vexed political, social and cultural theorists for some time now. There have been numerous attempts to define the core components of citizenship as it is inscribed in legal, political and civil discourses, as well as critical engagements which have sought to expand existing conceptions in the wake of broad transformations in those terrains. Attempts at definition are always flawed, in that they cannot fully account for the many different ways in which the notion of citizenship is mobilised; this often renders proposed definitions either overly prescriptive or

---

1 Weeks, J, 'The sexual citizen', in Featherstone, M (ed), *Love and Eroticism*, 1999, London: Sage, pp 35–52.
2 Richardson, D, 'Sexuality and citizenship' (1998) 32 Sociology 83.

overly vague. The concept is, without a doubt, inherently 'baggy', always subject to particular inflections in particular contexts. But, if we do have to settle on a working definition to guide our analysis, perhaps we should go with one provided in Engin Isin and Patricia Wood's recent book, *Citizenship and Identity*:

> Citizenship can be described as *both* a set of practices (cultural, symbolic and economic) and a bundle of rights and duties (civil, political and social) that define an individual's membership in a polity.[3]

This is a useful description, in that it brings together many different domains in which citizenship is enacted. It might be better to say, however, that those practices, rights and duties which together form the substance of citizenship define an individual's membership in a polity in both positive and negative ways: citizenship is an exclusionary concept, just as much as it is an inclusionary one. The grounds of exclusion are many-layered and often shifting in the context of specific articulations of citizenship; the boundaries of the included (citizens) and the excluded (non-citizens) are always on the move, expanding and contracting:

> Citizenship ... has always been a group concept – *but it has never been expanded to all members of any polity*. Still today, in modern democratic states there are many members who are denied the legal status of citizenship on the basis of their place of birth. Moreover, many members of polities are excluded from the scope of citizenship even if they are legally entitled to its benefits.[4]

There are, then, as Sarah Benton writes, two kinds of non-citizen to be considered: '... those who have never been admitted, and those who are exiled.'[5] What this exclusionary logic means, of course, is that battles around citizenship are battles to be recognised and included in the polity. Given the rights-duties coupling that citizenship invokes, fighting for inclusion often means conceding to perform certain duties or responsibilities in a barter for rights. As we shall see, this can usher in compromises that are often intensely problematic, both theoretically and politically. But, before we focus in on that aspect of the citizenship question, we should say a few short words about formulations of citizenship with different theoretical agendas.

The particular starting point for understandings of the modern condition of citizenship is the work of TH Marshall, especially his 1950 essay, *Citizenship and Social Class*.[6] Revisions, critiques and extensions of Marshall's theorising

---

3   Isin, E and Wood, P, *Citizenship and Identity*, 1999, London: Sage, p 4. Emphasis in original.

4   *Ibid*, p 20. Emphasis in original.

5   Benton, S, 'Gender, sexuality and citizenship', in Andrews, G (ed), *Citizenship*, 1991, London: Lawrence & Wishart, p 154.

6   Marshall, TH, *Citizenship and Social Class*, 1950, Cambridge: CUP.

have filled many volumes.[7] Subsequently, three broad perspectives have emerged in citizenship theory: civic liberalism; civic republicanism (often seen as manifest in communitarianism); and radical democracy. The civic liberalist tradition in citizenship theory is most closely aligned to Marshall, with its analysis of the State's paternal role in securing the welfare and rights of its citizens, as well as binding citizens together in sociality. Civic republicanism places more stress on obligation often mediated through 'political participation in communal affairs'.[8] The nation-State is placed centre stage in civic republicanist conceptions of citizenship, as is national identity. Pluralist, feminist and poststructuralist takes on citizenship, which we can (perhaps a little untidily, even uneasily) group under the banner of radical democratic citizenship theory, have become increasingly prominent in the academy, chiming as they do with the reinvention of politics under postmodernity.[9] Most commentators assert that there is something within the notion of citizenship that can further a radical democratic project, despite recuperation by 'New Right' politicians – mobilised in the UK, for example, around the figure of the 'active citizen' and in the drafting of a Citizens' Charter, and in the US through neoconservative discourses around welfare and the family.[10] By adding insights from poststructuralist and feminist theory – such as critiques of the gendered assumptions about citizenship's location in the public sphere and its simultaneous propagation in the private sphere (especially in the family) and work on the 'decentering' of the subject – these approaches seek to complicate (and simultaneously re-energise) the figure of the citizen and its relation to forms of 'identity politics'. As Anne Phillips writes: 'The value of citizenship lies in the way it restates the importance of political activity ... this might prove itself as a way of dealing with the politics of an extraordinary time.'[11] Reflecting the poststructuralist perspective, this 'extraordinary time' is described in Paul Clarke's *Deep Citizenship* as one of transformation:

> ... the world into which we are moving is fractured in multiple ways ... its meta-narratives have collapsed ... its old ideologies have fallen into disrepute and ... its old certainties have been transformed into new uncertainties.[12]

That sense of fragmentation, of 'new uncertainties', certainly provides one of the motor mechanisms for restating citizenship in political discourse. It also

---

7   See, eg, Turner, B, 'Outline of a theory of citizenship' (1990) 24 Sociology 187; Turner, B (ed), *Citizenship and Social Theory*, 1993, London: Sage. For Marshallian discussions of sexual citizenship, see, eg, Evans, D, *Sexual Citizenship*, 1993, London: Routledge; Sinfield, A, *Gay and After*, 1998, London: Serpent's Tail.

8   Ellison, N, 'Towards a new social politics: citizenship and reflexivity in late modernity' (1997) 31 Sociology 697.

9   See, eg, Yeatman, A, *Postmodern Revisionings of the Political*, 1994, New York: Routledge.

10 See, eg, Cooper, D, 'The Citizens' Charter and radical democracy: empowerment and exclusion within citizenship discourse' (1993) 2 SLS 149.

11 Phillips, A, *Democracy and Difference*, 1993, Cambridge: Polity, p 87.

12 Clarke, P, *Deep Citizenship*, 1996, London: Pluto, p 24.

affords the opportunity to radically rethink what being a citizen is all about; shifting the boundaries, then, of a particular form of political (but not only political) identity. This raises an important question about *how* citizens are engaged in politics – and about what we mean by *the politics of citizenship* itself.

A useful critical summary of the roles available to citizens in the current polity is offered by Holloway Sparks.[13] Sparks argues that the political role of citizens within current citizenship theory is both limited and limiting, and suggests the need to expand our conception of citizenship to incorporate dissent, which, she argues, has 'fallen through the cracks of much mainstream citizenship theory', which has focused on attempts to secure rights within the public sphere of advanced capitalist market societies.[14] This theorisation advances a model of 'participatory democracy', Sparks argues, that sidelines dissent as a political practice. Importantly, Sparks concludes that her revisioning of citizenship is valuable, in that it suggests that we must acknowledge 'the political agency of dissidents and "marginals" as the agency of *"citizens"*', as well as broadening our 'understanding of where political participation takes place'.[15] That these concepts have clear resonances with the kinds of politics mobilised by *sexual dissidents* will become clear later. With this in mind, we shall now turn our attention to attempts to mobilise the concept of citizenship specifically within the context of sexuality, offering a brief but critical reading of some recent contributions to the debate.

SEXUAL CITIZENSHIP

As the notion of citizenship re-emerged in political, academic and popular discourses in the 1980s – spurred on in the UK by the Conservative administration's notions of active citizenship, of a Citizens' Charter and of emphasising the flipsides of the equation of citizenship (rights *always* come with responsibilities), as well as by a brief flurry of excitement over communitarianism – so it entered the register of sexual politics. With its mobile combinations of the political, the economic, the social, the legal and the ethical, citizenship seemed to be a neat concept for articulating the field of sexual politics generally. In a period marked by countless transformations – the controversial appearance, negotiations and disputes around queer theory and queer politics; the centralising of the AIDS crisis in mobilising allying discourses and in homophobic discourses; continuing debate over the form

---

13 Sparks, H, 'Dissident citizenship: democratic theory, political courage, and activist women' (1997) 12 Hypatia 74.

14 *Ibid*, p 77.

15 *Ibid*, pp 100–01.

and status of the 'lesbian and gay community'; varieties of 'sex war' recasting notions of a politics rooted in desire; the solidifying of social constructionist notions of sexuality through theories of performativity, plus the contrary re-essentialising of 'gay' identity through biomedical researches; the intensified marketisation of sexualities, and so on – the field of sexual politics, in its broadest sense, seemed likewise to embody many of the debates activated by a focus on citizenship, with its crossing of boundaries between the public and the private, between the collective and the individual, and between entitlements and duties.

Diane Richardson has attempted to survey and summarise existing insights into sexual citizenship, and we would like to here sketch her argument, as well as that of Jeffrey Weeks. Both writers seek to explore how the notion of sexual citizenship is currently mobilised: Richardson's focus shadows that of feminist critiques of citizenship discourse, by exposing the heterosexualising of citizenship as an extension of exposing its gendering:

> My starting point is the argument that claims to citizenship status, at least in the West, are closely associated with the institutionalisation of heterosexual as well as male privilege.[16]

Following Marshall's delineation of the domains of citizenship – civil, political and social – she charts inequalities faced by two groups of sexual citizens, lesbians and gay men: lack of full equal rights; lack of full political participation and representation; and lack of access to welfare entitlements. While she acknowledges that lesbians and gay men are afforded certain rights – usually 'won' as a result of their designation as a 'minority group' – she argues that there is a very high price to pay: sexual citizenship is heavily circumscribed and simultaneously privatised, its limits set by the coupling of tolerance with assimilation: 'Lesbians and gay men are granted the right to be tolerated as long as they stay within the boundaries of that tolerance, whose borders are maintained through a heterosexist public/private divide.' This means that lesbians and gay men can only be citizens if they can be 'good' citizens.[17] This cost, in terms of performing 'good' sexual citizenship, is identified by Carl Stychin as one of the prime dangers in using citizenship as a model for advancing lesbian and gay rights claims:

> ... in attempting to achieve legal victories, lesbians and gays seeking rights may embrace an ideal of 'respectability', a construction that then perpetuates a division between 'good gays' and (disreputable) 'bad queers' ... The latter are then excluded from the discourse of citizenship.[18]

In addition, Richardson notes that limiting lesbians' and gay men's spaces of citizenship to the private has a contradictory logic to it, in that the private

---

16 *Op cit*, Richardson, fn 2, p 88.
17 *Op cit*, Richardson, fn 2, p 89.
18 Stychin, C, *A Nation by Rights*, 1998, Philadelphia: Temple UP, p 200.

sphere is constructed in a heterosexualised frame – as the space of the family. This helps to explain the enduring deployment of reformulations of 'family' in current sexual rights claims – in the notion of 'families we choose' and in arguments for lesbian and gay marriage and parenting: the model of the private into which sexual citizens are projected is one in which only certain articulations are conceivable. Further, as diverse cases including *Bowers v Hardwick* and *R v Brown*[19] have shown, the private is a precarious place for sexual citizens, one that is all too easily breached.[20]

In terms of social citizenship, Richardson defines this in the context of the nation-State, in terms of social membership or belonging. As the growing literature on the relationship between sexuality and the nation shows, despite the imperatives of globalisation and transnationalism, citizenship continues to be anchored in the nation, and the nation remains heterosexualised.[21] The arguments over military exclusion of sexual dissidents in the US and UK can be seen as emblematic of the tensions between sexual and national identity, as we shall see.

Finally, Richardson signals two domains of citizenship not considered by Marshall, but which have come to be seen as central to contemporary citizenship discourses: cultural citizenship and citizenship as consumerism. The first includes struggles over representation and 'symbolic rights', while the second centres on the economic and commercial power of groups to 'buy' themselves rights and recognition. The debates around the so called 'pink economy' here bring sexual citizens into the broader question of the commodification of citizenship: to what extent do our rights depend on our access to capital? Certainly, in the UK, the New Right's make-over of citizenship in the 1980s placed commercial power centre stage; this has been seized upon by some commentators as offering sexual dissidents ways to gain citizenship status that they have previously been denied. As we shall see, economic entryism into citizenship has provoked conflicting responses from commentators.

Jeffrey Weeks' essay, 'The sexual citizen', approaches the subject from a very different angle. Weeks' interest is in the broader social transformations which have created the preconditions for the figure of the sexual citizen to emerge on the landscape of citizenship:

> The sexual citizen, I want to argue, could be male or female, young or old, black or white, rich or poor, straight or gay: could be anyone, in fact, but for one key characteristic. The sexual citizen exists – or, perhaps better, wants to come into being – because of the new primacy given to sexual subjectivity in

---

19   *Bowers v Hardwick* 478 US 186 (1986); *R v Brown* [1993] 2 All ER 75.

20   See, eg, Halley, J, 'Sexual orientation and the politics of biology: a critique of the argument from immutability' (1994) 36 Stan L Rev 301; Moran, L, 'Violence and the law: the case of sado-masochism' (1995) 4 SLS 225.

21   *Op cit*, Stychin, fn 18.

the contemporary world ... this new personage is a harbinger of a new politics of intimacy and everyday life.[22]

Set against this backdrop of transformations in identity, intimacy and relationships, this 'new personage', the sexual citizen, is heroised as shifting the very grounds of politics through a version of Giddens' 'reflexive project of the self':[23]

> The idea of sexual or intimate citizenship is simply an index of the political space that needs to be developed rather than a conclusive answer to it. But in this new world of infinite possibility, but also ever-present uncertainty, we need pioneers, voyagers, experimenters with the self and with relationships. The would-be sexual citizen, I suggest, represents that spirit of searching and of adventure.[24]

In this sense, the sexual citizen, as Weeks conceives him or her, is a marker of transformations in the sphere of personal life, particularly in its politicisation, that have taken place in the West since the 1960s. Weeks identifies the 'moment of citizenship' as a claim for inclusion, arguing that this is often twinned with a 'moment of transgression' in sexual politics: transgressive acts, which Weeks labels 'carnivalesque displays' and 'exotic manifestations of difference', are equated with queer politics – with kiss-ins, mass die-ins, and so on – and make visible that which has otherwise been rendered invisible; but the moment of citizenship allows difference to find 'a proper home'.[25] This seems to infer a 'proper' politics, too; one centred on campaigns for welfare, employment and parenting rights, equal protection in law and domestic partnership or marriage. Here, in an echo of Stychin's critique of sexual citizenship, transgression can only be a temporary tactic on the path to 'good' citizenship.

Weeks sketches the transformations which have created the possibility of the sexual citizen as threefold: (a) the democratisation of relationships (new ways of living together); (b) new subjectivities (new forms of identity and new notions of the self); and (c) new stories (new ways of narrativising (a) and (b) in, for example, counterdiscourses). He ends with a list of issues that are 'likely to be central to post-millennial politics':

- achieving a new settlements between men and women;
- elaborating new ways of fulfilling the needs for autonomy and mutual involvement that the family can no longer (if it ever could) fulfil;

---

22 *Op cit*, Weeks, fn 1, p 35.
23 Giddens, A, *The Transformation of Intimacy*, 1992, Cambridge: Polity. See, also, Plummer, K, *Telling Sexual Stories*, 1995, London: Routledge.
24 *Op cit*, Weeks, fn 1, p 48.
25 *Op cit*, Weeks, fn 1, p 37.

- finding ways of dealing with the denaturalisation of the sexual – the end of the heterosexual/homosexual binary divide, the new reproductive technologies, the queering of identities;

- balancing the claims of different communities with constructing new common purposes, recognising the benefits of individual choice while affirming the importance of collective endeavours;

- learning to live with diversity at the same time as building our common humanity.[26]

While Weeks is keen to stress that this is neither an agenda nor a map, his utopian projection of 21st century politics clearly (whilst also rather vaguely) lists new domains of sexual citizenship without offering concrete proposals for the materialisation of his wishes. It is almost as if merely living as a sexual citizen will inevitably bring about these further transformations. In fact, in many ways, that kind of logic steers some of the current ways in which the rights claims of sexual citizens are argued: that lesbian and gay marriage, for example, could serve to undermine, even destroy, the whole institution of marriage and all its attendant privileges. We will return to that thread of argument later in the chapter; first, we want to sketch three current 'moments of sexual citizenship' and interrogate the ways in which each inflects the form of the debate as it stands.

SEXUAL CITIZENSHIP AND CONSUMPTION

One of the principal ways in which claims to sexual citizenship are currently articulated is via the market. Specifically, the power of the 'pink economy' is seen as offering possibilities for citizenship through consumer muscle.[27] Visible consumption spaces (such as gay villages) are, therefore, recast as *spaces of citizenship*. This obviously raises very real problems of social exclusion; moreover, the notion that citizenship can (or, indeed, must) be 'bought' has to throw into question the kinds of sexual citizenship opportunities which the market can offer.

In the late 1990s, one could be forgiven for thinking that lesbians and gay men were economic angels, blessing the recession with boundless and increasingly conspicuous consumption. It has now become a commonplace assumption that lesbians, and more notably gay men, are model consumers – miracle workers in the new urban service economy of post-industrial, post-Fordist, Western society. However, recent analytical work by economists has argued that the pink economy is nothing more than a myth. The discourses of

---

26 *Op cit*, Weeks, fn 1, p 49.
27 See, eg, *op cit*, Evans, fn 7.

sexual citizenship have become slotted in to this emerging debate on the political economy of sexuality, whilst also being inflected by the mythologising of the pink economy – often to contradictory effect. In part, of course, this is as an extension of the broader notion that citizenship is increasingly commodified, as we have already noted. However, the particular problems that this idea raises for the sexual citizen demand further attention.

Among the many commentators on 'queer consumption', there is a tendency either to demonise and pathologise gay men as shallow, passive consumers and as both victims and exploiters of capitalism, or to celebrate the creativity, radicality and innovatory nature of gay consumer culture:

> Recently, a new stereotype has crept into the antihomosexual literature of the right. In addition to being portrayed as immoral, disease-ridden child molesters, gay men and lesbians are now described as superwealthy, highly educated free spenders. The economic arguments that have begun to appear in the past few years are an important part of the same strategy: to split the gay community off from what might have appeared to be its natural allies in a broad, progressive civil-rights movement.[28]

Other commentators have argued that lesbian and gay rights can in fact be conceived as commodities to be bought and sold on the open market; thus, capitalism can actually secure lesbian and gay liberation. An important arm of this argument is that the visibility which economic muscle provides keeps gay communities in the limelight and makes them better able to resist marginalisation:

> The visible existence of gay and lesbian communities is an important bulwark against the tide of reaction; the economic vitality of contemporary lesbian and gay communities erodes the ability of conservatives to reconstruct the closet.[29]

However, while some commentators champion the growth of the gay market, many gay consumers themselves remain unmoved, even bemused, by all the targeting and niche marketing. In addition, the growth of new commercial venues (taken as a barometer of gay economic power – and of its exploitation) is not welcomed with open arms by all. The homogeneity, attitude and high price of some venues is surely nothing new to anyone on the gay scene. People are not duped by the hype surrounding new venues, but instead have a love/hate relationship with them. People know they are being targeted and exploited, but they do not stop using the scene just because they know that the rules of the game are rigged. While this sounds somewhat fatalistic – like admitting that citizenship is inevitably and irretrievably commodified, so we

---

28 Hardisty, J and Gluckman, A, 'The hoax of special rights: the right wing's attack on gay men and lesbians', in Gluckman, A and Reed, B (eds), *Homo Economics*, 1997, London: Routledge, p 218.

29 Escoffier, J, 'The political economy of the closet: notes towards an economic history of gay and lesbian life before Stonewall', in *ibid*, Gluckman and Reed, p 131.

just have to live with that as a 'market reality' – an understanding of the economic basis of sexual citizenship is essential as a counter to the reductive arguments thus far advanced either for or against gay consumer citizenship.

We need to move beyond rather simplistic discussions of why gay men (and lesbians) shop. Crucially, we need to trace the evolution of lesbian and gay consumption practices vis à vis the family orientation of the Welfare State. The major reason why the market has provided the stage for the realisation of lesbian and gay citizenship has been exclusion from the Welfare State. The Welfare State was constructed on the basis of heterosexual assumption and, until very recently, it sought to promote heterosexuality and to penalise sexual diversity. A more thorough examination of the heteronormativity of the Welfare State is long overdue and must serve as a counter to the rather misleading media and academic commentary on the state of the pink economy. Indeed, as the Welfare State itself becomes increasingly marketised, we need to examine the ways in which this impacts on the economics of citizenship in its broadest sense, promoting (and, indeed, producing) forms of social exclusion that further limit access to citizenship.

LESBIAN AND GAY MARRIAGE

Assimilationist claims to the right to same-sex marriage or registered partnership have been central to current lesbian and gay rights struggles. The arguments made centre on the right to publicly recognise same-sex partnerships in law (and also, related to consumer citizenship, to reap the financial benefits of partnership). At one level, denying the right to marriage limits the citizenship claims of sexual dissidents; on the other hand, marrying into citizenship means sanctioning certain kinds of relationship at the expense of others. While the notion of lesbian and gay marriage has been argued to denaturalise marriage as a heterosexual institution, it naturalises the stable, monogamous couple-form as the ideal-type of 'families we choose'.

Typical of the pro-registered partnership argument is Morris Kaplan's work on intimacy and privacy.[30] Kaplan claims that agitation for lesbian and gay marriage asserts 'the positive status of lesbian and gay citizenship' – they represent the 'demands of queer families to enjoy equal social and legal status with their straight counterparts'. Crucially for Kaplan, lesbian and gay marriage is central to attaining full citizenship and empowerment, since it offers such recognition as the freedom of intimate association, insulated by law. As he concludes:

---

30 Kaplan, M, 'Intimacy and equality: the question of lesbian and gay marriage', in Phelan, S (ed), *Playing with Fire*, 1997, New York: Routledge, pp 201–30.

Lesbian and gay marriages, domestic partnerships, and the reconceiving of family institutions as modes of intimate association among free and equal citizens all are efforts to appropriate, extend and transform the available possibilities.[31]

It might be instructive to read Kaplan's analysis alongside a number of other considerations of lesbian and gay marriage or registered partnerships. For example, Henning Bech's modest but insightful 'Report from a rotten State', a commentary on the Danish registered partnership law passed in 1989, distils the terms of the debate by proponents and opponents of the law to show the extent to which political and legal questions get framed in particular, contextualised ways – in this case, both sides argued that their stand on the law was important to say something about *Denmark* (either to protect it from international ridicule or to position it at the forefront of civilisation and human rights).[32] The limits of the Danish law reform – omitting adoption rights and the right to a church wedding – were seen by some activists to have 'cemented the status of homosexuals as second-rate citizens', while also advocating a fixed model of homosexual relationships which 'discouraged an acceptance of homosexuals in their difference and otherness'.[33] However, Bech notes that such oppositional critique was relatively marginal to the public debate in Denmark. In a similar vein, Angelia Wilson sketches a shift in British gay politics, from the GLF's revolutionary calls for the abolition of the family to present agitations based on the rhetorics of rights, justice and equality.[34] In the US, too, 1970s gay liberationists critiqued 'the elevation of the family to ideological pre-eminence', arguing that one task of gay liberation must be to support 'issues that broaden the opportunities for living outside traditional heterosexual family units' for gays and straights alike.[35] Most forcibly, John D'Emilio, writing in the early 1980s, urged that 'solutions should not come in the form of a radical version of the pro-family position'; rather, they should come by means of the building of an 'affectional community' in which 'the family will wane in significance' for all members of society.[36] The stark contrast between gay liberation's utopian social project (in which gay culture leads) and the 'pro-family' agenda of liberal reformism (where gay culture seeks to replicate heterosexual) is truly striking. By mainstreaming sexual politics, then, the radical edge is blunted and a 'back door revolution' advocated, with things like partnership registration held as 'tactical, practical

---

31 *Op cit*, Kaplan, fn 30, p 222.

32 Bech, H, 'Report from a rotten State: "marriage" and "homosexuality" in Denmark', in Plummer, K (ed), *Modern Homosexualities*, 1992, London: Routledge, pp 134–47.

33 *Ibid*, p 136.

34 Wilson, A (ed), Introduction in *A Simple Matter of Justice?*, 1995, London: Cassell.

35 D'Emilio, J, *Making Trouble*, 2nd edn, 1992, New York: Routledge, p 13.

36 *Ibid*, pp 13–14.

step[s] towards greater justice'.[37] Such moves tread a very fine line – which many of their advocates seem aware of, yet incapable of resolving – as well as revealing tensions within the agendas of different campaigning positions.

Opening up the question of 'lesbian and gay marriage', of course, *can* have far broader impacts, throwing light on both the constructions of homosexuality and heterosexuality in law, and the limitations of such constructions. Dennis Allen's discussion of the public debate on same-sex marriage in Hawaii in the light of a suit filed by two lesbian couples and one gay male couple[38] clearly illustrates the destabilising function of such appeals: as the Hawaii Supreme Court struggled to refine its definition of 'marriage' (by linking it irrevocably to heterosexuality through the dubious logic of reproductive biologism, whilst also trying to sidestep sexual discrimination), it revealed 'the logical difficulties, the internal gaps and fissures, not only in the "inevitable" linking of marriage to heterosexuality but within the very idea of heterosexuality itself'.[39] By having to draw a boundary around marriage as defined in relation to reproduction, it excluded involuntarily childless heterosexual couples; and its tortuous attempts to bring them in (by reference to medical technology and the *potential* for reproduction) threatened to open a door for same-sex couples (who could equally use medical technologies to overcome biological barriers to reproduction). As with legal definitions of sodomy (in *Bowers v Hardwick* (1986), for example, where the Georgia law defined sodomy as oral or anal sex, without explicitly demarcating the genders of participants), the precariousness of the homo/hetero binary is exposed; in this case, it is heterosexuality which comes to be defined by conduct – using a rather convoluted definition of 'natural' (or, at least, naturalised), *potential* reproductive conduct. Such problematic defining of sexuality exposes the constructedness of categories in law.

It is this kind of exposure which advocates of registered partnerships often point towards, and the 'broader agenda' behind such struggles for reform; far from assimilationist, then, same-sex marriage is held as capable of undermining the most solid of social structures ('the family') by infiltrating it and exposing its contradictory logics. The fact that the take-up rate for registered partnerships in Denmark has been very low is, thus, only of secondary importance when set alongside the bigger picture of both the fact of the *possibility* of partnership registration for those who may want it and the *threat* to marriage that registered partnerships purportedly pose.

This seems to be the currently dominant political methodology expressed in both academic and activist discourses: the 'quest for justice' within the broad equal rights/citizenship framework, with the suggestion that riding on

---

37 Tucker, S, *Fighting Words*, 1995, London: Cassell, p 12.

38 *Baehr v Lewin* 852 P2d 44 (1993).

39 Allen, D, 'Homosexuality and narrative' (1995) 41 Modern Fiction Studies 617.

the back of these claims are more troublesome 'hidden agendas' – of challenging structural homophobia and, thereby, questioning the foundational definitions of sexual citizenship. *Bowers v Hardwick* (1986), for example, challenged Georgia's sodomy laws through the lens of the right to privacy, whilst also navigating an uneasy path through the relation of homosexual identity to homosexual conduct. The framing of the challenge within 'rights discourse', which occupies a particular and sensitive place within US law and culture, opened up the terms of the debate in more far reaching ways, by raising questions about the immutability (or mutability) of homosexual identity (whether or not sexuality is legally analogous to 'race', thus opening up its eligibility for shelter under the Equal Protection Amendment) and about the extent of overlap between 'homosexual conduct' and 'homosexual identity'. The question remains, however, of whether reducing radical activism to claims under law has a positive impact. As Nan D Hunter says, for advocates of legal approaches, 'the process of organising and litigating empowers and emboldens', while, for its critics, 'the reduction of radical demands into claims of 'rights under the law' perpetuates belief systems that teach that other, more transformative modes of change are impossible, unnecessary, or both'.[40]

It is worth examining in more detail the logic of this methodology – and the argument over legal-reformist versus 'radical' action – through the debate on same-sex marriage, since advocates are keen to stress the subversive challenge posed by what can be read as an assimilationist strategy. As Hunter points out, the politics of the family have become 'a newly identified zone of social combat', central to agitations for lesbian and gay equality and citizenship.[41] In a sense, marriage is a useful cypher for the whole citizenship debate, since it is seen as a cohesive element of social life, straddling the public and the private, containing a mix of rights and duties and occupying a central position in political, legal and popular discourses of radically different orientations – from the petitions for the recognition of 'families we choose' to campaigns for a reinstatement of 'family values' as the heart of Christian-democratic political and moral culture. Agitation in the US for the rights of 'queer families' enables us to witness these competing discourses enacted on the political and legal stage. Like citizenship, then, marriage 'does not exist without the power of the State ... to establish, define, regulate and restrict it'.[42] Hunter suggests that same-sex marriage could potentially 'alter the fundamental concept of the particular institution of marriage', also sending out shockwaves that may shake the foundations of other social institutions

---

40 Hunter, N, 'Marriage, law and gender: a feminist enquiry', in Duggan, L and Hunter, N, *Sex Wars*, 1995, New York: Routledge, p 120.

41 Hunter, N, 'Identity, speech, and equality', in *ibid*, Duggan and Hunter, p 101.

42 *Ibid*, p 110.

that are presently loci of discrimination.[43] Part of Hunter's argument rests with the potential of same-sex marriage to destabilise the *gendered* structure of marriage, fracturing discourses of dependency and authority. It serves, then, to *denaturalise* marriage, to reveal its constructedness and, thereby, to 'democratise' it.[44]

Paradoxically, however, it seems that such a move could have the function of *reaffirming* marriage as an institution. There are a number of strands to this counter-argument. First, by further marginalising the unmarried, it perpetuates a two tier system in the recognition of relationship status. It also maintains the (long term, monogamous) bonds of coupledom as the most legitimate form of lovelife-choice. It 'liberalises' the institution of marriage, opening it up to those (heterosexual) people who currently oppose its inequalities, as well as comforting those married couples who are currently uneasy about their privileged status – again reinforcing (and relegitimising) marriage over and above nonmarried relationships. It puts people who are currently ineligible to marry under increased moral and legal pressure to wed (such as homosexual couples with children). Meanwhile, it fails to address economic aspects of marriage (whether positive, such as tax breaks, or negative, in terms of welfare and dependency); neither does it address the continuing links between marital status and other forms of legal rights (next of kin status, intestate inheritance, etc). Perhaps most significantly, it upholds the notions of a particular model of romantic love and commitment, which in many ways are more central to the meaning of marriage than (potentially) procreative coupling, at least outside of legal discourses. A focus exclusively on challenging the legal discourse around marriage, therefore, falls short of considering which aspects of *popular discourse* are contested or reaffirmed by such a move. Since popular discourses then spill over into political and legal process (the recent British moral panic over single mothers, for example), strategies for change need to consider the many meanings of marriage (and non-marriage) that contribute to its social (as well as legal) status. As Katherine O'Donovan rightly suggests, marriage retains such an iconic status in society that it is almost inconceivable to think outside its logics: 'There is a kind of uniform monotony to our fates. We are destined to marry or to enter similar relationships.'[45] From this perspective, demanding the right to join that uniform monotony starts to look like a strange political tactic for dissident sexual citizens.

Hunter, meanwhile, reviews calls for same-sex marriage law alongside the alternative strategy of registered partnership legislation, in part examining feminist arguments around both, as well as critiquing work from critical legal

---

43 *Op cit*, Hunter, fn 40, p 112.

44 *Op cit*, Hunter, fn 40, p 114.

45 O'Donovan, K, 'Marriage: a sacred or profane love machine?' (1993) 1 FLS 87.

studies which has focused on questioning the use of rights discourse in such mobilisations. Registered partnerships offer many practical advantages (and are not hidebound by 'tradition' to construct contractual obligations along marriage-like lines) but lack the status (in both legal and cultural sense) of marriage; unless marriage is abolished altogether and replaced by a single system of partnership registration, that distinction will remain, and will carry with it ideological and moral weight.

One aspect of lesbian and gay marriage that is not considered in discussions is the so called mutually beneficial arrangement – the marriage between a lesbian and a gay man for strategic reasons (often immigration status). While this is often portrayed as a desperate (not to mention dangerous) move, such 'marriages of convenience' could be seen as offering a further, more transgressive strategy. If gay men married lesbians *en masse* as a *political act*, then the status of marriage as the State-licensed public statement of romantic love and lifelong commitment would be exposed and undermined. The couple could then have a claim on all the benefits of marriage without having to bear the responsibilities, whilst also falling completely outside current discourses of what marriage means (or *is made to mean*).

The strategic claiming of the right of same-sex couples to marry also runs the risk of domesticating sexual practice, lending support to policies which seek to 'clean up' tabooed aspects of gay culture (principally public sex), as well as distancing 'assimilationist' agitation from radical activism – the moment of citizenship versus the moment of transgression. As Eva Pendleton suggests, the assimilationist agenda in American gay politics has a profoundly conservative orientation:

> These boys are anxious to recoup the white, middle class privilege that has previously been denied to openly gay men. Rather than challenge this hegemony, they will do what they can to overcome the political handicap that homosexuality has traditionally represented. The best way to do this, they argue, is to assimilate into Middle America as much as possible.[46]

Such a position leads, in Pendleton's words, to 'asexual political activism';[47] her reading of gay conservative texts such as Bruce Bawer's *A Place at the Table* uncovers the erotophobia inherent in demands for same-sex marriage.[48] Public sex is especially demonised as a *political* practice (in fact, its politics are erased under the trope of hedonism and irresponsibility). Bawer's take on gay marriage, as outlined by Pendleton, is to suggest that 'the most effective way

---

46 Pendleton, E, 'Domesticating partnerships', in Dangerous Bedfellows (eds), *Policing Public Sex*, 1996, Boston: South End, p 375.

47 *Ibid*, p 387.

48 Bawer, B, *A Place at the Table*, 1993, New York: Touchstone.

to preserve the heterosexual nuclear family is to grant homosexuals legal rights'.[49] The logic of this argument runs thus:

> ... closeted gay men often marry and have children in order to cover up their true desires. Thus it is actually the stigmatisation and secrecy of homosexuality that undermines 'the family'; if gay couples were given equal rights, the sham marriages that eventually destroy families would no longer be necessary. The socially responsible thing for conservatives to do is eliminate the need for homosexuals to use heterosexual marriage as a means of avoiding social stigma – by advocating gay marriage ... Groups like the Christian Coalition should join with gay conservatives to advance a truly conservative, pro-family agenda for gays and straights alike.[50]

What this exposes is precisely the dangers which assimilationist strategies are prone to their recuperation by conservative agendas and agenda setters. Activism based on rights agitation – especially around issues such as partnership/marriage or the right to privacy – can serve to erase aspects of sexual citizenship founded outside the narrow bounds of 'normalcy', reinstating the tension between definitions of the 'good homosexual' and the 'bad homosexual'. Pendleton is at pains to point out, however, that many radical (non-conservative) agitations also valorise monogamy as the 'responsible' mode of sexual citizenship in the time of AIDS. Pervasive sex-negativity can only be further enabled by demands for the right to marry, while arguments based around protecting privacy threaten to further domesticate sexual citizenship by undermining public articulations of sexual identity, such as public sex.[51] The call for registered partnerships, held by many as absolutely central to claims for sexual citizenship, is a strategy which must be viewed critically, for we must be aware of the kinds of citizens that such a move would produce – and the kinds of non-citizens it would exclude.

GAYS IN THE MILITARY

Equally prominent, and equally problematic, in recent arguments about sexual rights have been the military exclusion policies in the UK and US. Interrogating the logic of these policies affords a window into crucial aspects of the sexual citizenship debates – the relationship between acts and identities, notions of public and private, and the homosocial/homosexual binary. The compromise 'Don't ask, don't tell' stance in the US shows how these aspects of sexual citizenship are negotiated and contested, giving us an indication of

---

49 *Op cit*, Pendleton, fn 46, p 385.
50 *Op cit*, Pendleton, fn 46, p 385.
51 See, eg, *op cit*, Dangerous Bedfellows, fn 46.

how claims to sexual rights outside the context of the military are likely to fare in law.

The gays in the military debate in the US can be seen to instate *passing* as the only possible strategy for homosexuals serving in the forces, since any form of homosexual conduct (including coming out as an 'admitted homosexual' – a definition used in *Ben-Shalom v Marsh*)[52] contravenes the Defence Department's policy:

> The identity/conduct distinction that advocates for gay, lesbian and bisexual rights have been so eager to assert is collapsed, in this instance through the mediating category of speech: homosexuality is articulated through speech, and speech has been summarily defined, by the courts, and by the Clinton administration, as conduct.[53]

Even withholding homosexual identity – by passing – can, however, be used as grounds for dismissal. In fact, in *Steffan v Cheney*,[54] the full force of the Department of Defense's homophobia apparently centred on *the very act of passing*:

> Steffan was under a positive *duty* as a member of the military to come out because his gay identity was otherwise undetectable but contrary to regulations. The result of his coming out, though, was his expulsion as unfit for service. Paradoxically, however, in going public he revealed that his sexuality had not rendered him incapable of service. He demonstrated, instead, that absent a public declaration, he remained completely undetectable on the inside of what is, in the end, an institution forged with same-sex bonds.[55]

Steffan's presence in the Navy thus threatened to destabilise (or at least muddy) the distinction between a sanctioned homosociality and an outlawed homosexuality – a distinction which is actually very precariously enacted in institutions like the military. The Navy's fear, put simply, is of *contagion* (backed up by arguments upholding Steffan's expulsion, which are centred on the 'threat' of HIV and AIDS impacting on the 'healthy' military's abilities to defend the nation). Paradoxically, then, as Carl Stychin notes:

> Joseph Steffan was defined as an outsider because of his ability to pass – to reveal, through the articulation of a gay identity, that he was an insider all along. However, in assimilating the military with the nation, Steffan is further constructed, not as *being* an insider but as performing the role of the insider – as an espionage agent might perform a role to undermine national security. The underlying concern, then, is not simply that Steffan had successfully performed the role until his own revelation, but that his success had revealed the performativity of the military subject.[56]

---

52 *Ben-Shalom v Marsh* 881 F2d 454 (7th Cir 1989).

53 Currah, P, 'Searching for immutability: homosexuality, race and rights discourse', in Wilson, A (ed), *A Simple Matter of Justice?*, 1995, London: Cassell, p 66.

54 *Steffan v Cheney* 780 F Supp 1 (DDC 1991).

55 Stychin, C, *Law's Desire*, 1995, London: Routledge, p 94. Emphasis in original.

56 *Ibid*, p 99.

What the gays in the military issue also makes clear, as Nan Hunter points out, is the complex intertwining of privacy, equality and expression, which is central to current forms of sexual citizenship agitation (and to its regulation):

> The ban on military service by lesbians, gay men, and bisexuals ... renders identical conduct such as kissing permissible or punishable based on the sexual orientation of the actor. Moreover, the ban restricts self-identifying speech with the justification that homosexual 'conduct' is antithetical to morale, good order and discipline.[57]

Further, in order to prohibit the 'public' statement (by confession or coming out) of homosexuality by serving military personnel, the military must itself repeatedly speak the term – generating more of that 'sex-talk' which Davina Cooper identifies as central to the act of making things public so as to render them private;[58] this means constructing a 'homosexual military subject' in order to deny her or his existence. In Judith Butler's words, 'The regulation must conjure one who defines him or herself as a homosexual in order to make plain that no such self-definition is permissible within the military'; the definition of homosexuality must always come from outside (from the State, the law or the military), never from inside.[59] The debate becomes about not gays in the military, but what Butler calls 'gay speech in the military'.

The US military's 'Don't ask, don't tell' ruling, however, offers a strange opt-out clause, or 'rebuttal presumption' – the possibility of renunciation by unchaining identity from conduct (Butler writes it thus: 'I am a homosexual and I intend not to act on my desire'),[60] or the possibility of writing off an isolated incident of 'homosexual conduct' as a 'mistake' (an exit route also often routinely offered to politicians and other prominent public figures who are caught in compromising situations).

The debate in the UK has followed the path of that in the US to a large extent, ushering in the same arguments against homosexual presence in the military, especially the threat to what Derek McGhee terms the military's 'informal panoptic homosocial habitus'.[61] In addition, the phantom 'general public', always to be relied on as homophobic, is introduced into the debate, on the assumption that homosexual servicemen and women would dent the armed forces' image and reputation in the public's eyes (crucially, in the eyes of parents whose teenage children might be thinking of signing up). The

---

57 *Op cit*, Hunter, fn 41, p 139.

58 Cooper, D, 'An engaged state: sexuality, governance and the potential for change' (1993) 20 JLS 257.

59 Butler, J, *Excitable Speech*, 1997, New York: Routledge, p 104.

60 *Ibid*, p 116.

61 McGhee, D, 'Looking and acting the part: gays in the armed forces – a case of passing masculinity' (1998) 4 FLS 206.

evolving situation in the UK, that of the 'unbanning' of homosexuality in the military, will inevitably have to negotiate these spectres and problems. We await the final outcome of the manoeuvre.

In the meantime, we need to reflect on the relationship between the gays in the military debate and the wider question of sexual citizenship. At its simplest, of course, the argument is that denying homosexuals the right to fight for their country denies them full citizenship, given the continuing durability of the relationship between the citizen and the nation-State. This obviously sidesteps the crucial question of the legitimacy of such a strategy in the context of rights agitation. In the same manner as the debate on lesbian and gay marriage, the gays in the military debate is upheld by some as having a destabilising, radical function: opening up one of the most heteronormative State institutions to homosexuals begins the task of undermining heteronormativity itself. While there is something appealing about this line of argument, it also needs to be treated with some scepticism, as Carl Stychin notes:

> I remain convinced that the struggle for the inclusion of 'out' gays and lesbians in the US military, and the fight for same-sex marriage, *could* be discursively deployed to reimagine these central national institutions, and by extension, the ways in which the nation-State has been gendered and sexualised. Although I am very sceptical as to whether activism is interested in such a project, these struggles may contain within them the *potential* to destabilise the construction of the nation.[62]

The framing of Stychin's comment is important and leads us into our concluding discussion, which concerns theory and politics.

CONCLUSION (IN THEORY)

As part of his discussion of the UK ban on gays in the armed forces, Derek McGhee takes Carl Stychin to task. In McGhee's eyes, Stychin's 'deconstructive' reading of the US military exclusion policy overstresses 'epistemic panic' and discursive destabilising at the expense of a recognition of the 'materiality of practice':

> One could say, 'so what?' the heterosexualised, homosocial space [of the armed forces] has been denaturalised in a Queer Legal Theorist's article. But will this really change anything?[63]

McGhee's disquiet is symptomatic of a broader concern with the abstractions of 'theory' and the mismatch between 'theory' and 'politics'. This tension runs

---

62 *Op cit*, Stychin, fn 18, p 198.
63 *Op cit*, McGhee, fn 61, p 235.

through all the modalities of sexual citizenship that we have discussed in this chapter. We share McGhee's disquiet, in that theoretical readings might seem a million miles away from the concrete realities of the experience of sexual citizens and non-citizens. Individuals who lose legal cases make 'interesting' studies for theorists who wish to interrogate the inner workings of the law machine, but this cannot always be broadly productive. In the same way, the destabilising potential offered by same-sex marriage and gays in the military might never amount to more than *potential* – both areas of rights agitation could equally easily shore up the institutions they are supposed to corrode.

What this suggests, we think, is not that theory cannot play its part in sexual citizenship, but that we need ways in which to negotiate the void between theory and the 'materiality of practice'. The marketisation of sexual citizenship is something that we need to attend to with a critical insight, for sure, but one which does not write off the ambiguities inherent in the notions of the pink economy and the lesbian and gay community (and the relations between the two). Same-sex marriage must also be handled with care, and we must stop to think about the consequences of such rights claims, rather than accepting them as self-evident. And any reading of the gays in the military debate must tread a similarly careful path between the seductions of textual deconstruction and the material and social outcomes that policies can, and do, have. Obviously, we need 'theory' to aid us in these interrogations, but we must not lose sight of the lives and experiences of those we theorise about.

CHAPTER 10

ISLAMIC FEMINISM AND
THE EXEMPLARY PAST

Qudsia Mirza[1]

Modern Islamism's dependence upon the discursive *topos* of a 'return' to a pure originary, its reliance upon the restoration of a foundational verity untouched by chance, facilitates, in Al-Azmeh's memorable phrase, 'the elision of history'.[2] However, it is the moment of origin, and not subsequent elisions, that mainly preoccupies the Islamist mind. The Islamist's doctrinal absorption with the inception of Islam as an ideal past, as a 'luminous purity' that has arisen from the defining moment of Islam's origin, manifests itself in the contemporary accent on the trope of authenticity. Accordingly, the birth of Islam is viewed as having brought about the installation of an immaculate order, flawless in its depiction of the ideal society and claiming a fullness and totality which Islamists endeavour to re-institute. The original moment, both as repository of a former utopia and as ultimate reality, denotes an order which once was, and which now rests unequivocally upon, the promise of an authentic recreation.

Invariably, the production (and, indeed, reproduction) of religion rests upon a particular textual genealogy which can be traced back to this foundational moment. In the Islamist rendition of the past, history is channelled in two markedly separate and distinctly nuanced registers: one which possesses an inaugurating authority, is atemporal and gives rise to a pristine order established around the authentic Islamic self; the other – tainted, variable and shaped by contingency, prey to contamination by the non-Islamic other – is reduced to mere sequential history and branded insignificant. In this representation, 'contamination' by a non-Islamic other can be described in terms of both the past and the future. As far as the past is concerned, the original moment of purity is viewed by Islamists as bringing about the elimination of the corrupt *jahiliya*, the dystopian period which inhered prior to the institution of Islam, and converting this past into Islamic order. This is a temporality which stresses the contamination of the past and the revolutionary nature of the change – the erasure of impurity or contamination – effected by the establishment of a new Islamic ethos. In the same manner, the future Islamic self, after the period of the 'Golden Age'[3] of early Islam, is

---

1   My special thanks to Beverley Brown for her comments on earlier drafts of this essay.

2   Al-Azmeh, A, *Islams and Modernities*, 1993, London and New York: Verso, p 46.

3   See, also, *Conversation with Aziz Al-Azmeh, Political Islams: Modernities and Conservative-Populist Ideologies* (1997) 15–16 Iran Bulletin, for the ideal, and idealised, past of Islam.

viewed as having been corrupted by forces 'external' to it, by, for instance, the encounter with the West.[4] It is only by exorcising or cleansing itself of this pollution that the Islamic self can be revived. Thus, it is the nostalgia for an Islam determined by the former historical register that characterises much of contemporary Islamists' yearning for a return to the Golden Age of a 'true prior reality'.[5] The revival of a pure Islamic beginning can, therefore, commence by a renewed adherence to an 'authentic' Islam as outlined in its sacred texts, most notably the focal text of the *Qur'an*, and by emulating the template of the exemplary life of the Prophet Muhammad, recorded in the *hadith* literature.

The essence of the authentic beginning of Islam is unchanging and remains unaltered by the vagaries of time. Allied with this ahistoricity is a conception of the Islamic subject as weakened and undermined through time, yet one that retains an essential core which requires revival by a return to this pure beginning, which, throughout history, Al-Azmeh contends, 'flows as a subliminal impulse'.[6] In reverting back to this origin, the Islamist project is one which aims to resurrect the Islamic subject and restore this cultural self to its rightful place. Time, therefore, is measured as an uninterrupted continuum, in which the past is called upon in order to create the future, the present being but an imperfect interregnum that exists between the past of a sublime beginning and its reinauguration.[7] A 'new' social imaginary is created out of the nostalgia for the past and manifests itself in the application of a programmatic remedy, with law as its primary instrument. Islamic orthodoxy has held out this body of law, *shari'a*,[8] developed in the early period of Islam, as the eternal, complete and infallible expression of law, untainted by external influences and encapsulating a vision of an ethical Islam. The relationship between the authentic recreation of the ideal past of Islam with law is clear: as Al-Azmeh asserts, 'the most notable title under which this politics of nostalgia for an imagined past is officiated is of course the "application" of Islamic law'.[9]

The foundation of the vast corpus of Islamic law is the text of the *Qur'an*, *kalam Allah*, the eternal and absolute divine word, revealed over a number of years to the Prophet Muhammad, the 'instrumental cause'[10] of revelation. The

---

4   See, also, Al-Azmeh, A, *al-'Almaniyah fi manzur mukhtalif,* 1972, Beirut: Markaz Divasat al-Wahdah al-'Arabiyah.

5   *Op cit,* Al-Azmeh, fn 2, p 8.

6   *Op cit,* Al Azmeh, fn 2, p 47.

7   *Op cit,* Al-Azmeh, fn 2, p 49.

8   It is simplistic to define *shari'a* merely as Islamic law. It encompasses a great deal more – '... [it is] the body of rules guiding the life of a Muslim in law, ethics, and etiquette' Najmabadi, A, 'Feminism in an Islamic republic', in Yazbeck Haddad, Y and Esposito, JL (eds), *Islam, Gender, and Social Change,* 1998, Oxford: OUP, p 81.

9   *Op cit,* Al-Azmeh, fn 2, p 8.

10   Stowasser, B, 'Gender issues and contemporary *Qu'ran* interpretation', in *ibid,* Yazbeck Haddad and Esposito, p 31.

seriatim process by which revelation took place accords with the empirical method of its unveiling: many of the verses, including those considered to have legal or quasi-legal effect, were revealed in response to specific situations that arose during the Prophet's life.[11] The other main source of Islamic law is the voluminous compilation of *hadith* writings, traditions of the Prophet Muhammad and of the group of reputable epigones of the Prophet's time and of the period immediately after his death. The *hadith* is viewed as providing detailed scriptural understanding – an elaboration of the broad principles and norms of the *Qur'an*. Thus, the *hadith* is second in sanctity to the *Qur'an* and first in its role as the interpreter of scripture. This order is mirrored in the hierarchy of these texts as sources of law, with the *logos* of the *Qur'an* posited as the primary source of law. Finally, the (often inconsistent and conflicting) rulings of the early Muslim jurists also form an important part of Islamic law. These primary sources are all supported by a prodigious collection of exegetical texts, the *tafsir* literature, including the vast corpus of writing on *usul ul-fiqh*, Islamic jurisprudence.

Thus, 'authentic'[12] Islam is reinstituted, by a return to the sacred text and a recreation of the code of behaviour outlined in the traditions of the *hadith*. It is not, therefore, recreated in the form of a set of abstract norms, but by the recovery of a compendium of paradigmatic instances and standards. By selectively promoting a set of examples from the *Qur'an* and the *hadith* as archetypally constitutive of this utopian past order, and by naming such examples as 'Islamic' and conferring on them a sacred status – a 'moral inevitability',[13] contemporary Islamist discourse represents these paradigmatic acts as possessing a normative and timeless quality. Thus, it is in the 'authentic' re-creation of such exemplary acts that an ethically complete, definitive Islam can be re-enacted. The exemplary matters selected by Islamists as instances of Islamic righteousness are linked to Islam by virtue of a metonymic association which yokes the sacral property of the name 'Islam' with the particular example selected. In this manner, an extensive corpus of examples is collected which is deemed to constitute the essential Islamic discourses. There is, therefore, a core of examples of this kind which are central to the Islamist agenda, many of which are found in the quasi-sacred body of *hadith* literature, a corpus of writing which chronicles the paradigmatic acts, *dicta* and judgments of the Prophet Muhammad and his

---

11 However, although the *Qur'an* makes various statements which are based on historical fact, it is 'not a book of history': Zafrulla Khan, M, *The Qur'an: Introduction*, 1981, London: Curzon, p xxv.

12 For a fuller exposition of the trope of authenticity, see *op cit*, Al-Azmeh, fn 2, especially Chapter 2. See, also, Al-Azmeh, A, *al-'Arab wa-al-barabirah al-muslimun wa-al-hadarat al ukhra*, 1991, London: Riad el-Rayyes.

13 *Op cit*, Al-Azmeh, fn 2, p 25.

wives, immediate companions and successors. This collection is prolific and contains narratives – considered to be true renditions – which portray the life of the Prophet Muhammad and his companions. Thus, the narratives provide us with representations, a set of vivid images, which not only detail the life of the Prophet, but also provides us with a depiction of the ideal past of Islam: 'The order of perfection ... frozen in time.'[14]

These selected examples are sanctified by the linkage with the name 'Islam' and are imbued with qualities which render them prescriptive in their application, inviolable and wholly resistant to any form of censure. However, the pool of examples from which a potential selection can be made is vast, and only a small number is singled out as possessing this exemplary quality. Thus, for Al-Azmeh, this form of arbitrary selection is a matter of political ideology and is one rooted in an Islamist agenda which goes beyond the 'pietistic and ethical imperatives and nostalgias'[15] of Islam. Moreover, as Ahmed contends, it is at 'certain moments in history that the dominant, prescriptive terms of the core religious discourses were founded and institutionally and legally elaborated'.[16] The deconstructive project for Islamic feminism[17] entails identifying such key historical moments which have played such a profound role in influencing contemporary social and legal articulations of gender.

However, the question for feminists is not simply one of identification; it is one of determining how the associative link between certain examples from the *Qur'an* and the *hadith* have achieved this paradigmatic quality. Feminists also advocate that the selection of such examples and the sacral gloss that they are deemed to acquire by virtue of the association with the name 'Islam' is primarily a matter of Islamist ideology. A repertoire of arcane examples is disinterred from a history in which time is conceptualised as a series of frozen historical moments, linked, directly, with the period of Islam's inception by the material re-creation of these examples from that past. The Islamist reproduction of this memory of Islam's origin is cast as *the* Islamic memory, a recollection deemed to be both accurate, legitimate and beyond interrogation or any form of challenge. There is, therefore, a correlation between the determining position that the notion of temporality occupies for both Islamists and feminists and the manner in which each deploys time in their relative configurations of Islamic history. The difference lies, simply, in what each views as the content of that history and the specific loci in time from which the paradigmatic examples are obtained. Thus, the Islamist view of history is

---

14   *Op cit*, Al-Azmeh, fn 2, p 25.

15   *Op cit*, Al-Azmeh, fn 2, p 26.

16   Ahmed, L, *Women and Gender in Islam*, 1992, New Haven: Yale UP, p 3.

17   As Moghissi points out, 'Islamic feminism' is a problematic term for a number of reasons, not least of which is the perceived antinomy of these two terms: Moghissi, H, *Feminism and Islamic Fundamentalism: The Limits of Postmodern Analysis*, 1999, New York: Zed.

articulated with a conception of temporality that Al-Azmeh regards adversely as the 'elision of history'. Accordingly, Al-Azmeh's view that contemporary Islamist discourse rests upon an elliptical temporality also constitutes a fundamental dimension of the feminist critique of Islamism.

In laying claim to the notion of a paradigmatic past, Muslim feminists, despite fundamental differences that inhere between different strands of Islamic feminism, also profess an adherence to the importance of understanding the period of Islam's genesis. Correspondingly, there is an attachment to the Islamist rhetoric of authenticity and to the contemporary project of re-enacting the past utopian order. However, although the contours of the feminist counter-paradigm are shaped by a conception of the past which accords, fundamentally, with that of the Islamist model, the feminist framework differs radically in its understanding of that past. In other words, the discourse of the past is axial for both Islamist and feminist perspectives, in that both recognise that it is this moment that has determined the Muslim ethico-moral code that must be reconstituted in the present, primarily in the form of a legal order. It is also from this decisive moment of genesis that all future interpretations of Islam must commence. What divides them is the contrasting vision each possesses of the substantive content of that ethically correct past, resulting in the feminist quest for an authentic genealogy of women's legal and cultural rights in Islam.

Feminist historians of Islam, such as Leila Ahmed, challenge the accuracy of the Islamist version of history and point to a different trajectory, claiming that a fundamental part of the Islamist vision has been the structural institution of a sexual hierarchy. This feminist reinterpretive schema, which has produced a radical new configuration of Islam, reveals a schism in the emerging Islam, two tendencies that conflicted with each other and grappled for ascendancy. The first was the establishment of a male dominated sexual division, which may be termed the 'pragmatic voice' of Islam and which was intended to be temporary (binding for the extenuating circumstances of the early Islamic period) and largely contextual. In contrast, what feminists have identified as the *true* 'ethical voice'[18] of Islam clearly advocated the creation of a normative (and, therefore, timeless) sexual equality and pointed to women and men possessing an identical spiritual status with corresponding social, economic and political rights within society. Feminists point out that what is striking about the period of early Islam is that women, who had played a significant role as the creators of verbal texts (which were later transcribed by men), became invisible after the inception of Islam, both as creators and interpreters of such texts. Instead, these texts, such as the *Qur'anic* exegetical works and the vast *hadith* literature, which are considered the core prescriptive

---

18 The distinction between the 'ethical' and the 'pragmatic' voices of Islam is made by Leila Ahmed, *op cit*, fn 16.

texts of Islam, were now produced by men, who inscribed in them their own restrictive assumptions and understanding of gender relations. Legal texts, of what is now orthodox Islam, were also created in the above manner and the masculine rubric was inscribed into the literary, legal and institutional creations of that time, setting in motion the process by which the ethical voice became atrophied.[19]

The hierarchical relation between the sexes encoded in the structure of orthodox Islam, including the textual edifice of Islamic law, can be traced back to the paramountcy of this pragmatic voice and its concomitant androcentrism. The tension between the broader ethical vision that feminists claim Islam was designed to articulate, and which is premised unambiguously upon the principle of equality between the sexes, and the conflicting – and correspondingly non-ethical – regulatory pragmatism which resulted in the implementation of a gendered hierarchy and the consonant curtailment of women's rights, is one which is central to the contemporary feminist project. In focusing on this tension, feminists are referring back to an authentic, original Islam (the 'true' Golden Age) in their endeavour to recover the ethical voice of Islam. The ethical paradigm, therefore, is clearly equated with the feminine, whilst its pragmatic antithesis is marked as masculine. Thus, the versatility of the discourse of authenticity renders it open to an array of different interpretations – from the broad spectrum of Islamist to feminist.

However, a mapping of the diversity of contemporary feminist responses to the trope of authenticity reveals a more complex picture. Certain analyses are characterised by an ambivalence towards the notion of an Arcadian age of Islamic purity and the resulting (legal) rights for women that such a time gave rise to. In contrast to some reinterpretations which have appropriated the protean nature of authenticity, viewing it as a constructive force and pointing to a pure Islamic beginning which assigned positive rights to women, other versions have emphasised the highly speculative evidence upon which such a categorical assertion is based. The importance of any reversion to an authentic beginning lies in its significance as the base from which a reconfiguration of sexual difference may take place and, in structural terms, the role that the law plays in realising that difference. Related to this foundational problematic is the question of scriptural exegesis, specifically, the interpretation of the text of the *Qur'an*. By developing and supplementing the traditional interpretive techniques of classical theological elucidation (with the view that the '[propagation] of legal reform lies in the separation of the true *Shari'a* from its medieval juridic formulation'),[20] feminists have created new interpretations of the *Qur'an* and, in particular, *Qur'anic* verses that relate to women and which form the basis of rights enshrined in Islamic law. Therefore, the importance of

---

19 See, generally, *op cit*, Ahmed, fn 16.
20 *Op cit*, Stowasser, fn 10, p 34.

an authentic origin lies in its link with this 'reinterpretation' of the *Qur'an*; the textual creation of a new social imaginary is bound up with a myth of origin, of an 'authentic' past to which the present can be connected, a former age that can be regained.

Some feminist reimaginings are of an equivocal nature and, in part, envisage the future merely as a repetition of an already constituted past. Sexual difference, in this register, is the premise for the division of province and locale, and is directly derivative of the Islamist paradigm.[21] For some, it is the separation of spiritual essence from temporal being;[22] for others, it is the forensic unearthing and meticulous reconstitution of elliptical fragments left over from a verifiable history.[23] In all of these configurations, the return to the *reality* of an origin – however determined – is a vital part of the transformative enterprise. For Iqbal, the literal interpretation of the *Qur'an* is both clear and obvious: the text authorises a gender division which is premised upon a delineation between the public and the private, in which men and women inhabit different domains under the 'separate but equal' rubric. In this configuration, men are guardians of women ('men are appointed guardians over women, because of that in respect of which Allah has had some of them excel others, and because the men spend of their wealth')[24] and are therefore scripturally enjoined to occupy the public sphere, whilst women are commanded, as carers and nurturers of children, to occupy the private domain. In casting women and men as possessing different roles and inhabiting different spheres of life, Iqbal asserts that this (true) equality between the sexes deflects the orthodox representation of women as spiritually inferior to men. Thus, the text is distinct and unambiguous. The divisions between women and men in their temporal lives that Iqbal identifies and which, for Iqbal, do not point to inequality, do not, in any manner, compromise the equal spiritual status that each sex enjoys. In this rendition, as in that of Islamists, the accent is on the primacy of the sacred text, a probity of interpretation in which a proper construction of the divine word is arrived at only by a close, exact and, therefore, faithful reading. In this interpretation, the meaning of the sacred word is explicit: a literal interpretation of the *Qur'an* and a direct application of its precepts constitutes the recreation of Islam and an ethically correct gender paradigm.

---

21 See Iqbal, S, *Woman and Islamic Law*, 1991, Delhi: Adam.

22 See, eg, Engineer, AA, *The Rights of Women in Islam*, 1992, London: Hurst; Wadud-Muhsin, A, *Qur'an and Woman*, 1992, Kuala Lumpur: Penerbit Fajar Bakti Sdn, Bhd.

23 See *op cit*, Ahmed, fn 16; Mernissi, F, *Women and Islam*, 1992, Oxford: Blackwell; Yammani, M (ed), *Feminism and Islam: Legal and Literary Perspectives*, 1996, Reading: Ithaca, especially Pt 1.

24 *Op cit*, Zafrulla Khan, fn 11, *The Qur'an Al-Nisa*: 35. All quotations are from this translation.

The supreme defining feature of Islamic law is the endophytic relationship that it has with theological doctrine. The interdependence of law and theological principle and the representation of religious doctrine that textual law is perceived to contain is an association that has raised, throughout the history of Islamic theology and legal theory, the question of how the distinction between these two fundamental elements of Islam can be determined. In historical terms, it is the apparent convergence between law and religion that has prompted attempts to delineate the two in formulations such as the following: '[Law's] "essence" is its religion but its "expression" is a response to the formal exigencies of juristic style in language, logic and structure.'[25] However, the symbiotic relationship between religious doctrine and law indicates that the boundary between the two is not as easy to demarcate as this formulation indicates. It is the permeability between the two that allows Islamists to claim that, because law is the primary means of recreating the past of the Islamic utopia, the present establishment of a legal order can be equated directly with the reinstitution of that past. Consequently, the vagueness of the line between theological principle and law has been emphasised by Islamists in their call for the institution of a legal order based on *shari'a*, thus adroitly manufacturing a conflation between law and religion. It is this dynamic that transmutes Islamic doctrine into legal principle and, in a double movement, transforms legal principle into Islamic doctrine. The significance of this point lies in the fact that Islamic doctrine is cast, naturally, as possessing an ethical integrity. Islamist discourse asserts that *it* is the repository of Islamic doctrinal purity and, as such, articulates the correct configuration of ethical Islam. The feminist counter-argument is unequivocal:[26] this conflation is the result of an ideological move which equates Islamism with Islam, resulting in a misrepresentation of true or authentic Islam. Law is implicated in the Islamist account because of its ambiguous relationship with Islamic doctrine. Thus, Islamic law has become enmeshed with Islamist ideology and it is this plexus that feminist critics are endeavouring to unravel, as well as establishing a feminist and, therefore, ethical and authentic recreation of Islam.

The belief in *shari'a* as a unified corpus of law incorporating a set of unambiguous and fixed rulings that originated at the time of Islam's dawn as either divine *Qur'anic* revelation,[27] the 'moment of divinity'[28] or in the canonical *hadith* narratives of the Prophet Muhammad, is one invoked

---

25 Siddiqui, M, 'Law and the desire for social control: an insight into the Hanafi concept of *kafa'a* with reference to the *Fatawa 'Alamgiri* (1664–1672)', in *op cit*, Yammani, fn 23.

26 See, eg, one of the most outspoken critics of Islamism, Fatima Mernissi: *The Veil and the Male Elite: a Feminist Interpretation of Women's Rights in Islam*, Lakel, MJ (trans), 1991, Reading, Mass: Addison Wesley.

27 In numerical terms, the legislative content of the *Qur'an* is relatively small: less than 700 of the Quran's 6,000 verses contain legislative provisions. The remaining 5,300 verses are concerned mainly with the regulation of worship: Karmi, G, 'Women, Islam and patriarchalism', in *op cit*, Yammani, fn 23, p 81.

28 *Op cit*, Al-Azmeh, fn 2, p 93.

currently by both Islamist and feminist discourse. However, in claiming that law's provenance lies in these two sources, a particular fidelity to *usul* that Islamists cleave to, Islamists also contend that, methodologically, the process by which legal principles, exemplary standards and the paradigmatic norms of Islam can be ascertained is both clear and apparent. Quite simply, a literal reading of the *Qur'an* and the *hadith* literature provides a self-evident exposition of such principles. For Al-Azmeh, this literalism rests upon a denial of the 'translatability of [the] traditional texts'[29] of Islam. In assessing contemporary Islamist discourse, Al-Azmeh divides Islamism into two schools of thought: first, Islamist modernism or reformism, which allows for the conversion ('translation') of key features of Islamic rectitude into modern neoteric form; and, secondly, Islamist revivalism, which is predicated on the unequivocal belief that Islamic texts are not open to such an interpretation. Thus, for Islamist modernists, the process of conversion allows *shura* to be located in its contemporary configuration of parliamentary democracy, the past of original Islam becomes a flawless augury of socialism and the catalogue of vatic events detailed in the first section of the *Qur'an* become portents of modern scientific discoveries.[30]

This interpretation views the text of the *Qur'an* and the corpus of *hadith* literature as containing a number of paradigmatic examples, representative of early Islam in a particular form, but also organic in their ability to take on a different guise when 'translated' into different forms, in periods subsequent to the time of original Islam. In contrast, Islamist revivalism or salafism, the exponent of a particular *intégrisme*,[31] views Islam as 'untranslatable', as uniquely singular and distinct in its depiction of the paradigmatic examples of original Islam, inscribed in the focal texts of Islam. Consequently, the singularity of these exemplary instances means that they are viewed as being entirely unconnected to developments such as parliamentary democracy or socialism and, of course, feminism; developments considered to be 'modern' and, therefore, un-Islamic. Developments such as feminism belong to the second of the two historical registers that history is divided into by Islamists: contingent, contaminated and entirely unconnected to the pure beginning of Islam. For this element of Islamic orthodoxy, the reinstitution of the 'legalistic utopia'[32] of early Islam rests, unequivocally, upon a literal recreation of the paradigmatic elements of the past, both in terms of the form that these instances took at the time of early Islam as well as their substantive content. The revivalist project turns on the notion of a reinstitution that can only be

---

29 *Op cit*, Al-Azmeh, fn 2, p 79.

30 *Op cit*, Al-Azmeh, fn 2, p 79.

31 Salafism calls for a return to the text of the *Qur'an* and the traditions of the Prophet Muhammad and his companions and immediate successors. The contemporary manifestation of this doctrinal position is found in Wahhabite discourse.

32 *Op cit*, Al-Azmeh, fn 2, p 95.

effected by an authentic re-creation of the paradigmatic elements of Islam, with 'authenticity' as the key determinant of the efficacy of this project.

Critics of the revivalist exposition draw attention to its over-simplicity. In particular, Al-Azmeh's critique centres on the fact that this rendition portrays *shari'a* in a superficial and reductionist manner and is the result of Islamism's deliberate disregard of the true nature of *shari'a*. The complexity of interpretive methods and techniques that constitute the way in which change is effected is an important element of Islamic law. For Al-Azmeh, the methodology outlined above is utilised by Islamist orthodoxy as a means by which the core tenets of Islamic law are obtained, and, critically, is reliant upon 'scriptural statements without the mediation of legal reason'.[33] By this, he is alluding to the importance of interpretive methods or rules as a medium by which radical innovation may take place, resulting in the reinterpretation of Islamic law. The allusion to the complexity of Islamic law refers to the fact that the rules that constitute legal methodology are of a highly sophisticated and intricate nature ('deontic logic, analogical connections, rhetorical methods, philological and lexical procedures'),[34] often garnered from esoteric and arcane exegetical and hermeneutic sources of Islamic jurisprudence. This has led one writer to suggest that Islamic law is so highly technical that it has 'but a ... tangential connection with ethical or dogmatic considerations'.[35] Thus, the Islamist description of *shari'a* as a codified system of law which can be easily and literally applied is a view that is countered by feminist and other reformist writers as one contrary to the true nature of Islamic law.

In one significant respect, a parallel may be drawn between Islamic law and English law, in that both types of law accord a central role to the concept of precedent. In *shari'a*, great reliance is placed upon precedent as a primary means by which legal innovation occurs. It is utilised in a manner which allows law to be highly flexible and variable – rather than immutable and inflexible, the representation of perennial fixity expounded by contemporary Islamist ideologues. This fixity is linked to the stagnation of Islamic jurisprudential thought that occurred at the time of the collapse of the Abbasid dynasty in the 13th century. The closing of the 'gates of *ijtihad*'[36] (individual interpretation of scripture leading to innovation) and the restricted use of *rai* ('reasonable' interpretation), the two key hermeneutic methods by which reinterpretation took place, have led directly to this reduction in progressive interpretations of Islamic law. Furthermore, the heuristic device of *ikhtilaf*, or the scope allowed for difference of opinion on specific points of law, is a key tool of interpretation, which, in classical Islamic jurisprudence, has been a

---

33 *Op cit*, Al-Azmeh, fn 2, p 11.

34 *Op cit*, Al-Azmeh, fn 2, p 11.

35 *Op cit*, Al-Azmeh, fn 2, p 11, quoting the jurist Sarakhsi.

36 For a comprehensive analysis of *ijtihad*, see Hallaq, W, 'Was the Gate of Ijtihad closed?' (1984) 16 Int J Middle Eastern Studies 3.

primary channel of legal innovation. The use of *ikhtilaf* and its recognition of diversity of opinion is an important element of legal methodology and one which, throughout the history of Islamic jurisprudence, has been employed as a means of legitimising inconsistent and even contradictory opinions on points of law. Thus, key elements of legal methodology demonstrate that the nature of Islamic law is one of mutability, neoterism and heterogeneity, a rendition which again conflicts with that described by contemporary Islamist discourse. Such discourse expounds a version of *shari'a* that attributes a certitude and finality to law,[37] an understanding which is articulated with the Islamist notion of temporality and, in particular, the period of original Islam. The Islamist project is based upon the exact recreation of that past, frozen in time; correspondingly, the reinstitution of Islamic law entails the precise recreation of law found at the time of Islam's inception. Thus, Islamism's heterophobic conception of law precludes the reformulation of law, based as it is upon a reinterpretation of scripture.

In developing a new approach to scriptural interpretation, 'opening the gates of *ijtihad*', Muslim feminists such as Amina Wadud-Muhsin[38] are said to have created a new Islamic epistemology.[39] However, because feminist discourse is predicated not upon an abandonment of *shari'a*, but upon a reformulation, feminists are concerned primarily with developing a new interpretive methodology and a radical reinterpretation of the tenets of Islam. This results in a recasting of *shari'a*, one that incorporates the concept of gender equality, considered to have been jettisoned by much of classical Islamic jurisprudential thought. In spite of this important departure, the feminist theoretical approach – an important facet of the wider contemporary 'reformist' trend in Islamic discourse – shares a number of key characteristics with Islamist thought.[40] Both are anchored in the focal texts of the *Qur'an* and the *hadith* literature; both represent their own interpretation as the expression of authentic 'true' Islam – in this respect, they enjoy a parallactic relationship with the trope of authenticity; and both discourses are predicated upon the notion of the ideal past of Islam as the foundation of law. However, the fundamental distinction between the two discourses lies in their differing approaches to the relationship between religious doctrine and law. To reiterate, the Islamist accent is on the abstraction of legal principle from a literal interpretation of the text of the *Qur'an*. This misplaced conflation between hierological doctrine and legal rule is one that has well established antecedents in Islamic legal history and has led reformist writers such as

---

37   *Op cit*, Al-Azmeh, fn 2, p 12. See, also, Al-Azmeh, A (ed), *Islamic Law: Social and Historical Contexts*, 1988, London: Routledge.

38   In the resourceful *Qur'an and Woman*, *op cit*, fn 22.

39   *Op cit*, Stowasser, fn 10, p 30.

40   For a historical summary of the relationship between Islamist and feminist discourse, see *op cit*, Moghissi, fn 17.

Fazlur Rahman to comment that, throughout the history of Islamic legal theory, jurists and commentators have 'regarded the *Qur'an* as a lawbook and not the religious source of the law'.[41] In accordance with this statement, feminist discourse is also predicated upon a separation between the sacred text as a repository of religious principle and this text as a distinct charter of legislative provisions, given flesh by unmediated literal application.

One of Islamic feminism's main concerns, and a central component of the new methodology that is being developed, is the relationship between the absolute and aeonian nature of the *Qur'an* and its application in specific historical and cultural contexts. If the *Qur'an*, as *kalam Allah*, is viewed as atemporal and ahistorical, eternally relevant at all times and in all contexts, how can this be reconciled with the idea of historical change and social and cultural specificity? This is also a central question for much of contemporary reformist discourse, but is particularly pertinent for feminist critics. This is because it is precisely this decontextualised application of the *Qur'an*,[42] particularly those verses of the *Qur'an* which, on a literal reading, appear to discriminate against women, that has resulted in the biased scriptural interpretations[43] that are so deeply embedded in Islamic legal and theological literature. The development of the feminist argument is, of course, motivated by the need to redress this inequality. However, it is not simply this objective that drives the development of the feminist argument. It is motivated by a greater impulse: the need to represent authentic Islam. Feminists believe that it is only in their reinterpretation of scripture that true, authentic Islam can be recreated and an ethically correct legal order can be erected. Furthermore, there is a recognition that traditional interpretive literature has obscured the interpretation of the *Qur'an*, as the focus has been on understanding the exegetical literature itself rather than the text of the *Qur'an*. As Wadud-Muhsin observes, the result has been 'a disconnection from the original text and its intent'.[44]

Wadud-Muhsin, one of the foremost proponents of a feminist hermeneutics, identifies three main types of *Qur'anic* interpretive

---

41 Rahman, F, *Major Themes of the Qur'an*, 1980, Chicago: Bibliotheca Islamica, p 47. See, also, Rahman, F, *Islam and Modernity: Transformation of an Intellectual Tradition*, 1981, Chicago: Chicago UP; Ragi al-Faruqi, I, 'Towards a new methodology for Qur'anic exegesis' [1962] Islamic Studies 35; Ahmad An-Na'im, A, *Toward an Islamic Reformation: Civil Liberties, Human Rights, and International Law*, 1990, Syracuse: Syracuse UP; Stowasser, B, *Women in the Qur'an, Traditions, and Interpretation*, 1994, New York: OUP; Esposito, JL, *Women in Muslim Family Law*, 1982, Syracuse: Syracuse UP.

42 This criticism is also relevant to the application of the *hadith* literature.

43 One of the criticisms that is often made by feminists is that, historically, most of the exegetical literature has been written by men, resulting in the bias that we see today. See, eg, Wadud-Muhsin's trenchant criticism in *op cit*, fn 22, pp 95–96.

methodology: traditional, reactive and holistic. Traditional *tafsir* (both modern and classical) has the disadvantage that it is based upon an 'atomistic methodology'[45] which analyses the text of the *Qur'an* in a linear manner, proceeding from the first verse and moving on to the second, and so on. This methodology omits to take into account the structure and thematic coherence of the *Qur'an* and results in an interpretation that offers an insufficient analysis. Furthermore, it is a methodology which has traditionally been utilised by men and has, therefore, advanced interpretations which are disadvantageous to women. The second methodology is the 'reactive' method, developed by ideologically motivated writers primarily as a reaction to the position of women in poor Islamic societies, to advance a *Qur'anic* interpretation which attributes the inferior position of women in these societies to the text. Finally, the 'holistic' method, the comprehensive interpretive system that Wadud-Muhsin favours, is based on a contextualised analysis of *Qur'anic* verses, one which also takes into account the lexiomatic, grammatical and semantic structure of the text itself placed in the wider context of the *Qur'anic* 'worldview'.[46]

Wadud-Muhsin's methodology incorporates the notion of determining the hierarchy of *Qur'anic* verses, a method propounded by reformist writers such as Islamil Ragi al-Faruqi. He contends that it is necessary not only to discover the intent or purpose of the *Qur'anic* verse(s); it is also essential to differentiate between textual levels of the *Qur'an*. This results in the identification of two types of scriptural text: first, the historically specific which has to be distinguished from the 'eternally valid'; and, secondly, those verses that are socially and culturally specific, as opposed to those that demonstrate a universal ethical principle.[47] This is a methodology that is very similar to Asghar Ali Engineer's differentiation between the 'normative' and 'contextual' verses of the *Qur'an*.[48] Engineer suggests that certain statements in the *Qur'an* should be viewed as possessing normative effect, that is, they are universal in nature and their applicability inheres at all times and in all circumstances. In contrast, contextual verses have cultural and historical specificity and are viewed as having application only in limited periods of time and social contexts.

Applying this methodology to the question of gender in the *Qur'an*, Engineer considers verses which point clearly to gender equality,[49] in

---

44 *Op cit*, Wadud-Muhsin, fn 22, p iv.

45 *Op cit*, Wadud-Muhsin, fn 22, p 2.

46 *Op cit*, Wadud-Muhsin, fn 22, pp 1–5. This notion of an Islamic worldview incorporates the idea of core ethical norms of Islam, deduced from verses such as those expounding gender equality.

47 This demarcation, a somewhat artificial 'space' and 'time' differentiation, gives rise to some overlap.

48 *Op cit*, Engineer, fn 22, p 42.

particular those that point to the spiritual equality and dignity of each of the sexes. In addition, Engineer locates verses which describe the religious equality of women and men and, importantly, actually name both women and men when listing the religious duties that are incumbent on them ('Lo, men who surrender unto Allah and women who surrender, and men who believe and women who believe, and men who obey, and women who obey, and men who speak the truth, and women who speak the truth ...').[50] Engineer then analyses those verses which demonstrate inequality between men and women, particularly verses which evince a distinct superiority of men over women. Such verses range from general statements that position men as the 'maintainers' or 'guardians' of women, to one which asserts that men are a degree above women. There are also specific verses detailing, for instance, laws of inheritance which stipulate the lesser share that women, as compared to men, are permitted to receive. Engineer concludes that these verses should be divided into the two categories described above, a classification in which the scriptural passages that describe inequality must be seen as merely contextual and inhering for only limited periods and particular contexts. In contrast, those verses which are unequivocal in their affirmation of equality must be viewed as possessing normative quality and as expressing the 'ethical' voice of Islam.

A similar 'hierarchisation' of *Qur'anic* verses[51] has been proposed by the reformist Abdullahi An-Na'im, who has developed an analysis based on that advanced by Mahmoud Mohamed Taha.[52] An-Na'im begins by suggesting that the stagnation in *Qur'anic* interpretation and the resulting fixity in *shari'a* must be countered by a radical reform of *Qur'anic* interpretive methodologies.[53] In addition, the use of such methodologies must yield new interpretations of the canonical texts of Islam, which, in turn, produce a *shari'a* framework that clearly incorporates the concept of gender equality. An-Na'im advocates a methodology based upon the juristic principle of *naksh* and the abrogation or suspension of specific verses of the *Qur'an*.[54] In his appraisal of the *Qur'an*, An-Nai'm follows Taha's differentiation of verses into the earlier Meccan verses, which are viewed as embodying general principles of justice and equality and as enunciating an ethically correct vision of Islamic principles. The later verses, revealed after the Prophet Muhammad's migration to Medina, are characterised as having been revealed in response to

---

49 *Op cit*, Engineer, fn 22, especially Chapter 3.

50 *Al-Baqarah*: 224.

51 See *op cit*, Stowasser, fn 10, p 40.

52 See Mohamed Taha, M, *The Second Message of Islam*, Ahmed An-Na'im, A (trans), 1987, Syracuse: Syracuse UP.

53 *Op cit*, Ahmed An-Na'im, fn 41.

54 *Op cit*, Ahmed An-Na'im, fn 41.

social and cultural situations or specific problems that the Prophet Muhammad encountered. This separation of the *Qur'an* is developed by An-Nai'm, who contends that it is the earlier Meccan verses which should form the theological base from which a new *shari'a* is fashioned.

Furthermore, in a move which is considered to be radical[55] in its implicit challenge to the traditional understanding of the *Qur'an* as *kalam Allah*, An-Nai'm proposes that those later Medinan verses, which conflict with the Meccan verses, should be abrogated.[56] This is a recommendation which indicates a fundamental 'break with history', as it would result in the creation of a modern *shari'a* that is not based, as has been the case in the past, upon the later Medinan verses. The radical nature of this proposal should not be under estimated. The implementation of this recommendation would mean the abandonment of a *shari'a* that has inhered for much of the past 1,400 years of Islamic legal history and would result in a reconfiguration of Islamic law that would bear little resemblance to that propounded by contemporary Islamist orthodoxy. An-Naim's proposal has great implications for gender equality, as it is these later Medinan verses upon which the majority of discriminatory legal provisions on women have been based. An example of this is *Al-Nisa*: 35 in the *Qu'ran*,[57] which posits men as the 'guardians' of women and is a verse revealed to the Prophet Muhammad in the later Medinan period. This is a verse which has been inscribed into the canon of Islamic law, constituting the basis of many well established discriminatory legal provisions against women.

The reformist Nasr Hamid Abu Zayd has developed a methodology[58] based, again, on formulating a distinction between different parts of the *Qur'anic* text. Central, or core, verses incorporating gender equality are contrasted with exceptional verses which are considered to be irregular or anomalous because they articulate a gender bias. For Abu Zayd, this differentiation must be utilised to contextualise those verses considered to be irregular, as verses revealed in the specific environment of Arabic society at the particular historical time of the Prophet Muhammad. Such verses are considered secondary to those which evince gender equality and must have limited application in view of these core verses of the *Qur'an*. Abu Zayd's scriptural hermeneutic is, thus, similar to that advanced by Engineer in his demarcation of normative and contextual *Qur'anic* verses and the weight that

---

55 This is a development that, in some quarters, is considered apostical. See, eg, the charge of apostasy made against the radical Egyptian theologian Nasr Hamid Abu Zayd.

56 *Op cit*, Ahmed An-Na'im, fn 41, p 56.

57 A verse which has taxed many reformist writers who consider this verse to be particularly problematic in its explicit articulation of gender inequality.

58 See, particularly, Abu Zayd, NH, *Naqd al-Khitab*, 1994, Cairo: Sina lil-Nashr; *Mafhum al-Nass: Dirasah fi 'Ulum al'Qur'an*, 1990, Beirut: al-Marquaz al Thaqafi al-'Arabi.

he accords to the former, verses which are based, clearly, on sexual difference but are explicit in their incorporation of gender equality.

In order to understand fully the contrast between Islamist and feminist discourses of 'authentic' Islam, it is necessary to return to the period of Islam's inception and the differing visions of early Islam that these discourses contain. *Jahiliya*, the pre-Islamic period which Islamic orthodoxy terms the dystopian 'age of ignorance', was the referent against which the new, emerging Islam defined itself. The rhetoric of Islamism asserts that, before the arrival of Islam, the strictures that women were forced to endure, in the form of traditions and customs that inhered at the time, and which formed the basis of their oppression, was unlimited. Women enjoyed no rights: they were found to be in positions of enslavement; they were inherited as possessions; they were often one of many wives or concubines and were subjected to detrimental forms of marriage; as victims of divorce, they were exposed to precarious marriages in which the cursory granting of a *tal'aq* was firmly in the hands of their husbands. Most importantly, the right to life itself was denied, as female infanticide was a common practice in the period immediately prior to the advent of Islam.[59] The phenomenon of infanticide plays a key role in the Islamic consciousness, as it is the leading example cited by many Islamists when contrasting the inferior position of women in *jahiliya* and the subsequent improvement in their position brought about by the Islamic prohibition of the practice. The pre-Islamic custom of female deities, the most famous of which were al-Lat, ul-Uzzah and Manat,[60] who were referred to as God's daughters, were important figures in the divine hierarchy and, although they were not worshipped directly, they played a significant role as deities who interceded with God on behalf of their followers. In sharp contrast, as Engineer points out, whilst followers considered these deities eminent figures in the divine pantheon, their social attitude towards female children and women was quite different. In addressing each of these issues, nascent Islam presented itself as the deliverer and custodian of women's rights by instituting injunctions against such customs and establishing a new set of ethical norms, which, both Islamists and feminists claim, in another point of convergence for these oppositional discourses, led directly to the emancipation of women.[61]

---

59 Amongst the sayings of the Prophet Muhammad detailed in the *hadith* literature: 'He who has a female infant and he does not bury her alive, does not insult her, and does not prefer sons over her, will be ushered into paradise.' (Al-Afghani, S, *Al-Islam wal Mar'ah*, 1945, Damascus: Tarakki, p 59.) There is evidence to indicate that three pre-Islamic tribes were known particularly for this practice: *Tamim, Rabi'ah*, and *Kindah*: Mahmasani, S, *The Legal Systems in the Arab States*, 1965, Beirut: Dar al'Ilm lil Malayin, pp 54–56, quoted in Al-Hibrih, A, 'A study of Islamic herstory: or, how did we get into this mess?' (1982) 5(2) Women's Studies Int Forum 207, p 209.

60 Famously resurrected by Salman Rushdie in *The Satanic Verses*, 1988, London: Jonathan Cape.

61 According to writers such as Kah-haleh in *Al-Mar'ah* Vol VI, 1978, Beirut: Risalah Institiute, Islam prohibited a great number of discriminatory and oppressive practices. These ranged from matters such as how long a husband was permitted to abstain from sexual relations with his wife to making the murder of a woman a crime in the same manner as the murder of a man.

Marriage and divorce, and the laws that were introduced in respect of these, are presented as salutary examples of Islam's reformist power. They are also useful in demonstrating the contrasting visions that feminists and Islamists possess of the period of early Islam and the substantial differences that exist between various feminist interpretations. In the *jahiliya* period, various forms of marriage existed,[62] all of which were based on the subservience of women. *Nikah al-dayzan* was a common form of marriage, in which the eldest son of a woman's husband would inherit her when his father died. By throwing a cloth over her, his possession of her would be complete; his inheritance of her also meant that he acquired the right to marry her or prevent her from marrying another. He was also entitled to claim *mahr*, a dowry payment from her prospective husband, if he decided to allow her to marry again. Islam prohibited this practice by the revelation of a verse of the *Qur'an*: 'Marry not women whom your fathers had married ... It was a foul and hateful practice and an evil way.'[63] Similarly, another form of marriage considered to be oppressive was the *mut'a*,[64] which conferred legitimacy on temporary unions, which expired automatically on the stipulated date. Again, Islam soon condemned the *mut'a* as permitting sexual relations which were considered illicit or *zina*, and asserted that it was a form of marriage which viewed women merely as sexual objects, to be abandoned at will. Islam proscribed it as a valid form of marriage, claiming that this privilege of men oppressed women. *Zawaj al-badal* entailed the mutual exchange of wives between men, in which there was no requirement to obtain the consent of the women involved. A similar arrangement was *zawaj al-shighar*, in which men were sanctioned to marry off their immediate female relatives to other men who would reciprocate by giving their own female relatives in marriage. Both were condemned by the emancipatory message of Islam as oppressive to women and were proscribed as legitimate forms of marriage, becoming central doctrinal points which were soon 'translated' into legal form.

Divorce during *jahiliya* was as well established as marriage.[65] The power of repudiation lay, as in the case of marriage, in the hands of husbands, and could be exercised with relative ease. In such cases, the words 'I separate you' or 'I liberate you' were deemed to be sufficient to effect divorce. One form of repudiation in particular – *zihar* – was widely prevalent. Here, the husband would state to his wife that she was like his mother's back or his aunt's womb,

---

62 For a selection of analyses of pre-Islamic forms of marriage, see *op cit*, Engineer, fn 22; *op cit*, Ahmed, fn 16; *op cit*, Karmi, fn 27.

63 *Al-Nisa*: 23.

64 A form of marriage that is still practised by Shi'i Muslims.

65 See *op cit*, Engineer, fn 22, p 26.

or like his sister's sexual organ. By likening his wife, by analogy, to a relative of his to whom marriage was prohibited, the husband was able to dissolve the marriage. This was a practice that was considered to be exceptionally opprobrious by the *Qur'an*: 'Those among you who put away their wives by calling them mothers are surely guilty of uttering words that are manifestly evil and untrue.'[66] Similarly, al-'ila, the form of divorce in which the husband would assert that he was leaving his wife for a period of time, ranging from a number of months to many years, was judged to be unjust and its draconian effect was reduced by restricting the period that a wife was forced to wait to four months, after which the husband would be compelled to decide whether to divorce his wife or continue the marriage. *Al-'adl*, a form of divorce in which a husband would divorce his wife by imposing a condition that she could not re-marry without his consent, was also prohibited by the *Qur'an* as an oppressive custom which unjustifiably restricted a woman's right to marry again.[67]

However, in her reappraisal of this period, Ahmed asserts that, during the period of *jahiliya*, there were two trends that dominated marriage customs in the period immediately preceding the advent of Islam in the 7th century.[68] Dividing these traditions into the matrilineal and the patrilineal, Ahmed argues that these two tendencies sat uneasily with each other and reflected contrasting views of the position of women in society, as well as different – and oppositional – configurations of social relations. The matrilineal system allowed for the marriage to take place at the woman's house and classified any children she may have as belonging to her kin group with whom she resided. In addition, the question of paternity was considered to be insignificant and there was an almost total lack of emphasis placed upon the issue of female chastity. In a contrast that was the reverse of this in virtually every respect, the patrilineal system commanded that a woman had to leave her kin group and follow her husband upon marriage and that any children she bore belonged to his family. As the woman would normally have been a spoil of war or purchased from her father, her husband could divorce her unilaterally; he was also able to exercise complete authority over her, a development that appears to have laid the foundation for the type of gender hierarchy that very quickly became entrenched in Islamic doctrine. In contrast to the view of *mut'a* as oppressive to women, feminists such as Mernissi contend that it is a form of marriage that cannot be classified as belonging to either the patrilineal or the matrilineal system, as it appears to accord equal

---

66 *Al-Mujadilah*: 2.

67 'When you divorce your wives and they reach the end of their waiting period and the divorce becomes irrevocable, do not hinder them from marrying their chosen husbands.' (*Al- Baqarah*: 232.)

68 For an early study of marriage in this period, see Stern, G, *Marriage in Early Islam*, 1939, London: Royal Asiatic Society.

rights to men and women.[69] There is also a view that the eventual dominance of the patrilineal over the matrilineal system was guaranteed by the outlawing of the egalitarian *mut'a*,[70] a view in accordance with that of historians who have identified *mut'a* as belonging to a transitional period in which overtly matriarchal features were eliminated while society evolved to a largely patriarchal system.

Writers commenting on the position of women in Arabian society at the time that the *Qur'an* was revealed have concluded that, while it is probable that the *Qur'an* did improve the position of women somewhat, 'it does not seem that the *Qur'an* meant any dramatic upward change for women';[71] others have pointed to the fact that women of certain tribes, who had enjoyed customary rights before, became less free after the imposition of *Qur'anic* law. Furthermore, even in those areas where *Qur'anic* rights were favourable to women, because there was not a universal adoption of these new legal innovations by societies, it has been suggested that women's position did not visibly alter after the emergence of Islam.[72] Keddie and Beck argue that the Arab Muslim conquest of the Middle East resulted in the rapid development of a corpus of Islamic law, which, by incorporating *Qur'anic*, interpretative and older Near Eastern concepts, and by embodying discriminatory customs which pre-dated Islam, gave rise to the subsequent codification of the secondary position of women.[73] A different analysis is offered by Coulsen and Hinchcliffe, who argue, as outlined above, that, under customary tribal law existing at the advent of Islam, women were virtually without status and could be sold into marriage by their guardians, be divorced by their husbands at will and possessed little or no succession rights.[74] Insofar as the rights of

---

69   The *mut'a* was liberating for men and women, as it gave both the freedom to contract such a marriage. It also appears to be associated with a canon of paternity rules that differed from those associated with traditional Muslim marriages: Mernissi, F, *Beyond the Veil: Male-Female Dynamics in a Modern Muslim Society*, 1975, Cambridge, Mass: Shenkman, p 37.

70   See Robertson Smith, W, *Kinship and Marriage in Early Arabia*, 1885, Cambridge: CUP.

71   Keddie, N and Beck, L (eds), *Women in the Muslim World*, 1978, Cambridge, Mass: Harvard UP, p 26.

72   As Mernissi asks: 'Is it possible that Islam's message had only a limited and superficial effect on deeply superstitious 7th century Arabs who failed to integrate its novel approaches to the world and women? Is it possible that the *hijab*, the attempt to veil women, that is claimed today to be basic to Muslim identity, is nothing but the expression of the persistence of the pre-Islamic mentality, the *jahiliyya* mentality that Islam was supposed to annihilate?' (*Op cit*, Mernissi, fn 23, p 81.)

73   Quoted in *op cit*, Ahmed, fn 16, Chapter 3.

74   Coulsen, N and Hinchcliffe, D, 'Women and law reform in contemporary Islam', in *ibid*, Keddie and Beck. Coulsen and Hinchcliffe do acknowledge, however, that there is some controversy attached to this point. Nevertheless, they maintain that the weight of evidence supports their analysis.

women on marriage were concerned, the *Qur'an*[75] radically modified tribal law by introducing innovations such as the direct payment of dower to the wife by the husband, in consideration of the marriage. This change introduced a dramatic change to pre-Islamic society, as, previously, the dower had been paid to the wife's guardian, resulting in the loss of this important payment to the wife. This development had wider implications than the immediate effect of making the wife the sole beneficiary of the dower: it also resulted in a shift in the process of marriage. The parties to the marriage now also became the parties to the marriage contract, allowing the woman to gain important contractual rights. This is in dramatic contrast to the former position, which provided for the husband and the woman's guardian to be parties to the marriage contract, with the wife placed in the position of the object of the contract.

Ahmed[76] argues that, although there was great diversity in the range of marriage practices dominant in 6th century Arabian society, one predominant practice appears to have been the matrilineal uxorilocal marriage. However, despite the existence of this type of marriage and other customs which were advantageous to women, such customs did not connote that women occupied a superior position in society, in terms of either power or economic resources; instead, there is much evidence to point to a highly misogynistic society, of which the most extreme example was the common occurrence of infanticide. The *Qur'anic* prohibition on infanticide is frequently cited as unequivocal evidence, not only of the right to life that Islam bestowed on women, but also for the claim that the position of women *generally* was dramatically improved by the advent of Islam. This is a contentious point for Ahmed, as there is evidence to indicate that women in the *jahiliya* period enjoyed greater sexual autonomy, as shown in such practices as polyandry, and an independence which allowed them to become active participants and, in some cases, leaders in a wide range of community activities. As such, it has been argued that Islam displaced a matriarchal order with a patriarchal one.[77] Alternatively, it has been argued that the tracing of certain pre-Islamic traditions reveals a society that was not explicitly matriarchal in nature, but one which was clearly matrilineal[78] and undergoing a change towards patriliney – a change which

---

75 Indeed, a whole chapter is devoted to the rights and duties of women (*Sura 4, An-Nisa*) and covers, amongst others, issues such as the (then radical) laws on inheritance which deprived men of their former privileges of inheritance. In this respect, men were doubly affected: their inherited goods were reduced as women could no longer be inherited, and their share of lawful inheritance was diminished, as they now had to divide this between themselves and female beneficiaries.

76 *Op cit*, Ahmed, fn 16, Chapter 4.

77 See *op cit*, Robertson Smith, fn 70, cited in *op cit*, Ahmed, fn 16, p 43.

78 See Montgomery Watt, W, *Muhammad at Medina*, 1956, Oxford: Clarendon, cited in *op cit*, Ahmed, fn 16, p 43.

was consolidated by the advent of Islam. In this respect, Islam was a regressive, rather than a liberating, force and brought about a social transformation which severely restricted women's independence by, *inter alia*, establishing patrilineal, patriarchal marriage as the only legitimate form of marriage.

Other, external factors also played a part in shaping the contours of early Islamic marriage. These included the dissolution of the old nomadic order as a result of commercial expansion, the exposure to, and infiltration of, other cultural influences from neighbouring societies as diverse as Iran, Yemen and Ethiopia, and the presence of monotheistic religions. These other religions, which had gained some predominance in adjoining regions, meant that the movement towards monotheism, patrilineal marriage, male control of women's sexuality and the accompanying exclusion of women from public affairs were all manifestations of a process which had been developing well before the introduction of Islam. In this context, the laws that were instigated in the centuries immediately after the inception of Islam, far from bringing about an improvement for women, marked a decline in the rights and egalitarian conditions enjoyed by women. However, it is important to note that this decline constituted a continuing trend which had already been established by other socio-religious systems, in particular, Christianity. Islam, therefore, acted as a crystallising force for such developments by selectively legitimising or prohibiting existing customs which accorded with the emerging values and institutions of Islam. Of central importance to the 'new' Islamic institution of marriage were relatively well established customs such as polygyny and, perhaps most importantly, the question of paternity, which was to become a fundamental tenet of the Islamic message. These developments re-drew dramatically the contours of the relationship between the sexes and laid the foundation for the subsequent inequality, enshrined in law, that came to characterise the hierarchical structure of marriage.[79]

This historical analysis of the development of marriage and the attendant ambiguity of early Islam must be set against those *Qur'anic* verses dealing with marriage. These can be divided into two main categories. First, there are those that clearly envisage marriage as an institution which affords equal rights to men and women and, thus, implement a vision of marriage which corresponds with the 'ethical voice' expounded by feminists such as Ahmed. An example of this is the following unequivocal verse: 'Wives have rights corresponding to those which the husbands have, in equitable reciprocity.'[80] In a similar vein are those related verses which allow polygyny in such circumscribed circumstances as to virtually outlaw it, and other verses which

79 *Op cit*, Ahmed, fn 16, p 45.
80 *Al-Baqarah*: 229.

explicitly condemn the practice of male unilateral divorce. In contrast are those verses privileging men, which appear to contradict and even subvert this ethical vision of equality by sanctioning unconditional polygyny ('marry of other women as may be agreeable to you, two or three, or four')[81] and sexual relations (without marriage) with slave girls and allow men the prerogative to divorce at will. These latter, conflicting sections of the *Qur'an* are infused with the 'pragmatism' that was considered necessary at the time in order to deflect opposition and appease influential detractors who were critical of the loss of their rights over marriage and sexual relations and of the granting of new, extensive rights to women on marriage. Applying the new interpretive methodologies, outlined above, offers an interpretation of the *Qur'an* which allows feminists to re-evaluate the scriptural basis of the law of marriage. The variety of feminist interpretations, incorporating new historical analyses, improved textual approaches and methodologies, are testimony to the plurality of contemporary Islamic feminist debates. The objective of developing a scripture-based interpretation, which incorporates gender equality as an integral aspect of new configurations of Islamic law, is an important facet of Muslim feminist debate, placing feminist discourse at the heart of contemporary Islamic reformism.

---

81 *Al-Nisa*: 5.

CHAPTER 11

JUDGING WOMEN: RETHINKING SHAME THROUGH CORPOREALITY

Judy Purdom

shame	ignominy or disgrace; a painful emotion resulting from having done something dishonourable, unworthy, degrading ... indecent (Collins English Dictionary)
awra	shameful, imperfect, female genitals, female hair, female voice ... something that must be covered, indecent (Arabic)
scham	shame, modesty ... indecent (German)
scham-haare	pubic hair (German)
scham-lippen	the lips of the vulva (German)

INTRODUCTION

Rape trials are horrible. So is non-consensual penetration of the vagina by the penis. It is assault. Violation. And yet, it is the victim of rape who feels ashamed. Dirty. Why is it that rape is equated with degradation and shame? What conception of women and the body does such shame assume? These questions are central to the issue of how women are judged, and point to rape as a concern of standards as much as of assault. Shame is an implicit judgment against the complainant who is made to feel dishonourable, unworthy ... indecent. Tart. This is particularly obvious in the humiliation that women so often suffer in rape trials; trials which, as the case of Julia Mason demonstrates, become as much a judgment of the woman complainant and her honour as of the man and rape.[1]

In 1996, Julia Mason waived her right to anonymity in order to challenge the treatment she had received in court, and provoked a barrage of reports, comments and discussion, including the Home Office Report, *Speaking Up for*

---

1   This case, and the ensuing debate on rape trials, was widely discussed in the national newspapers. See, eg, Langdon-Down, G (1998) *The Guardian,* 21 July; Birkett, D (1998) *The Guardian,* 4 August; (1998) *The Guardian,* 27 October, where Jennifer Temkin (Professor of Law, University of Sussex) gives a summary of her public lecture, 'Justice in rape trials'. The humiliation of rape victims is not a new issue. Indeed, it was more than 20 years ago that public concern prompted an inquiry, chaired by High Court Judge Dame Rose Heilbron, and then the Sexual Offences (Amendment) Act 1976. This aimed at safeguarding women against 'irrelevant' questioning on their sexual history and provided anonymity for victims.

Justice,[2] and a critique of rape trials by barrister Vera Baird.[3] The Julia Mason case was, it would seem, a most straightforward case: the nightmare scenario of rape by a complete stranger. *R v Edwards*. Innocent v Monster. Mason was approached by Ralston Edwards at a bus stop, bundled into an alleyway and raped. There was no question of consent, and no 'grey' areas of familiarity or provocation. Even so, Mason was questioned for six days by Edwards, who defended himself, and subjected her to such an ordeal of questioning that Mason summarised the trial with the question, 'Why did they let him rape me again?'. It was not a rhetorical question, as the extensive news coverage and subsequent reports show. An interesting debate ensued, and questions were raised which complicate the stereotypical 'innocent v monster' model of rape and which disrupt the positioning of both 'innocent' and 'monster'. Rape is not so simple.

In her report, Baird noted that most rapes are perpetrated by people known to the victim: friends or relatives. Indeed, Baird records that half of the rapes in her study of 1998 were within intimate relationships, compared with only 35% in 1985. Again, the stereotype is by no means standard. 'Date rape', rape within marriage and male rape all complicate the model. But, what is indisputable is that women are not being protected by the law. Baird admitted that wrong acquittals are systemic in rape trials. Judgment is loaded against women. Women, it seems, are the ones who are being judged and who carry the burden of shame. If she is not innocent, she is slut and whore. She should be ashamed of herself.

A second point made in the report is perhaps the more crucial. The Baird report argued that the complainant's past history may be relevant and must be allowed in evidence, in order to forestall the very assumptions about women which position her as innocent, vulnerable and in need of protection – like the equation of youth with virginity, or of marriage with monogamy – and which might undermine the defence.[4] The danger is that if she is not positioned as child, she is temptress. Indecent. Never an independent woman with a voice of her own. Always either ashamed or shameful.

---

2 *Report of the Interdepartmental Working Group on the Treatment of Vulnerable or Intimidated Witnesses in Criminal Justice*, 1998, London: HMSO. The Report, produced by a Working Party set up by Jack Straw, Home Secretary, puts forward proposals to improve the treatment of rape complainants in court.

3 Baird, V, *Rape in Court*, 1998, London: Society for Labour Lawyers.

4 The Court of Appeal overturned a conviction against the rape of a 14 year old girl because her defence depended on the assumption of her virginity. New South Wales operates a 'rape shield', setting down specific occasions for such cross-examination. In Canada, the Criminal Code bans questions about reputation but sets judicial guidelines aimed at balancing the rights of defence against rights of privacy and dignity.

Women are not necessarily models of femininity; chaste, faithful or pure. Men are not all monsters. This point was reiterated by journalist Dea Birkett in an article for *The Guardian*, in which she argued that the protection against intrusive questioning and of anonymity afforded by the Sexual Offences (Amendment) Act 1976 worked against women being recognised as full and equal citizens.[5] Are women too feeble to stand up to the adversarial process? Too pathetic to face their alleged attacker? When women are excused from the trawl of cross-questioning; or when they remain silent, too traumatised to give evidence; or, as proposed by the Home Office Report of June 1998, they give evidence by video link, they are situated as 'damaged, blubbering women, pitched against hardened rapists'. They are positioned as children – 'incapable, vulnerable, needing guidance', and the accused is portrayed as monster. This, Birkett claims, compromises the defence. The accused must be assumed innocent until proved guilty, so let both parties have their say, and let the jury decide. But, that is not so easy. What Birkett fails to recognise is that, as I hope to demonstrate, equal citizenship is just what women don't have. They remain under the 'protection' and definition of the standard of men. As 'child', she is ashamed and silent; as whore, she is shameful, and that indecency tempers her complaint of rape. There is both the shame *for* women and the shame *of* women. On both counts she is sub-standard. Where is her voice?

In her extensive work on feminism and sociability, notably in the collection of essays, *Imaginary Bodies*, philosopher and feminist theorist Moira Gatens identifies the paradox of women's position in liberal democratic societies. They are at once free citizens, members of the body politic and under the 'natural' authority of men, a paradox which goes some way to explaining the continuing denigration of women and their equation with shame.[6] Gatens observes that, whilst human rights determines women to be free and rational members of the political body, the very structure of democratic liberal sociability determines women as subordinate to the 'standard' man. Women are by no means equal.

In my discussion of shame here, I extend Gatens' argument to show how the shame of being a woman, a shame that is a shame of the body as much as of behaviour, doubles women's already subordinate position as pre-rational and unsociable. I go on, using Deleuze, to explore how that shame is implicit in the shame of being human, by which I mean the shame that what we glibly call 'democracy' requires the dominance of a majority and, thus, a collusion and compromise of that democracy in the exclusion of the minority. Women are one of the excluded.

---

5   (1998) *The Guardian*, 4 August.

6   See Gatens, M, 'Power, ethics and sexual imaginaries', in *Imaginary Bodies*, 1996, London: Routledge, p 136.

The paradox of democracy might help us to understand why, when a woman such as Julia Mason has been undoubtedly raped, she is 'raped again' in court. The fact is, as Gatens points out, women are not full members of the body politic and do not have equal political right. That prejudice allows men to assert what she calls 'an unequal natural right'.[7] Gatens illustrates this with a rape case of 1992, this time a case of marital rape.[8] Summing up this case, Bollen J advised the jury that 'experience has taught the judges that there have been cases where women have manufactured or invented false allegations'.[9] Two key issues then emerged: the generalisation of women as a class of witness, and a disreputable one at that; and the fine line between persuasion and coercion, between intercourse and rape. The ensuing furore led the Australian Court of Criminal Appeal to rebuke Bollen's warning of possible false allegation with a direction that it is indeed erroneous in law for the judge to position the complainant as a member of a 'class of suspect witnesses'. Women's individual right, as citizens, to a fair and unprejudiced trial was upheld. However, at the same time, man's 'natural' right was defended. Bollen J's decision that 'rougher than usual handling' was an acceptable 'persuasion' to intercourse was upheld and the husband was acquitted of rape. 'No' means 'yes', and the husband's right over his wife remains sacrosanct. As Gatens stresses, what is clear here is that it is the experience of the judge that is binding, and that experience prevails as the normative attitude towards women and sets the standard by which women are judged. Women are classed as sub-standard and are under the 'natural' authority of men, and shame is symptomatic of the parallel exclusion from the body politic.

In an adversarial system which is adjudicated in line with the 'experience' of the judge, an experience which, after all, is an exclusively male experience, women as complainants have to prove not only the guilt of the defendant, but their own 'innocence'. That innocence is equated with a certain normative perception of woman, a norm that situates woman as being under man's natural right. Judgment is made on two levels. 'Within' the system, she is shamed and silenced as a dubious witness and a vulnerable being in need of protection; if she dares to speak up, she is brazen hussy or disrespectful wife, and undeserving of a place within the body politic. The fact of assault is weighed against the culpability of the woman. She is shamed, not because she has been violated, but because she has failed to live up to the expected behavioural norms of femininity expected of her sex: modesty and compliance, decency and chastity. Wifeliness. As a free citizen, she has the

---

7   *Op cit*, Gatens, fn 6, p 136.
8   *R v Johns* (1993) 59 SASR 214; (1993) 66 A Crim R 259.
9   *Op cit*, Gatens, fn 6, p 137.

right to privacy and dignity; under the authority of men, she has neither. Even her body is not her own.[10]

But, why should women be shamed or ashamed? Need shame only be a mark of suppression? Maybe that shame could be a source of strength and a possible impetus to exposing and then resisting the paradoxical exclusion of women from the body politic. Shame typifies that exclusion because of its equation of women with all that is indecent or unworthy and, importantly, with an unsociability that is not admitted into human rights. That unsociability is also equated with the pre-rational and with the body. That body must be covered and the voice silent as the price of women's tacit inclusion in the body politic. The association of shame with the female body leaves us in no doubt as to what is indecent. The immodest; the female voice, the female body. Already, women are judged. Her body covered and her voice silenced. Shame is being humiliated – and excluded. But does it have to be this way? What if women won't keep quiet?

There are, I suggest, two sides to shame. Shame that keeps women hidden, and shame that begs the question of a possible political resistance to the norms and standards that regulate and exclude women from the body politic. Using the work of Gatens and Deleuze, I propose that shame could be a catalyst in creating a new way of thinking about women, where women are understood as autonomous and free from the male domination standards of our so called democracies.

Gatens' project centres on a consideration of the representation of the human body and how that is played out in social, moral and political theory. She successfully exposes the structural bias against women and how her sexual, social and political possibilities are captured and curtailed, and she goes on to consider the possibility of a more ethical sociability. Shame may be a useful impetus to that liberation.

In both *What is Philosophy?* and the collection of conversations, *Negotiations*, Deleuze puts forward shame as one of the most powerful motifs of philosophy. He goes so far as to claim that it is shame that forces philosophy to be political philosophy: 'This is one of the most powerful incentives towards philosophy, and it's what makes all philosophy political.'[11] There is no way to escape shame and the 'ignoble', but philosophy might set up a resistance to that ignominy by thinking *before* shame. The aim is to critique the structure that produces shame and to construct a model that, because it is active *before* shame, does not allow that degradation. This is what

---

10 It might be interesting to compare cases of male rape. Does a man provoke rape by being insufficiently masculine? Or by being too feminine and making himself vulnerable to the to the right of male domination? I would suggest that, in both female and male rape, the issue is one of gender misplacement.

11 Deleuze, G and Guattari, F, *What is Philosophy?*, 1994, London: Verso, p 110; Deleuze, G, *Negotiations 1972–1990*, 1995, New York: Columbia UP, p 172.

liberation really means – to be unashamed. Shame is to be a slave; to be unashamed is to be free. Indeed, Nietzsche already defines liberation with a reference to shame: '"What is the seal of liberation?" – No longer being ashamed in front of oneself.'[12] Perhaps feminist theory should also reference shame. The starting point is the return to the voice of women and a corporeality that is covered and indecent – that is shamed.

THE SHAME OF WOMAN

There are many shames. Deleuze lists several in his own short essay on shame in literature.[13] There is the shame of dependence and of servitude; the shame of the body; and the shame of the democrat whose 'glory' is snatched from him by the suffering of the compromised. There is a shame that haunts democracies.[14] There is always shame, always that which is not fitting and indecent, apartheid being perhaps the most grotesque and overt example of the compromise of democracy; the shame of women being another. As we shall see, shame reflects the perversity of democracy – that a fraternity of citizens dominates the mass of common people. However, as the language of shame so clearly demonstrates, the most essential shame is the shame that women are bound to, the shame of the body. The dishonourable, the indecent and the improper are not only social and political positions but a judgment against corporeality – the voice, the hair, the genitals. The female body.

Shame is indicative of what Gatens signals as the 'juridical view' of sociability. It is a hierarchical organisation, where powers and capacities are compounded by social norms and moral judgments. Everyone in their place. Everyone a type. What kind of judgment can women expect under such a system? Deleuze links judgment with the Judeo-Christian tradition, a human tradition obsessed by moralism:

> At bottom, a doctrine of judgment presumes that the gods give *lots* to men, and that men, depending on their lots, are fit for some particular *form*, for some particular organic *end*.[15]

He cites Nietzsche, DH Lawrence, Kafka and Artaud as authors who defy this moralism and who resist judgment in order to move beyond such a restrictive human form. Part of that project is a certain immoralism and a different understanding of the body. Gatens takes up the challenge in relation to feminism.

---

12 Nietzsche, F, *The Gay Science*, 1974, New York: Random House.
13 Deleuze, G, 'The shame and the glory: TE Lawrence', in *Essays Critical and Clinical*, 1998, London: Verso.
14 *Op cit*, Deleuze and Guattari, fn 11, p 107.
15 Deleuze, G, 'To have done with judgement', in *ibid*, fn 13, p 128. Emphasis in original.

Clearly, the juridical model of sociability expresses a peculiarly human concept of the body. Briefly, it is one that privileges the mind over the body and one where the body is positioned as a pre-representational 'chaotic' nature that must be tamed. The particular alignment of women with that nature inevitably situates her, too, as essentially indecent, even inhuman. And, when women do not shape up to their allotted form and do not fulfil their function within the prescribed human organisation, they are shamed. Indecent. The denigration of women in rape cases is an unsavoury reminder of that positioning. Gatens usefully summarises this juridical model as one of 'capture' and 'utility'.[16] Women are 'captured' within a peculiarly human organisation that aligns man with the rational mind and woman with a pre-representational body. She is 'utilised' under male authority and given a specific form and function that defines her in relation to men: she is wife or mother, virgin or whore. Inspired by Deleuze's question, 'What is the difference between the society of human beings and the community of rational beings?', Gatens takes up Deleuze's interest in an ethical sociability, a sociability which does not depend on heirarchical relations that serve some 'organic end'. She critiques liberal democracy and then goes on to develop a more equitable political model.

The foundation of the juridical view is liberal humanism; a liberalism which, despite the Enlightenment cry of 'Liberty! Equality! Fraternity!', depends on a violence against the body and against women. It depends on shame. The conception of the body at work here is one where the body is understood as a 'natural' that must be overcome. It depends on an essentially dualist conception of being: on the one hand, there is a 'bodily' nature that is self-interested, envious and competitive, unsociable, individualistic and disorganised; on the other, man's superior rationality. There is nature, and there is a transcendent plane that organises and socialises that nature.[17] The unsociable acts as a drive to rationalisation, so that democratic agreements and compromises are made for the sake of stability and 'progress'. In short, the pre-human unsociability, of which women are a part, is overcome by dint of reason, and thus man is a self-determined product of his own organisation. This is what being human means: civilisation, organisation and the suppression of the specificity of the body. The privilege of the mind over body. The democratic organisation of society. Rules, norms and the penal code are informed by this particular human ontology and thus reflect the hierarchy of mind over body, man over woman and, backed up by the 'truths' of biological norms and other discursive sciences, civil, social and economic structures are all equally 'reasonable' – and equally unequal. We can see, then, that, within the juridical model, sociability is driven by the compromises that govern

---

16 *Op cit*, Gatens, fn 6, p 108.
17 Gatens, M, 'Through a Spinozist lens: ethology, difference, power', in Patton, P (ed), *Deleuze: A Critical Reader*, 1996, Oxford: Blackwell, p 165.

'human' democratic society. One of those compromises is woman, and it is as such that she is judged. The organisation demands it.

Within this discursive sociability, judgment always relates to the pre-existing values of the humanist liberal tradition and is necessarily sexist. The experience of the judge is likewise governed by the sexist precedent of the 'reasonable' overlay of norms and functions. Following this precedent, the formal judgment of the court cannot but replicate the positioning of women in other discursive 'democratic' constructions – civil, social and economic. What is being judged? Conformity to the organisation and its organic end. And conformity requires that women be modest, decent and quiet. She is tamed; like the body. That is her lot, and judgment proceeds within that human order. It is essentially reactive.

François Zourabichvili traces Deleuze's renunciation of judgment as reactive and as nihilism: judgment, he says:

> ... consists in treating the entirety of the visible as material for surveying rather than educating, always relating it to something else, the memory of the latent content that explains it, the pre-existent values according to which it is assessed.[18]

Understanding judgment as surveying is useful and might go some way to understanding the judicial obsession with the most minute of evidence and the consequent harassment of women in rape cases. It is as if the more one surveys, the more one knows, the more accurate the assessment of the individual against transcendent norms and the more 'reasonable' the judgment. But what is clear from the institutionalisation of sexism within liberal democracy is that such 'surveying' is an inquisition that can only exacerbate women's failings. Within this system, the penal code and judgment is an agent of social control which reinforces democratic norms and functions, and then somehow penalises women for failing in their responsibility towards a body politic that they are already compromised by.

Man is the model. The female remains unsociable and unorganised. She is silenced by her reduction to the unreasonable, the pre-human and the animal; she is vixen, bitch, shrew ... tart. As an example of this gagging, Gatens cites Mary Wollstonecraft (1792), who, in trying to address the issue of women's political rights, was called a 'hyena in petticoats' by Walpole.[19] Liberal politics is built on the subordination of woman and her exclusion from its organisation, so, obviously, any bid for rights that admits that sexism is a compromise on equality. How does feminism deal with this situation? From the point of view of feminist theory, there are three distinct waves of feminism, but all work within a body/mind binary that shames the body as

---

18 Zourabichvili, F, 'Notes on the percept (on the relation between the critical and the clinical', in *op cit*, Patton, fn 17, p 124.

19 Gatens, M, 'Corporeal representation', in *op cit*, fn 6, p 24.

pre-rational and, therefore, pre-representational. This model assumes that the body is something that must be overcome and covered, and in this sense it maintains a juridical view. It is this scenario that Gatens challenges.

The juridical view maintains a strict body/mind binary. This is reflected in the sex/gender distinction that maps gender onto sex, the male onto the masculine and the female onto the feminine. The body is thus understood as a pre-representational body and this materialism, even biologism, is perpetuated by feminist theory in both the bid for equality and the bid for difference. The bid for equality which was characteristic of first wave feminism demanded that feminists free themselves from any essential sexed determination and asserted the sex/gender distinction in order to theorise gender differences as a representational overlay imposed on otherwise equal bodies. This analysis held onto the notion of mind/body split and the Enlightenment idea of the essential pre-representational body being overlayed by transcendental values. What it failed to do was understand the point that Gatens forcefully makes: that gendering is rooted in the sexed sociability of the modern political structure and the 'masculine confederation', or, as Carol Pateman neatly calls it, the 'fraternal patriarchy'.[20] As we have seen, those values privileged a 'male' rationality, and, by outlawing any essential bodily difference, feminists played into the hand of the dominant rationale. The second wave feminist theory, with its emphasis of 'different but equal', returns to the question of the body but still works with a model of the pre-representational body. Again, the emphasis is on representation, rights and equality, and continues the debate about the sex/gender distinction and the mechanism of gendering. Diametrically opposed approaches emerge; either the body and sex is an independent determining essence or sex is a product of the mind and an effect of an idealist representation. In either case, the body marks the polarity between materialism and representation.

The notion of a pre-representational body has been challenged by a third wave feminism, as in the work of Judith Butler, for instance, which attempts to think the beyond notions of sameness and difference and to understand the body as having a force which marks that representation. Again, the attention is on language and representation. Where gender is a function of self-determination, gender, rather than sex, is central, and sex becomes an effect of an ideal, disembodied, voluntary and arbitrary representation. This third

---

20 Gatens, M, 'Sociability and inclusion', in Caine, B *et al* (eds), *Australian Feminism: A Companion*, 1999, Melbourne: OUP, p 302. This article includes a section headed 'The sexual contract', where Gatens discusses Pateman's response (*The Sexual Contract*, 1988, Cambridge: Polity) to Rousseau's text, *The Social Contract*, in which Rousseau conflates the liberal individual with the masculine individual. For a discussion of the way that new moves in Australian feminism radicalise the sex/gender distinction, see Colebrook, C, 'From radical representations to corporeal becomings: the feminist philosophy of Lloyd, Grosz and Gatens' (2000) 15(2) Hypatia (special issue).

model shows up the human as a peculiarly fragile construct and begs the question of what expression the body might take when it is not subject to an oppressive organisation. However, it fails to extricate women from the shame of the body.

Butler develops her work on performativity as a critique of the sex/gender distinction. In Butler's model, the body exists before, but is only thought after, the event of representation. The thought of the body is, then, not so much as an effect of the event of discourse, but the representational as *performative* and productive. Its status as non-discursive is a logical effect of positing, and it is perceived as material through an idealist positing and known through language as a material reality 'outside' the ideality of representation. The issue of the body therefore remains one of language and maintains a matter/representation dichotomy, where sex is understood as a product of gender attribution subsequent to the performance of those attributes. Gender remains an ideality and sex a material reality. The feminist concern is, again, the question of gender and representation – of rights. As Claire Colebrook astutely points out in her review of moves in Australian feminist philosophy, this idealist model has the same political and ontological problems as biologism/materialism.[21] There is still the sexed sociability that underpins the hierarchical sexism of liberal politics. The body is a function of the mind, and how you represent the body is a mark of your sociability. The body, and women, are still shamed, still covered, still 'captured' and 'utilised'. It is still a juridical system, and the paradox of women's position as both inside and outside the body politic still holds. Feminism has failed to disentangle itself from an essentially sexist model of liberal democracy. So much for rights.

As Colebrook notes, there is a parallel to the body/mind dualism in the sex/gender distinction that has preoccupied, even grounded, feminist thinking. The denial of the specificity of nature has led to a philosophy focused on questions of reason, of language and representation and the discourses of gender, and an ethics of autonomy and self-determination. The concern is with rights, emancipation and equality. The human body is a disembodied body and a consideration of corporeality bypassed. When liberal values are proved to be governed by a male dominated reason, it is clear that women are precisely what the language of Old English tells us: wife – *wifmann*, *wimman* or wo-man. Along with nature and corporeality, woman is that which is refused, shamed and veiled.[22] The long fought for democratic right of women to be full and active members of the body politic is countered by the 'natural', or, more accurately, the 'reasonable', right of man's authority. Gatens' paradox holds.

---

21 *Op cit*, Colebrook, fn 20.

22 The Old English *wif* is related to the Old Norse *vif*, a word possibly derived from *vifathr*, 'veiled'.

What is interesting is the irony that, in a democratic sociability that is rigidly organised and kept under strict surveillance, it is the male majority that is subservient to peculiarly human hierarchies and values. It is the majority that is dominated, while, as we shall see, the minority that falls outside this organisation because of its association with a body or nature that is overcome by reason are the ones who are curiously free.

SHAME AT BEING HUMAN

Deleuze argues that there is great shame at being human. The shame of the spectacular failure of the democratic State and of human rights. The shame of an exclusory body politic. The shame of the poor, the illiterate, the Indian, the Arab; the shame of women, and the Jew. Shame for those who have no voice; the aphasic and the acephalous.[23]

Deleuze cites Primo Levi, who, in his many autobiographical novels and poems, so keenly articulates his shame of having survived the Holocaust. Levi describes shame as a composite feeling: shame that men could have done this, shame that we haven't prevented it, shame at having been demeaned and diminished, shame at having survived. Shame of having colluded and compromised oneself in order to survive. Shame at being human.[24] Each democrat, though not responsible for Nazism, is nevertheless, by their very survival, tainted by it.

Deleuze is quick to point out that it is not just the extreme situation of the Holocaust that prompts this shame at being human, but the everyday 'meanness and vulgarity' of society:

> We also experience it in insignificant conditions, before the meanness and vulgarity of existence that haunts democracies, before the propagation of these modes of existence and of thought-for-the-market, and before the values, ideals, and opinions of our time.[25]

This thought is supplemented by a further discussion of shame in *Negotiations*, in the interview entitled 'Control and becoming', where he finds shame in the derisory circumstances that haunt our times; in the vulgarity of thought; in popular television; in the speeches of government ministers; and in talk of the good things in life.[26] Shame in a life driven by the market. Clearly, shame is a

---

23 For Deleuze's references to shame, see *op cit*, Deleuze and Guattari, fn 11, p 107 *et seq*. See, also, *op cit*, Deleuze, fn 10, p 115. Deleuze references Artaud as a voice 'for' minorities: 'Artaud said: to write *for* the illiterate – to speak for the aphasic, to think for the acephalous.' (Page 109.)

24 Levi, P, *The Drowned and the Saved*, 1986, London: Abacus. See *op cit*, Deleuze and Guattari, fn 11, pp 107, 225 fn 17.

25 *Op cit*, Deleuze and Guattari, fn 11, p 107.

26 *Op cit*, Deleuze, fn 11, p 172.

political issue. The 'success', even the livelihood, of some demanding the 'failure', even the exclusion, of others. Hence the control and management of the poor, of ghettoisation and shanty-towns; of the police and armies who secure the rights or, should we say, comfort of the 'majority'.[27] Shame at our collusion.

What is clear in these examples is that it is the survival and comfort of the few that this exclusory sociability defends. The determining 'majority', the white-Western-Christian-heterosexual-adult-male, so often 'the American', is far outnumbered by the suffering, vulgar 'minority'.[28] The 'vulgar' are the mass of common people.[29] So much for democracy. As Deleuze and Guattari stress in the plateau 'Postulates of linguistics' in *A Thousand Plateaus*, the opposition between majority and minority is not an issue of quantity. The majority holds the weight of determination. It serves as the standard measure. So, where the standard is the 'white-Western-Christian- …', that man holds the majority, 'even if he is less numerous than mosquitos, children, women, blacks, homosexuals, etc'.[30] This 'normalisation' creeps into and pervades the everyday. For example, Gatens observes that, though human bodies are diverse, many anatomical illustrations of the human body turn out to be depictions of white, male bodies; a standard enshrined in language, in the indiscriminate use of the pronoun 'he', in terms such as chairman, and, indeed, in the very word woman. Philosophers are certainly always assumed to be men! The majority dictates 'the order of things'; it 'implies a constant of expression and content serving as a standard measure by which to evaluate it'.[31] The minority is, then, that which is different and constitutes a sub-system or 'outsystem'. Deviation. Unsociability. It is not just that these people are segregated; they are missing. Inhuman. Missing precisely because they exist as a minority. Like stolen children.[32]

Free from the axiomatic of the majority, the minority, as an 'outsystem', might be in a position of strength. Ironically, it is the majority that is dominated because they are the ones subjected to the model. They are the ones under pressure from the market and subject to the heinous values and

---

27 *Op cit*, Deleuze and Guattari, fn 11, p 107.

28 (1999) *The Observer*, 5 September reports that 'California will next year become the first "minority-majority" US State, with white people in the minority'.

29 From the Latin *vulgus*, 'the common people'; *vulgaris*, 'belonging to the multitude'.

30 Deleuze, G and Guattari, F, *A Thousand Plateaus*, 1988, London: Althone, p 105.

31 *Ibid*.

32 Lloyd, G, 'No-one's land: Australia and the philosophical imagination' (2000) 15(2) Hypatia (special issue) 26. The State Children's Act 1895 recommended that children who were 'neglected' or 'destitute' would be removed from their families. Under this provision, thousands of Aboriginal children were 'stolen' and placed with non-indigenous families or in homes. This policy of 'protection' amounted to cultural genocide; the stolen children meant that Aboriginal peoples were not only missing but exterminated.

opinions of current times. The minority, by definition, escape that model and subjection. They are the autonomous ones. Here, then, is here the potential for political resistance. Deleuze and Guattari propose the 'minorisation' of politics. As Daniel Smith explains in his excellent introduction to Deleuze's *Essays Critical and Clinical*, 'Minorities have the potential of promoting compositions (connections, convergences, divergences) that do not pass by way of the capitalist economy any more that they do the State formation'.[33] What do Deleuze and Guattari mean by this?

Being rent from the standard and refusing to be an aggregate or State in relation to the majority, the minority resist complicity in the homogeneity and universality of the human – and thus resist positioning as other to the dominant model of the human as male, white and heterosexual. We can see this policy of political resistance in recent moves in feminism which reject separatism in favour of alliances with other minority groups who are, like women, excluded from liberal politics – gays, greens, indigenous peoples, etc. These new alliances re-focus the whole issue of rights. Gatens identifies this move as a move from a politics of individual rights to a radical rethinking of the idea of the body politic. As she explains in her article, 'Sociability and inclusion', rather than work for inclusion within what is historically an exclusive democratic organisation, feminists are now looking for a model which does not depend on the *a priori* exclusion on which liberalism depends:

> [Rather,] they refuse a set of ideas (rather than a type of person) that selfishly seeks to enhance the freedoms at the expense of others. Put differently, it could be said that some persons, through their subscription to an unsociable politics, voluntary exclude themselves from those social movements striving to attain an inclusive form of sociability.[34]

Gatens, like Deleuze and Guattari, now understands exclusion as a position of strength, precisely because the very unsociability of exclusion is a variable that threatens the stability of juridical organisation, norms and functions. Rather than grounding feminism on the sex/gender distinction and developing strategies of sociability and inclusion, the new Australian feminism of Gatens and of Genevieve Lloyd questions the usefulness of that sex/gender distinction and develops a Spinozist/Deleuzian model of the body for which unsociability is productive because it forces new 'ethical' compositions of the body politic.[35]

---

33 *Op cit*, Deleuze, fn 13, p xviii.

34 *Op cit*, Gatens, fn 20, p 302.

35 For an overview of new moves in Australian philosophy and feminism, see (2000) 15(2) *Hypatia* (special issue). This issue includes important work by Genevieve Lloyd, Moira Gatens and Ros Diprose, as well as contributions from a new generation of thinkers, including Linnell Secomb, Claire Colebrook and Barb Bolt.

However, an unsociable, 'minority' politics of resistance does not mean that we should dismiss the struggle for political recognition, even the struggle to become a majority. Yes, fight 'as a woman' for work rights and status: for the vote, for abortion, for jobs and childcare. Claim a status, history and subjectivity 'as women'. But, remember that these campaigns are for a heterosociable 'equality' that will always be a compromise with the exclusory, male dominàted concept of the human. Human rights are man's right. For Deleuze and Guattari, these 'sociable' struggles are an index of a more profound, unsociable 'subterranean combat' and the promotion of a more equitable, autonomous body. The minoritisation of politics.

Alongside the fight for rights 'as women', Deleuze and Guattari advocate the more radical women's politics that disrupts the organisation of woman into the prescribed norms and functions characterised by her designation as 'virgin' or 'whore', or as animal and unsociable body. This politics usurps those standards and 'slips into a molar confrontation, and passes under or through them'.[36] Rather than be controlled, woman must use her unsociability to become uncontrollable and autonomous. This movement is the creation of what Deleuze and Guattari enigmatically call becoming-woman.

The task is not to be woman, because that can only mean denigration and domination, and to be ashamed *of* the body and *for* the body, *of* woman and *for* woman. The task is to create a body *before* woman, before her capture, organisation and utility *as* woman. This is what Deleuze and Guattari mean when, in *A Thousand Plateaus*, they challenge us to make ourselves a 'Body without Organs' (BwO). It is, after Artaud, a war on the organs: 'To be done with the judgment of God.'[37] Without organisation and the judgment that regulates and confirms norms and functions, the BwO cannot be a concept or a being. It is a practice or set of practices and the process that Deleuze and Guattari call deterritorialisation. The first stage of becoming a BwO is becoming-woman: resisting, disorganising and deterritorialising the status of women 'as woman' in order to think *before* woman.

SHAME BEFORE WOMAN

As in their discussion of minorisation, the examples that Deleuze and Guattari give of becoming-woman are literary examples: DH Lawrence, Henry Miller and Virginia Woolf. 'In writing, they become-women.'[38] Apparently, Woolf was appalled at the idea of writing 'as a woman'. After all, her quest for a 'a room of one's own' is precisely a bid for an identity and a place not

---

36 *Op cit*, Deleuze and Guattari, fn 30, p 276.
37 *Op cit*, Deleuze and Guattari, fn 30, p 150.
38 *Op cit*, Deleuze and Guattari, fn 30, p 276.

determined by man. With that autonomy comes 'a voice of one's own'. Woolf's use of language, her 'stream of consciousness', is read by Deleuze and Guattari as a minor language, by which they mean that she puts standard English, the major language, into variation. Kafka does the same to German. He uses it creatively, causing it to stammer and wail, 'constructing a continuum of variation, negotiating all of the variables both to constrict the constants and to expand the variables'.[39] An important point is that this variation is not in opposition to the majority, but disruptive of it, because it sets up a model which would never produce such dominance. '*Constant is not opposed to variable*; it is a treatment of the variable opposed to the other kind of treatment, or continuous variation.'[40] It is a movement of deterritorialisation that varies the standard. It makes it tremble, and creates new non-standard 'connections, convergences and divergences', and draws from it new compositions: 'cries, shouts, pitches, durations, timbres, accents, intensities.'[41] Instead of the variable being extracted from, universalised, standardised and made constant, the variable is kept in continuous variation. Writing such as that of Woolf takes up the inconstancy of 'womanhood', keeping it in variation and producing a becoming that is a woman. Instead of a concept of woman that only finds meaning in opposition to the standard 'man', the variable is a molecular woman, a practice of becoming-woman 'capable of crossing and impregnating an entire social field, and of contaminating men, of sweeping them up in that becoming'.[42] The variable puts the standard in turmoil. It is anti-juridical.

With the minorisation of language in mind, I want now to turn to the task of political philosophy; in particular, of feminist theory. As we saw earlier, the focus on language and representation characteristic of second and third wave feminism, and its bid for women as 'different but equal', fails to deliver because it remains within the binary of body/mind that aligns woman with the body and the essentially pre-human. To summarise: this model, despite its pretension to democracy and liberalism, puts women in a position of shame. Shame that she is unworthy, shame that she is indecent. The 'majority' is responsible for that designation and, in a 'egalitarian' liberal democracy, feels shame. It admits the shame of woman and feels shame for women in the same way as it is shamed by its exclusion of other 'minorities': the poor, the Indian, the Arab ... the mob. The shamed do not need representation. They need to resist representation. To resist the juridical. And it is resistance that we lack. '*We lack resistance to the present*.'[43] The responsibility of philosophy, as Deleuze understands it, is to create that resistance and to make the standard tremble.

---

39 *Op cit*, Deleuze and Guattari, fn 30, p 104.
40 *Op cit*, Deleuze and Guattari, fn 30, p 103. Emphasis in original.
41 *Op cit*, Deleuze and Guattari, fn 30, p 104.
42 *Op cit*, Deleuze and Guattari, fn 30, p 276.
43 *Op cit*, Deleuze and Guattari, fn 11, p 108. Emphasis in original.

The task, then, is not to speak for women, but to speak *before* them. To produce a becoming-woman. To keep the variable in play and to resist organisation and shame.

It seems that, despite the degradation of shame, shame has a particular place in the task of becoming-woman because it takes us back to the body as something which is uncontrollable and variable. The agony and suffering of woman might yet be her glory, if she is torn away from that shame and freed from the state of affairs which positions and subjects. Clearly, this demands that we rethink the body and understand it, not as an unsociable whose variability must be rationalised, but as a becoming or variable that deterritorialises the sex/gender binary of representation. Instead of an ontology of being and the human, we need an ontology of becoming.

Gatens tries to find a way out of the cul de sac of binarism by rethinking the sex/gender boundary. She takes ontology and the body/corporeality seriously and addresses a key question: 'What is it that gender re-presents?'[44] What is it that is being sexed and gendered? What about the body that is not overlayed? Not subject to organisation? Not shamed?

This return to the body is a response to what she understands, after Deleuze and Guattari, as the 'theft' of the body, a theft achieved through 'the transcendental organisation of her organs into a functional form: receptacle for male desire and progeny which are now conveniently co-implicated'.[45] But, as the original Deleuzian text in *A Thousand Plateaus* makes clear, this is not an issue of the organisational and representational overlay of gender which opposes masculine and feminine, but of the body: 'The question is fundamentally that of the body – the body they steal from us in order to fabricate opposable organs.'[46] This is an issue of a return to the body, but the body rethought beyond the binary that pits body against mind.

After a long incubation, in her later work, Gatens turns to Spinoza and reconsiders the body 'in order to develop a notion of embodiment that posits multiple and historically specific social imaginaries'.[47] This is the notion of embodiment as a variable that we need if we are to produce a becoming-woman that is an active and full member of the body politic. Using a Spinozist model of the body, Gatens rethinks the body/mind opposition that has dominated humanist thinking and denigrated women. Her aim is to develop a

---

44 This question is identified by Claire Colebrook as the question which sets Gatens' critique against other criticisms of the sex/gender distinction, such as that of Judith Butler. See *op cit*, Colebrook, fn 20.

45 *Op cit*, Patton, fn 17, p 176.

46 *Op cit*, Deleuze and Guattari, fn 30, p 276.

47 'The power of Spinoza: feminist conjunctions: Susan James talks to Genevieve Lloyd and Moira Gatens' (1998) 19 WPR 6; (2000) 15(2) Hypatia (special issue) 40. See, also, *op cit*, Gatens, fn 6, p x and Chapter 4.

notion of embodiment that allows us to keep hold of the 'sexual, political or ethical particularity of different bodies'.[48]

Spinoza has a monist model of the body and understands 'the mind as an idea of the body'.[49] So, rethinking the sex/gender distinction through Spinozist monism is an attempt to think through how the body becomes sexed, and how the subject emerges as a subject as a function or production of the body. However, it is not the individual body that we are talking about here. The Spinozist model is a model of the body as a network that extends to legal, social and civic bodies. This body is not an unsociable entity, to be overcome or overlayed by representation, but an embodied body. The model locates sense and meaning at the level of the corporeal, not as the transcendent form that is the disembodied mind of idealism. Here, the body is its modes of practices and engagement; its activity a 'way of life'. The body is a particular bodily existence. The mind is the idea of that body and the affirmation of the actual existence of the body. There is no truth of the body, only a dynamic articulation of the character and manner of its participation. Mobile and variable, it is always becoming; thus fulfilling Gatens' requirement for an embodiment that 'posits multiple and historically specific social imaginaries'.[50] The 'identity' of this body, of becoming-woman, for instance, is, then, a mode of relation and not a passive product of a transcendental overlay. The body is a variable, heterogeneous reality without being a constant or identity. To ask the question of being, 'What?' or 'Who is woman?' no longer makes sense, because there is no fixed reference. The body is not pre-human or pre-political, or an effect of political representation. The body is political. As such, it is anti-juridical. We can only explore the configuration of particular networks that are becoming-woman and ask if they are working or not. Are they ethical? Are they productive? Are they protective of organisation or liberation? Judgment then becomes an issue of ethics rather than morals; and of evaluation, not surveying. What it evaluates is the effectiveness of the civil body, not the individual.[51]

Key to Gatens' new model of the body politic is the idea that the body is always already in a social context and that that context is crucial to how the body can function. There is a shift here from the idea of the body as individual to the body as social and collective, so that freedom and responsibility become a function of the collective, not of the individual. This does not mean that there are no 'standards' or values, only that those values refer to the well being of all its members, not the success of the dominant 'majority'. Where responsibility is not attributed to individuals, the notions of blame and shame

---

48 *Op cit*, WPR, fn 47, p vii.
49 *Op cit*, WPR, fn 47, p 7.
50 *Op cit*, Gatens, fn 4, p 57.
51 See *op cit*, Zourabichvili, fn 18, p 208 for further discussion of the notion of evaluation.

are transferred to the civil body, and it is that body that has the responsibility for the sociability of all its members. This model thus takes the idea of sociability beyond the human.

Two recent cases might serve to illustrate how this model works. As I write, the newspapers report of one case of a 12 year old girl who recently had a baby by her mother's lover, and of another 12 year old who became pregnant by her 14 year old boyfriend.[52] Not surprisingly, the response is outrage. Both are cases of statutory rape. And it is perhaps in response to the fact that children under 13 are not legally able to consent to sex that the broadsheets have been quick to condemn, not the individuals, but the paucity of a social and educational structure that makes pregnancy an attractive proposition for a 12 year old. It seems that the children's very 'innocence' has forced the shame of rape onto the civic body. In an interview with Andrew Rawnsley for *The Observer*, Prime Minister Tony Blair brushed aside the question of prosecution, saying that he did not think that legal authority was the issue:

> The issue is how you could get to a situation where you have 12 year old girls becoming pregnant by 14 year old fathers. That's not in their interests or the interests of the child. We should be asking, 'Why?'.

Indeed we should. But, does Tony Blair recognise social responsibility over that of the individual? Or is it the individual, or their parents, who are culpable? There are two levels of responsibility here: the issue of a 12 year old becoming pregnant in the first place; and the question of their wanting to have and keep the children. On the first count, Tony Blair initiated a 'moral manifesto' and revived the 'traditional family', 'parental responsibility' and the 'practical issues' of sex education, parenting helplines and the like. All solutions that support individual responsibility with Government initiative and which maintain a governmental moral and juridical authority. It seems that one girl wanted to get pregnant and that both girls chose motherhood over abortion – 'to have something to love', said one – decisions that prompted a cutting and perceptive question of responsibility from Carol Sarler writing in *The Observer*: 'The question for the rest of us is this: if 12 year old motherhood is the choice they are making, then what are the options they are rejecting?' This is the question that opens up these rape cases to the broader and more radical concern of social responsibility and the kind of body politic that we want to create. It is something that the Labour Government should take seriously, if it is to achieve what Tony Blair calls the 'social imperative': 'to develop a modern, responsible notion of citizenship.' This cannot be the historical exclusory citizenship of liberalism. To paraphrase Deleuze's *dictum*, 'We are not responsible for the victims, but before them'; we

---

52 All quotes from (1999) *The Observer*, 5 September. The father of the one child was subsequently charged and bailed.

are not responsible for these pregnant girls, but responsible *before* them.[53] In other words, we are responsible for the situation where to have a child at 12 is even a consideration. We are responsible for a body politic that not only admits the rape of children, but makes pregnancy the choice of little girls.

These cases are prime targets for Deleuze's notion of 'clinical' evaluation, an ethical approach that he distinguishes from an authoritative and moralising 'critical' judgment. The idea is to take a symptomatological approach, like a doctor examining a new case: study the signs; distinguish cases and isolate symptoms; and then bring new workable structures of sociability into play.[54] Certainly; a creative solution is what is needed if girls are to become unashamed, by which I mean become free of finding their meaning and purpose, and love only as lovers or as mothers. To become liberated. Education is one such solution; as the adage goes, ambition is a great contraceptive.

Gatens takes an even more pragmatic approach to finding a new sociability, by recognising the problem of unravelling the historical legacy of suppression. Remembering Bollen J's resort to the 'experience' of the judges in adjudicating a case of marital rape in 1992, she firmly believes that women must become full members of the body politic, so that their experience is represented within the collective beliefs, habits and customs that are included in that embodiment:

> The [more] obvious response to the poor treatment that women often receive at the hands of the judiciary is to ensure that the experiences of women are represented at all levels of legal, social and political life. If Spinoza's views on knowledge and imagination are correct, the only means to ensure genuine representation, given our history, is the presence of women from various walks of life.[55]

Her idea is that generalisations, like the stereotype victim v monster model of rape, can be undone by a consideration of multiple, and even contradictory, experiences of the body politic, and it seems that, here, the aspirations of women fighting for individual rights, and those seeking a new model of collective sociability, come together.

The task is to deterritorialise an entrenched system of judgment, where women are degraded, shamed and excluded from the body politic because they are represented as unsociable. They must act before that shame and create a becoming-woman. Certainly, recent statistics show that women are indeed succeeding in that task: more women than men now file for divorce; the number of rapes (not male rape) recorded by the police has gone up

---

53 *Op cit*, Deleuze and Guattari, fn 11, p 108.
54 See Smith's Introduction to *op cit*, Deleuze, fn 10 for further discussion of the symptomatological approach to critique.
55 *Op cit*, Gatens, fn 6, pp 140, 141.

threefold in the last 10 years.[56] In defiance of their shame as women, women are taking a responsibility *before* victimisation. They are resisting the present. They are unashamed.

---

56 The conviction rate over the same period has dropped from 24% to 10%: (1998) *The Guardian*, 21 July.

BIBLIOGRAPHY

Abu Zayd, NH, *Naqd al-Khitab*, 1994, Cairo: Sina lil-Nashr

Adorno, TW and Horkheimer, M, *Dialectic of Enlightenment*, 1973, London: Verso

Ahmad An-Na'im, A, *Toward an Islamic Reformation: Civil Liberties, Human Rights, and International Law*, 1990, Syracuse: Syracuse UP

Ahmed, L, *Women and Gender in Islam*, 1992, New Haven: Yale UP

Ahmed, S *et al* (eds), *Transformations: Thinking Through Feminism*, 2000, London: Routledge

Ahmed, S, 'Intimate touches; proximity and distance in international feminist dialogues' (1997) 19 Oxford Lit Rev 19

Ahmed, S, *Differences that Matter: Feminist Theory and Postmodernism*, 1998, Cambridge: CUP

Al-Afghani, S, *Al-Islam wal Mar'ah*, 1945, Damascus: Tarakki

Al-Azmeh, A (ed), *Islamic Law: Social and Historical Contexts*, 1988, London: Routledge

Al-Azmeh, A, *al-'Almaniyah fi manzur mukhtalif*, 1972, Beirut: Markaz Divasat al-Wahdah al-'Arabiyah

Al-Azmeh, A, *al-'Arab wa-al-barabirah al-muslimun wa-al-hadarat al ukhra*, 1991, London: Riad el-Rayyes

Al-Azmeh, A, *Islams and Modernities*, 1993, London and New York: Verso

Al-Hibrih, A, 'A study of Islamic herstory: or, how did we get into this mess?' (1982) 5(2) Women's Studies Int Forum 207

Alexander, MJ and Mohanty, CT, *Feminist Genealogies, Colonial Legacies, Democratic Futures*, 1997, London: Routledge

Allen, D, 'Homosexuality and narrative' (1995) 41 Modern Fiction Studies 617

al-Nass, M, *Dirasah fi 'Ulum al'Qur'an*, 1990, Beirut: al-Marquaz al Thaqafi al-'Arabi

Andrews, G (ed), *Citizenship*, 1991, London: Lawrence & Wishart

Anscombe, E and Geach, P (ed and trans), *Descartes' Philosophical Writings*, 1972, London: Nelson

Armour, ET, *Deconstruction, Feminist Theology and the Problem of Difference*, 1999, Chicago: Chicago UP

Asher-Greve, JM, 'The essential body: Mesopotamian conceptions of the gendered body' (1997) 9(1) Gender and History 432

Assiter, A, *Althusser and Feminism*, 1990, London: Pluto

Baird, V, *Rape in Court*, 1998, London: Society for Labour Lawyers

Barnett, H, *Sourcebook on Feminist Jurisprudence*, 1997, London: Cavendish Publishing

Barry, B, *Political Argument*, 1976, Atlantic Highlands: New Jersey Humanities

Battersby, C, *Gender and Genius: Towards a Feminist Aesthetics*, 1989, London: The Women's Press

Battersby, C, *The Phenomenal Woman: Metaphysics and the Patterns of Identity*, 1998, Cambridge: Polity

Bawer, B, *A Place at the Table*, 1993, New York: Touchstone

Benhabib, S, Butler, J, Cornell, D and Fraser, N, *Feminist Contentions: A Philosophical Exchange*, 1995, London: Routledge

Benn, SI and Peters, RS, *Social Principles and the Democratic State*, 1959, London: Allen & Unwin

Blond, P (ed), *Post-Secular Philosophy*, 1998, London: Routledge

Bottomley, A and Conaghan, J (eds), *Feminist Theory and Legal Strategy*, 1993, Oxford: Blackwell

Bottomley, A et al, 'Dworkin: which Dworkin?' [1987] JLS 47

Boundas, C and Olkowski, D (eds), *Gilles Deleuze and the Theater of Philosophy*, 1994, New York and London: Routledge

Braidotti, R, *Nomadic Subjects*, 1994, New York: Colombia UP

Braidotti, R, *Patterns of Dissonance*, 1991, Cambridge: Polity

Brecher, B et al, *Nationalism and Racism in the Liberal Order*, 1998, Avebury: Ashgate

Bridgeman, J and Millns, S, *Feminist Perspectives on Law: Law's Engagement with the Female Body*, 1998, London: Sweet & Maxwell

Bright, S and Dewar, J (eds), *Land Law: Themes and Perspectives*, 1998, Oxford: OUP

Burchell, G et al, *The Foucault Effect: Studies in Governmentality*, 1991, Exeter: Harvester Wheatsheaf

Burke, C, Schor N and Whitford, M, *Engaging With Irigaray*, 1994, New York: Columbia UP

Butler, J, *Bodies that Matter: On the Discursive Limits of 'Sex'*, 1993, London: Routledge

Butler, J, *Excitable Speech: A Politics of the Performative*, 1997, London: Routledge

Butler, J and Scott, JW (eds), *Feminists Theorize the Political*, 1992, New York and London: Routledge

Butler, J *et al*, 'The future of sexual difference: an interview with Judith Butler and Drucilla Cornell' (1998) 28(1) Diacritics: A Review of Contemporary Criticism 20

Caine, B *et al* (eds), *Australian Feminism: A Companion*, 1999, Melbourne: OUP

Calder, C (ed), *Liberalism and the Limits of Justice*, 2000, Aldershot: Avebury

Cheah, P and Grosz, E, 'Of being-two: introduction' (1998) 28(1) Diacritics: A Review of Contemporary Criticism 5

Clarke, P, *Deep Citizenship*, 1996, London: Pluto

Clinton, H, 'Remarks for the United Nations: Fourth World Conference on Women', Beijing, China, 5 September 1998, available at www.whitehouse.gov/WH/EOP/First_Lady/9-5-95html

Colebrook, C, 'From radical representations to corporeal becomings: the feminist philosophy of Lloyd, Grosz and Gatens' (2000) 15(2) Hypatia (special issue)

Conaghan, J, 'Revisiting the feminist theoretical project' (2000) 27 JLS 351

Coole, D, 'Is class a difference that makes a difference?' (1996) 77 Radical Philosophy 17

Cooper, D, 'An engaged state: sexuality, governance and the potential for change' (1993) 20 JLS 257

Cooper, D, 'Fiduciary government: decentering property and taxpayers' interests' (1997) 6(2) SLI 235

Cooper, D, 'The Citizens' Charter and radical democracy: empowerment and exclusion within citizenship discourse' (1993) 2 SLS 149

Cornell, D, *At the Heart of Freedom: Feminism, Sex and Equality*, 1998, Chichester: Princeton UP

Cornell, D, *Beyond Accomodation: Ethical Feminism, Deconstruction and the Law*, 1991, New York and London: Routledge

Cornell, D, *The Imaginary Domain: Abortion, Pornography and Sexual Harassment*, 1995, New York and London: Routledge

Cornell, D, *The Philosophy of the Limit*, 1992, New York and London: Routledge

Cornell, D, *Transformations*, 1993, London: Routledge

D'Emilio, J, *Making Trouble*, 2nd edn, 1992, New York: Routledge

Dangerous Bedfellows (eds), *Policing Public Sex*, 1996, Boston: South End

De Beauvoir, S, *The Second Sex*, 1953, London: Cape

Deleuze, G and Guattari, F, *A Thousand Plateaus*, 1988, London: Althone

Deleuze, G and Guattari, F, *Capitalism and Schizophrenia: A Thousand Plateaus*, 1987, Minneapolis: Minneapolis UP

Deleuze, G and Guattari, F, *What is Philosophy?*, 1994, London: Verso

Deleuze, G, *Essays Critical and Clinical*, 1998, London: Verso

Deleuze, G, *Negotiations 1972–1990*, 1995, New York: Columbia UP

Deleuze, G, *The Fold, Leibniz and the Baroque*, 1993, Minneapolis: Minneapolis UP

Derrida, J, 'Declarations of independence' (1982) 15 New Political Science

Derrida, J, 'Force of law: the mystical foundation of authority' (1990) 11 Cardoza L Rev 921

Derrida, J, '*Geschlecht*: sexual difference, ontological difference' (1983) 13 Research in Phenomenology 65

Derrida, J, *Positions*, 1981, Chicago: Chicago UP

Derrida, J, *The Other Heading: Reflections on Today's Europe*, 1992, Bloomington: Indiana UP

Deutscher, P, *Yielding Gender: Feminism, Deconstruction and the History of Philosophy*, 1997, London: Routledge

Drakopoulou, M, 'Law, Crime and Sexuality' (1997) 5(1) FLS 107

Drakopoulou, M, 'Women's resolutions of laws reconsidered: epistemic shifts and the emergence of feminist legal discourse' (2000) 11 LC 47

Duggan, L and Hunter, N, *Sex Wars*, 1995, New York: Routledge

Edwards, S, *Sex, Gender and the Legal Process*, 1996, London: Blackstone

Ellison, N, 'Towards a new social politics: citizenship and reflexivity in late modernity' (1997) 31 Sociology 697

Engineer, AA, *The Rights of Women in Islam*, 1992, London: Hurst

Esposito, JL, *Women in Muslim Family Law*, 1982, Syracuse: Syracuse UP

Evans, D, *Sexual Citizenship*, 1993, London: Routledge

Featherstone, M (ed), *Love and Eroticism*, 1999, London: Sage

Feder, EK, Rawlinson, MC and Zakin, E (eds), *Derrida and Feminism: Recasting the Question of Woman*, 1997, London: Routledge

Fegan, EV, '"Subjects" of regulation/resistance? Post-modern feminism and agency in abortion-decision-making' (1999) 7(3) FLS 241

Fermon, N, 'Women on the global market: Irigaray and the democratic State' (1998) 28(1) Diacritics: A Review of Contemporary Criticism 3

Florence, P and Cornell, D, 'Towards the domain of freedom' (1997) 17 WPR 8

Foucault, M, *Herculine Barbin: Being the Recently Discovered Memoirs of a Nineteenth Century French Hermaphrodite*, McDougall, R (trans), 1980, London: Harvester

Fraser, N, *Justice Interruptus: Critical Reflections on the 'Postsocialist' Condition*, 1997, New York and London: Routledge

Fraser, N and Bartky, S, *Revaluing French Feminism*, 1992, Bloomington: Indiana UP

Frug, MJ, *Postmodern Legal Feminism*, 1992, London: Routledge

Gatens, M, *Imaginary Bodies: Ethics, Power and Corporeality*, 1996, London: Routledge

Gewirth, A, 'Is cultural pluralism relevant to moral knowledge?' (1994) 11 SPP 22

Giddens, A, *The Transformation of Intimacy*, 1992, Cambridge: Polity

Gilligan, C, *In a Different Voice: Psychological Theory and Women's Development*, 1982, Cambridge, Mass: Harvard UP

Gilroy, P, *The Black Atlantic, Modernity and Double Consciousness*, 1993, London: Verso

Gluckman, A and Reed, B (eds), *Homo Economics*, 1997, London: Routledge

Goldstein, J (ed), *Foucault and the Writing of History*, 1994, Oxford: Blackwell

Goodrich, P, 'The critic's love of the law: intimate observations on an insular jurisdiction' (1999) 10(3) LC 343

Guttman, A (ed), *Multiculturalism: Examining the Politics of Recognition*, 1994, Princeton: Princeton UP

Graham, K (ed), *Contemporary Political Philosophy*, 1982, Cambridge: CUP

Grosz, E, *Jacques Lacan: A Feminist Introduction*, 1990, London: Routledge

Grosz, E, *Space, Time and Perversion*, 1995, London: Routledge

Grosz, E, *Volatile Bodies, Towards a Corporeal Feminism*, 1994, Bloomington: Indiana UP

Hallaq, W, 'Was the Gate of Ijtihad closed?' (1984) 16 Int J Middle Eastern Studies 3

Halley, J, 'Sexual orientation and the politics of biology: a critique of the argument from immutability' (1994) 36 Stan L Rev 301

Hegel, GW, *Hegel's Philosophy of Right*, Knox, TM (trans), 1967, Oxford: OUP

Herman, D and Stychin, C (eds), *Legal Inversions: Lesbians, Gay Men and the Politics of the Law*, 1995, Philadelphia: Temple UP

hooks, b, *Ain't I a Woman: Black Women and Feminism*, 1982, London: Pluto

Huffer, L, 'Luce *et veritas*: toward an ethics of performance' (1995) Yale French Studies 87

Hunt, A and Wickham, G, *Foucault and Law: Towards a Sociology of Governance*, 1994, London: Pluto

Iqbal, S, *Woman and Islamic Law*, 1991, Delhi: Adam

Irigaray, L, *I Love To You*, Martin, A (trans), 1996, London: Routledge

Irigaray, L, *je, tu, nous: Toward a Culture of Difference*, Martin, A (trans), 1993, London: Routledge

Irigaray, L, *Sexes and Genealogies*, Gill, G (trans), 1993, New York: Columbia UP

Irigaray, L, *Speculum of the Other Woman*, Gill, G (trans), 1985, Ithaca: Cornell UP

Irigaray, L, *This Sex Which Is Not One*, Porter, C (trans), 1985, Ithaca: Cornell UP

Isin, E and Wood, P, *Citizenship and Identity*, 1999, London: Sage

Jackson, E, 'The problem with pornography: a critical survey of the current debate' (1995) 3(1) FLS 49

Jardine, A, *Gynesis: Configurations of Women and Modernity*, 1985, Ithaca: Cornell UP

Jay, M, *Downcast Eyes: The Denigration of Vision in Twentieth Century French Thought*, 1993, California: California UP

Kabeer, N, *Reversed Realities: Gender Hierarchies in Development*, 1995, London: Verso

Kant, I, *Anthropology from a Pragmatic Point of View*, Gregor, M (trans), 1974, The Hague: Martinus Nijhoff

Kant, I, *Grounding for the Metaphysics of Morals: On a Supposed Right to Lie Because of Philanthropic Concerns*, 1993, Indiana: Hackett

Kant, I, *Observations on the Feeling of the Beautiful and Sublime*, Goldthwaite, JT (trans), 1960, California: California UP

Kant, I, *The Metaphysics of Morals*, Gregor, M (ed and trans), 1996, Cambridge: CUP

Keddie, N and Beck, L (eds), *Women in the Muslim World*, 1978, Cambridge, Mass: Harvard UP

Kennedy, R and Bartlett, K (eds), *Feminist Legal Theory*, 1991, Boulder: Westview, p 44

Lacey, N, 'Feminist legal theory beyond neutrality' (1995) 48(2) CLP 1

Lacey, N, 'Normative reconstruction in socio-legal theory' (1996) 5(2) SLS 131

Lacey, N, *Unspeakable Subjects: Feminist Essays in Legal and Social Theory*, 1998, Oxford: Hart

Laqueur, T, *Making Sex: Body and Gender from the Greeks to Freud*, 1990, Cambridge, Mass: Harvard UP

Lawrence, P, 'War and exclusion: the aesthetics of modernist violence' (1998) 12(1) Global Society 103

Le Doeuff, M, *The Philosophical Imaginary*, Gordon, C (trans), 1989, London: Athlone

Ledger, S *et al*, *Political Gender: Texts and Contexts*, 1994, London: Harvester Wheatsheaf

Levi, P, *The Drowned and the Saved*, 1986, London: Abacus

Lim, H, 'Caesereans and cyborgs' (1999) 7(2) FLS 133

Lloyd, G, 'No-one's land: Australia and the philosophical imagination' (2000) 15(2) Hypatia (special issue) 26

Lloyd, G, *The Man of Reason: Male and Female in Western Philosophy*, 1984, London: Methuen

Loizidou, E, 'Sex at the end of the 20th century – some re-marks on a minor jurisprudence' (1999) 10(1) LC 71

Lotringer, S (ed), *Foucault Live: Collected Interviews 1961–84,* Hochroth, L and Johnston, J (trans), 1989, New York: Semiotex[e]

Lukes, S, *Power: A Radical View,* 1976, London: Macmillan

Mahmasani, S, *The Legal Systems in the Arab States,* 1965, Beirut: Dar al'Ilm lil Malayin

Marshall, TH, *Citizenship and Social Class,* 1950, Cambridge: CUP

Marx, K, *Grundrisse,* 1973, Harmondsworth: Penguin

Marx, K, *Selected Works in One Volume,* 1971, London: Lawrence & Wishart

McColgan, A, *Women Under the Law: The False Promise of Human Rights,* 2000, Harlow: Pearson

McGhee, D, 'Looking and acting the part: gays in the armed forces – a case of passing masculinity' (1998) 4 FLS 206

Mernissi, F, *Beyond the Veil: Male-Female Dynamics in a Modern Muslim Society,* 1975, Cambridge, Mass: Shenkman

Mernissi, F, *The Veil and the Male Elite: a Feminist Interpretation of Women's Rights in Islam,* Lakel, MJ (trans), 1991, Reading, Mass: Addison Wesley

Mernissi, F, *Women and Islam,* 1992, Oxford: Blackwell

Midgley, M, *Utopias, Dolphins and Computers: Problems of Philosophical Plumbing,* 1996, London: Routledge

Miller, D, *Social Justice,* 1976, Oxford: Clarendon

Moghissi, H, *Feminism and Islamic Fundamentalism: The Limits of Postmodern Analysis,* 1999, New York: Zed

Mohamed Taha, M, *The Second Message of Islam,* Ahmed An-Na'im, A (trans), 1987, Syracuse: Syracuse UP

Mohanty, C, Russo, A and Torres, L (eds), *Third World Women and the Politics of Western Feminism,* 1991, Bloomington: Indiana UP

Montgomery Watt, W, *Muhammad at Medina,* 1956, Oxford: Clarendon

Moran, L, 'Violence and the law: the case of sado-masochism' (1995) 4 SLS 225

Murphy, T, 'Britcrits: subversion and submission, past, present and future' (1999) 10(3) LC 237

Murphy, T, 'Feminism on flesh' (1997) 8(1) LC 37

Naffine, N and Owens, RJ, *Sexing the Subject of Law*, 1997, London: Sweet & Maxwell

Naffine, N, *Law and the Sexes*, 1990, Sydney: Allen & Unwin

Nietzsche, F, *The Gay Science*, 1974, New York: Random House

O'Donovan, K, 'Marriage: a sacred or profane love machine?' (1993) 1 FLS 87

Pather, P, 'On foreign ground: grand narratives, situated specificities, and the praxis of critical theory and law' (1999) 10(3) LC 211

Patton, P (ed), *Deleuze; A Critical Reader*, 1996, Oxford: Blackwell

Phelan, S (ed), *Playing with Fire*, 1997, New York: Routledge

Phillips, A, *Democracy and Difference*, 1993, Cambridge: Polity

Plummer, K (ed), *Modern Homosexualities*, 1992, London: Routledge

Plummer, K, *Telling Sexual Stories*, 1995, London: Routledge

Rabnow, P (ed), *The Foucault Reader*, 1991, London: Penguin

Ragi al-Faruqi, I, 'Towards a new methodology for *Qur'anic* exegesis' [1962] Islamic Studies 35

Rahman, F, *Islam and Modernity: Transformation of an Intellectual Tradition*, 1981, Chicago: Chicago UP

Rahman, F, *Major Themes of the Qur'an*, 1980, Chicago: Bibliotheca Islamica

Richardson, D, 'Sexuality and citizenship' (1998) 32 Sociology 83

Richardson, J, 'A burglar in the house of philosophy: Theodor Adorno, Drucilla Cornell and hate speech' (1999) 7 FLS 3

Richardson, J, 'Jamming the machines: "woman" in the work of Irigaray and Deleuze' (1998) 9(1) LC 89

Robertson Smith, W, *Kinship and Marriage in Early Arabia*, 1885, Cambridge: CUP

Rose, G, *Feminism and Geography*, 1993, Cambridge: Polity

Rushdie, S, *The Satanic Verses*, 1988, London: Jonathan Cape

Sachs, A and Wilson, JH, *Sexism and the Law*, 1978, Oxford: Martin Robertson

Said, E, *The Culture of Imperialism*, 1992, London: Chatto and Windus

Sallis, J (ed), *Deconstruction and Philosophy: The Texts of Jacques Derrida*, 1987, Chicago: Chicago UP

Sandel, M, *Liberalism and the Limit of Justice*, 1982, Cambridge: CUP

Sandland, R, 'Between "truth" and "difference": poststructuralism, law and the power of feminism' (1995) 3(1) FLS 3

Sandland, R, 'Seeing double? Or, why "to be or not to be" is (not) the question for feminist legal studies' (1998) 7(3) SLS 307

Sandland, R, 'The Housing Association, the judges, the tenant, and his lover' (2000) 8(2) FLS 227

Sandland, R, 'The mirror and the veil: reading the imaginary domain' (1998) 6(1) FLS 33

Sarggisson, L, *Feminist Utopias*, 1996, London: Routledge

Schwab, G, 'Women and the law in Irigarayan theory' (1996) 27 Metaphilosophy 152

Scott, JW, 'Deconstructing equality-versus-difference; or, the uses of poststructuralist theory for feminism' (1988) 14(1) FS 34

Sinfield, A, *Gay and After*, 1998, London: Serpent's Tail

Smart C, 'The women of legal discourse' (1992) SLS 29

Smart, C, *Feminism and the Power of Law*, 1989, London: Routledge

Smart, C, *The Ties That Bind: Law, Marriage and the Reproduction of Patriarchal Relations*, 1984, London: Routledge

Soper, K, *On Human Needs*, 1981, Brighton: Harvester

Sparks, H, 'Dissident citizenship: democratic theory, political courage, and activist women' (1997) 12 Hypatia 74

Spivak, GC, *Imaginary Maps*, 1995, New York: Routledge

Stern, G, *Marriage in Early Islam*, 1939, London: Royal Asiatic Society

Stowasser, B, *Women in the Qur'an, Traditions, and Interpretation*, 1994, New York: OUP

Stychin, C, *A Nation by Rights*, 1998, Philadelphia: Temple UP

Stychin, C, *Law's Desire*, 1995, London: Routledge

Synnott, A, 'Tomb, temple, machine and self: the social construction of the body' (1992) 43(1) Br J Soc 79

Temkin, J, 'Justice in rape trials' (1998) *The Guardian*, 27 October

Thomas, P (ed), *Socio-Legal Studies*, 1997, Aldershot: Dartmouth

Tucker, S, *Fighting Words*, 1995, London: Cassell

Tully, J, *Strange Multiplicity: Constitutionalism in an Age of Diversity*, 1995, Cambridge: CUP

Turner, B (ed), *Citizenship and Social Theory*, 1993, London: Sage

Turner, B, 'Outline of a theory of citizenship' (1990) 24 Sociology 187

Turner, B, *The Body and Society*, 1984, Oxford: Blackwell

Wadud-Muhsin, A, *Qur'an and Woman*, 1992, Kuala Lumpur: Penerbit Fajar Bakti Sdn, Bhd

Warnock, M (ed), *Women Philosophers*, 1996, London: Everyman

Whitford, M, *Luce Irigaray – Philosophy in the Feminine*, 1991, London and New York: Routledge

Williams, P, *The Alchemy of Race and Rights*, 1991, Cambridge, Mass: Harvard UP

Wilson, A (ed), *A Simple Matter of Justice?*, 1995, London: Cassell

Yammani, M (ed), *Feminism and Islam: Legal and Literary Perspectives*, 1996, Reading: Ithaca

Yazbeck Haddad, Y and Esposito, JL (eds), *Islam, Gender, and Social Change*, 1998, Oxford: OUP

Yeatman, A, *Postmodern Revisionings of the Political*, 1994, New York: Routledge

Young, IM, *Throwing Like a Girl and Other Essays in Feminist Philosophy and Social Theory*, 1990, Bloomington and Indianapolis: Indiana UP

Young, IM, 'Two concepts of self-determination', conference presentation, University of Bristol, September 1999

Zack, N, Shrage, L and Sartwell, C (eds), *Race, Class, Gender and Sexuality: The Big Questions*, 1998, Oxford: Blackwell

Zafrulla Khan, M, *The Qur'an: Introduction*, 1981, London: Curzon

Zubaida, S (ed), *Race and Racialism*, 1970, London: Tavistock

INDEX